# Wild New Jersey

# Wild
# New Jersey
## NATURE ADVENTURES
## IN THE GARDEN STATE

DAVID WHEELER

FOREWORD BY MARGARET O'GORMAN

**Rivergate Books**
An imprint of Rutgers University Press

NEW BRUNSWICK, NEW JERSEY, AND LONDON

LIBRARY OF CONGRESS CATALOGING-IN-PUBLICATION DATA

Wheeler, David.

Wild New Jersey : nature adventures in the Garden State / David Wheeler ; foreword by
Margaret O'Gorman.

     p.   cm.

Includes bibliographical references and index.

ISBN 978–0–8135–4921–7 (pbk. : alk. paper)

1. Natural history—New Jersey.  2. Natural areas—New Jersey.  3. Landscapes—New
Jersey.  4. Animals—New Jersey.  5. Outdoor life—New Jersey.  6. New Jersey—Environmental conditions.  7. Wheeler, David—Travel—New Jersey.  8. New Jersey—Description and
travel.  I. Title.

QH105.N5W47  2011

508.749—dc22

2010013764

A British Cataloging-in-Publication record for this book is available from the British Library.

Visit our Web site: http://rutgerspress.rutgers.edu

Manufactured in the United States of America

For my dad, Bill Wheeler
In memory of my beloved grandmother, Agnes Mellendick

# CONTENTS

# ILLUSTRATIONS

# FOREWORD

Wildlife, or its approximation, surrounds us in so many ways. We call our subdivisions Deer Run and Bear Preserve. We name our sports teams Eagles, Cardinals, and Panthers. We wear crocodile logos and aspire to drive cars called Jaguar. Avatars of wildlife are always present in our daily lives, but the real thing is just as close—and many times more fascinating than anything conceived by the marketing minds of Madison Avenue.

The contrast between New Jersey's urban reputation and its more complex reality is well known and much discussed in our state. We prepare "litanies of the positive" to be pulled from our hats like magic tricks in Atlantic City. We talk about the wonderful diversity of our state, its great cultural amenities, its top-class universities, the proximity to two great cities, the shore, the mountains, and the celebrated, protected regions of the Highlands and the Pine Barrens. We are stout defenders of the Garden State and we can, with David Wheeler's *Wild New Jersey*, add another boast—the rich and fascinating diversity of wildlife that lives in, and migrates through, our state.

More than 870 species of wildlife live in New Jersey, of which 70 some are considered rare enough here to be protected by the federal Endangered Species Act. Between the common species of wildlife and their rarer cousins, there are very few places in the Garden State where wildlife cannot be observed and quite a lot of places where high-quality wildlife watching can take place. This book takes the reader across the breadth of experiences possible in our great but underappreciated state.

At Conserve Wildlife Foundation of New Jersey, we seek to bring knowledge about rare wildlife into classrooms across the state and instill in New Jersey's schoolchildren a sense of place tied to these species. We want our children to know as much about the endangered forms of wildlife that live within our borders as they do about the endangered species in the Arctic or the rainforest. We ask them to get out, look, listen, and learn about our rich natural heritage, and through this work we observe and celebrate their sense of wonder. We do this for many reasons but mostly because we know the future of our wildlife will one day be in their hands. Today, we are responsible for ensuring they value it.

With this entertaining and insightful book, David Wheeler clearly illustrates the wonder of our wildlife, the need to celebrate it, and the ease with which we can engage with it. From the world-famous bird migration in Cape May to the less well-known joys of urban birding, from bears to bats, and from the mountains of the north to the shores of the south, he engages his subject with joy and enthusiasm. He shows, through his yearlong adventure, that New Jersey remains a wild place worth exploring and protecting.

It is only through ongoing protection that our children will continue to hear the spring peepers herald the change in season, marvel at the red-tailed hawks hovering over our highways, or throw a line to catch a crab at the Jersey Shore. Learning to value and protect our wildlife and wild places will enable our children to bring their children to the Delaware Bayshore to witness the shorebird migration.

So, whether you drive a Rabbit, a Ram, or a Road Runner, cheer for the Bobcats, the Bulls, or the Bucks, or live in Hawk Hills or Bluebird Brook, you, too, should take advantage of this great book and get outside to look, listen, and learn. Have fun and experience New Jersey's rich biodiversity and the wild legacy we can, and must, pass to future generations.

Margaret O'Gorman
Executive Director
Conserve Wildlife Foundation of New Jersey

# ACKNOWLEDGMENTS

My year-long journey through New Jersey's natural wonders was book-ended by another year of research and writing—and it all occurred only through the help and guidance of so many. I set out on my voyage with various destinations in mind, but many more revealed themselves to me as the journey continued. Each expert guide introduced me to three other naturalists I needed to know. Each place highlighted three other hotspots I had to visit. Each wildlife species brought to mind three others that couldn't be overlooked. Yet somehow, when my book was done, I had an even longer list of New Jersey places I still need to experience.

The highlight, for me, was the privilege of joining so many biologists, scientists, and naturalists in the field, exploring the places and species they have devoted their lives to studying and protecting. I am particularly indebted to those who contributed their own insights on wildlife events while also helping to put me in touch with their peers: MacKenzie Hall from Conserve Wildlife Foundation, Greg Remaud from NY/NJ Baykeeper, Christina Fehre from Palisades Interstate Park, and Cindy Zipf of Clean Ocean Action.

My wildlife experiences would have been far less "wild" without: Mick Valent, Kathy Clark, Amanda Dey, Kris Schantz, David Golden, Paul Tarlowe, and Charles Hofer of New Jersey Fish and Wildlife; Larry Niles, Todd Pover, and Gretchen Fowles from Conserve Wildlife Foundation; Scott Barnes, Linda Mack, Mike Anderson, Nellie Tsipoura, Kristin Mylecraine, Melissa Craddock, Hal Miller, Sean Fitzgerald, and Jessica Donahue from New Jersey Audubon Society; Charles Kontos; Nancy Slowik of Greenbrook Sanctuary; Captain Bill Sheehan and Nick Vos-Wein of Hackensack Riverkeeper; Debbie Mans, Andy Willner, and Rick Jacks of NY/NJ Baykeeper; Bill Schultz of Raritan Riverkeeper; Jim and April Faczak of Cheesequake State Park; John Shersick; Dominic Rizzo of Rizzo's Wildlife; Frank Gallagher of Liberty State Park; Kathy Murarik, Patty Bryce, Jeanette Lamphere, Cindy Geertsema, and Andy Bankendorf of New Jersey Sled Dog Club; Ray Lewis and family; Paul Guris, Ray

Duffy, and Heidi Petri for their pelagic guidance; Maurice Tremblay of Marine Mammal Stranding Center; Captain Jeff Stewart of Cape May Whale Watcher; Captain David Githens of Bald Eagle Boat Tours; David Moskowitz and Rich Wolfert of the East Brunswick Environmental Commission; David Burkett of Herpetological Associates; Harold Scaff of the Warren Rod and Gun Club; and Walt Steele of the Bethlehem Environmental Commission.

So many others shared their time for interviews and discussions, including the late Dery Bennett; Pete Dunne, Don Freiday, Vince Elia, Sean Grace, and Kim Hannum of New Jersey Audubon Society; Emile Devito of New Jersey Conservation Foundation; Margaret O'Gorman of Conserve Wildlife Foundation; Kelcey Burguess, Andrew Burnett, and Darlene Yuhas of New Jersey Fish and Wildlife; John Fletcher of the Appalachian Trail Conservancy; Len Wolgast and Joanna Burger of Rutgers University; Chris Spatz of the Eastern Cougar Foundation; Jim Stein of Lakota Wolf; coyote researcher Jon Way; Eric Nelsen of Palisades Interstate Park; Michael Newhouse of New Jersey Meadowlands Commission; Mark Gallagher of Princeton Hydro; Fred Virrazzi of National Biodiversity Parks; Glenn Phillips and Susan Elbin of New York City Audubon; David Parris of the New Jersey State Museum; Howie Cohn of New Jersey Paleontological Society; Dr. Leonard Compagno of the Shark Research Institute; Sheila Dean of the Marine Mammal Stranding Center; Ed Lippincott of Shark River Coalition; Eleanor Swanson of Wreck Pond Watershed Association; Kevin Holcomb of the U.S. Fish and Wildlife Service; Joe Roman of the Gund Institute for Ecological Economics; Valerie Montecalvo and Cynthia Fair of Bayshore Recycling; Noella Girard; Dave Coyle; Dr. Len Soucy of the Raptor Trust; Jane Galetto and Renee Brecht of Citizens United to Protect the Maurice River; Joanne Williams; Assemblyman Peter Barnes; Mickey Quinn; Judy Schmidt of Friends of the Great Swamp; Stephanie Fox of the Delaware and Raritan Canal; Cathy Blumig; Maya Van Rossum of Delaware Riverkeeper; Jeremy Phillips of the Pocono Environmental Education Center; Wayne Mann and Albert Sheehan of the Ramapough Mountain Indian Tribe; Alan Ambler of the National Park Service; Joe Reynolds; Michael Britt; Bill Lynch; Captain Darren Volker; William Boyle Jr.; Paul Kerlinger; Richard Fernicola; Barbara Deen; Caroline Ratti; Barry Knisley; Howard Sefton; Jack Whitman; Robert Wilenker; Volker Schmidt; red knot volunteers Diane Amico, Elisa Perez, and Susan Taylor; Susan Ritacco; Mike McGraw and Scott Quitel of Applied Ecological Services; Michael Rehman; Joe Seebode; Tom Oates; Hans Karlson; and Howard Chew.

I offer the gift of an oil change to my 2002 Toyota truck, which got me through thousands of miles of Garden State safari road trips, ice storms, and off-road mud trails without a major problem. Now if I can only get that heat and air conditioning to find a level between 0 and 100. I also appreciate the isolation I found for the bulk of the writing at my "mountain retreat" at Appalachian Motel in Vernon, and a one-room off-season studio in Bay Head a block from the Atlantic Ocean.

I thank my agent, Kathi Paton, for helping me get this project off the ground and finding the ideal publisher for *Wild New Jersey*. At Rutgers University Press, I thank Marlie Wasserman and Doreen Valentine for their expert guidance on the manuscript and their patience in answering the many questions of a first-time author. I also appreciate the hard work of Allyson Fields, Marilyn Campbell, Karen Baliff Ornstein, and Peter Mikulas at Rutgers, and the expert copyediting of Gretchen Oberfranc. And I learned much from the craftsmanship of editors Matt Dowling of the *Star-Ledger*, Phil Hartman of the *Home News Tribune*, Gail Robinson of *Gotham Gazette*, and Jennifer Weiss of *Green Jersey* in working on previous nature stories.

My heartfelt thanks go to those who reviewed my manuscript and provided helpful advice, especially my dad, Bill Wheeler, who also designed the superb maps and offered me an ever-steady sounding board throughout the entire journey. I also gratefully thank Michael Carroll for his perceptive editing advice on early drafts, as well as Dana Patterson, Craig Hunsinger, Sara Imperiale, Stephanie Wood, and Joann Chavelle Flynn for their valuable contributions to fine-tuning my manuscript in its various forms.

I have been fortunate to receive the direct and indirect support of many people on this project, and in some cases they joined me on wildlife tours. I especially appreciate the support of Bob Spiegel, whose stalwart activism and dedication makes any goal appear reachable. I also thank James Johnson and his family, Melanie Worob, Katrina Baptista, Jill Weislo, Mayble Abraham, Brad Van Arnum, Diana Lentzsch, Roger Donnan, Krystina Sabins, Frank Ettinger, Shannon Storey, Angela Gorczyca, Grace Lawrence, Bosh Keller, Jim Ward, Jeff Suto, Corey Ross, the Lewis family, Dr. George Mellendick, Amy and Ron Nobile, Carol Mellendick, the Readlinger family, and Sally-Cat (for her reminder that wild lurks even in the friendly backyard stray). And I lovingly thank my mom, Barbara Wheeler, for her unwavering support and encouragement, and my late grandparents for their unmatched devotion.

I owe an eternal debt of gratitude to my wife, Claudia, whose oft-tested patience allowed me to devote every weekend and weeknight to this near-obsession, at the cost of transforming all possible counter space into makeshift libraries and file centers. Without her commitment, I could never have experienced or written *Wild New Jersey*.

Lastly, my daughter Kayla and son William allowed me to refresh my mind when I needed it most, serving as the most enthusiastic and inquisitive travel companions I could have asked for on some of these journeys. I can only hope that their generation will have the same chance to enjoy New Jersey's wildest places and fascinating wildlife that my generation does today.

# **Wild** New Jersey

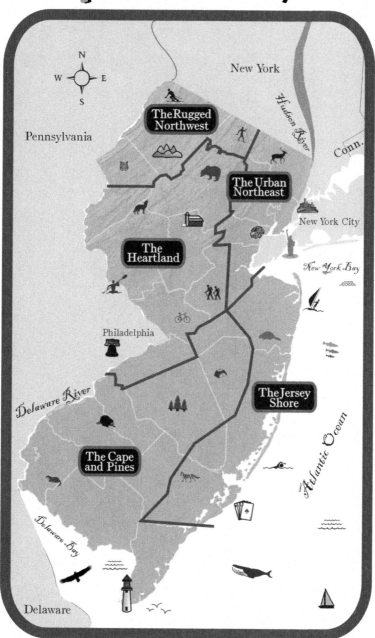

O Earth, O Earth, return!
Arise from the dewy grass;
Night is worn,
And the morn
Rises from the slumberous mass.

Turn away no more;
Why wilt thou turn away?
The starry floor,
The wat'ry shore
Is giv'n thee till the break of day.

—William Blake, "Introduction,"
from *Songs of Experience*, 1794

I was in the bush looking for turtles when not five feet away, a turkey popped out, screamed at me, defecated on the ground, and then walked away.

—Dominic Rizzo, New Jersey naturalist

# Introduction

Poisonous snakes at arm's length. Pods of dolphins swimming past by the score. A thousand bats careening past my head in a pitch-black roost. The Arctic sky's fiercest predator surveying its hunting grounds before me. A young black bear bounding up a mountain trail ahead of me. The fastest animal on earth—the peregrine falcon—dive-bombing me from the skies.

I have just concluded a year's journey encountering wildlife scenes I had never imagined. I explored mountains, valleys, beaches, pine barrens, caves, rivers, and more. And I did it all in New Jersey—a state home to more than 8.7 million residents, more densely populated than India and Japan.

Yes, New Jersey.

Let's be frank: it would be difficult to ignore the Garden State's reputation. Its toxic-spewing smokestacks, oil tank fields, and towering industrial cranes have made New Jersey the butt of countless jokes from stand-up comedians and talk-show hosts. The "New Jersey Turnpike industrial skyline"—so vividly captured in all its one-of-a-kind ugly glory by native son Bruce Springsteen—defines the state for many outsiders.

That reputation notwithstanding, wildlife is steadily reclaiming what industry and suburban sprawl pilfered from New Jersey during the past two centuries. The "harbor herons" in the metropolitan waterways of New York/New Jersey Harbor have expanded from an anemic 170 nests in 1982 to more than 1,600 in 2009. Bobcats and coyotes roam our forests, and at least two dozen species of sharks patrol our seas. Raptors—bald eagles, ospreys, and peregrine falcons—are making all-American comebacks from the brink of extinction to again fill our riverfront skies. New Jersey was home to only one nesting pair of bald eagles in the early 1980s; in January 2010 a two-day state survey found over 325 eagles. Peregrines were extinct east of the Rocky Mountains as of 1970, yet 39 hatched in New Jersey in 2009 alone; osprey expanded from 60 to 485 pairs during that same time period. And New Jersey's black bears—a historic symbol of America's eastern wilderness—have increased in number from fewer than 100 in 1970 to more than 3,000 today.

How can this possibly be?

Despite being smaller than some *counties* in the larger states, New Jersey supports an inordinate number of wildlife species. Its 465 species of birds include the largest concentration of shorebirds in America every spring. More migrating birds fly through Cape May each fall than anywhere else on the East Coast. Close to a million seabirds fly over the Avalon peninsula on the Jersey Shore each winter. An incredible 90 species of mammals share the land with 79 species of reptiles and amphibians.

New Jersey's unique location offers a home to both northern and southern United States species, with hemlock ravines and glacial bogs in the north giving way to southern coastal plains and hardwood swamps. Representing an ecological Mason-Dixon Line, the Garden State attracts the best of both worlds—rare visitors from the north like the beluga whale and snowy owl, and summer voyagers from the south like the manatee and roseate spoonbill. And for all its legendary suburban sprawl, more than half of New Jersey is either forest or wetlands.

I have been fortunate enough to experience all this by joining the pros who know each locale and each species best. But you don't have to embark on a latter-day Lewis and Clark expedition or be a world traveler like the late Steve Irwin to share the adventure that is New Jersey. Nearly all of these experiences are open to anyone with a joy for nature and the willingness to get out there and find it. Without leaving the state, you can view scenic mountain ridges, hike through vast pinelands, and observe birds in timeless tidal marshes—all in a single day.

Some tours require little more than taking a seat outdoors and watching the show unfold as nature intended it. After a hectic week of urban hustle and bustle, relax—there are whale-watching tours in Cape May and tube floats down the Delaware River. You can sit back and watch wildlife from just about anywhere, including your own kitchen window. There are literally lifetimes of adventures to experience out there—in Wild New Jersey.

Growing up in New Jersey, I never thought too much about our state's reputation. Once I moved away, first for college and then for a career, the state's stereotypes came up regularly. Many took the form of that timeless query: "What exit are you from?" I recall getting a ride back from college on a holiday break, and a Long Island girl in the car was afraid when we pulled off the Garden State Parkway—and I was being dropped off in Westfield!

I never kidded myself about my home state's image. Still, I always felt a strong pride for what we have here. In no other state can you wake up on a given day and get to a pristine Atlantic Ocean beach, a breathtaking cliff-top overlook—or a Manhattan nightclub—within an hour. It is that duality that always fascinated me: the pairing of stark industrial skylines with serene salt marshes and rugged mountains, of extraordinary numbers of people sharing space with an extraordinary diversity of species.

As a boy, I spent endless hours swimming in the ocean, exploring the suburban woods, and hiking with my dad, Bill Wheeler, who cherished time outdoors away from the office. Fortunately, the outdoorsman in him rubbed off plenty on me. They say some things never change: when I began the year of adventures that would become *Wild New Jersey*, my dad jumped at the chance to join me on much of the journey. Though he's sixty now, he's sixty going on thirty—and it was my honor to show him around this time.

After working in the corporate world for several years, I began to renew my interest in the outdoors and nature, thanks in large part to distant travel to places as diverse as Iceland, Egypt, Antigua, Istanbul, Norway, Palestine, and Scotland's Loch Ness. On American soil, a thrilling fifty-day cross-country trip found me camping at the Grand Canyon, pontooning the Louisiana bayou, night-hiking Yellowstone, surfing Maui, swimming the Pacific's Muir Beach, and hiking the Rockies.

Strangely enough, it was living and working in New York City that really shifted my passions back to nature. Surrounded as I was by pavement, any foray out of the city felt like something very special. By train, the drainage canals of the Meadowlands seemed like wild, untrammeled rivers, and the egrets and turtles lining the ponds might well have been the rarest of fauna. Manhattan has its natural side, too—and a fascinating one at that—but you really have to seek it out to uncover it.

In New Jersey, that wild side is all around us. It is in the suburbs, where an evening walk around the block can bring bats, owls, and a chance encounter with a flying squirrel. It is beside our highways, where each mile might reveal a woodchuck peering off its back legs, a herd of white-tailed deer foraging the forest edges, or a vulture gliding overhead. It is along our sandy shore, where beachgoers share the water with more than 400 species of fish and an astounding array of dolphins, whales, seals, crustaceans, sea turtles, and shorebirds. It is in our most urban of cities, where raptors hunt from skyline perches. And of course, it is in our wilder areas, where a list of our state's more charismatic species—bobcat, golden eagle, eastern coyote, porcupine, hammerhead shark, beaver, pileated woodpecker, black bear, snowy owl, river otter, tiger salamander, octopus, brown pelican, mink, and timber rattlesnake—reads like a promotional brochure for such national treasures as Yellowstone and the Everglades.

You can go to those far-off places—and you should—but you can also find all these critters in the Garden State. For the next few pages, let's experience the wonders of Wild New Jersey together.

Our journey will chart a clockwise course around New Jersey, beginning in the mountainous northwest. From there, we will explore the urban jungles and skyline peaks of the Hudson and Meadowlands, America's greatest metropolitan wilderness. We will then take a trip "down the Jersey Shore," where coastal species thrive along the Atlantic Ocean and back bays. Moving farther south, we will enjoy the globally significant wildlife spectacles and timeless migrations of Cape May and the Delaware Bayshore. And we will conclude our quest with a journey back in time through New Jersey's rural heartland, from the mysterious Pine Barrens right on up to the geological marvel that is the Delaware Water Gap. These captivating places harbor a veritable Noah's Ark of wildlife. And the highlights are endless.

We will track a family of black bears in the mountain wilderness.

We will fight off the aerial attacks of peregrine falcons on a skyscraper roof.

We will pan for cretaceous fossils in a hidden brook once home to mastodons and giant sloths.

We will dogsled across windswept alpine slopes in the haunts of porcupine and bobcat.

Best of all, we will enjoy these adventures in the Garden State. After all, this is Wild New Jersey.

# Part One

## The Rugged Northwest

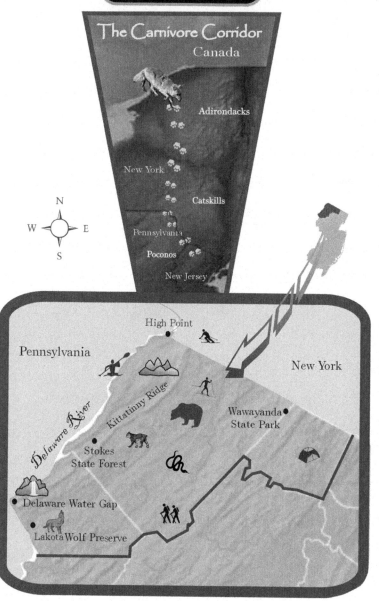

The Carnivore Corridor
Canada

Adirondacks

New York

Catskills

Pennsylvania

Poconos

New Jersey

N
W · E
S

High Point

Pennsylvania

New York

Kittatinny Ridge

Delaware River

Wawayanda
State Park

Stokes
State Forest

Delaware Water Gap

Lakota Wolf Preserve

# Wawayanda Wilderness 1
## A QUEST FOR BLACK BEARS

Climb the mountains and get
their good tidings. Nature's
peace will flow into you as
sunshine flows into trees.

—John Muir

**M**y dad and I walked up the mountain trail on a chilly autumn morning. Laurel and wild cherry and rhododendron cloaked the narrow boulder-strewn path, limiting our visibility to just a few yards ahead. We were the first hikers out that morning—but we were not alone. That was apparent right away. Fresh claw marks scarred the fallen tree trunks lining the trail; the parallel incisions on the logs left wood shavings in the dirt. Patties of bear scat greeted us every few minutes, the highbush blueberries still apparent in the droppings. With each bend in the trail, our anticipation grew.

*Will this be the day? Will we finally encounter a black bear in the wild?*

Step after step, my eyes focused on the trail. A sudden grip on my shoulder brought me to a halt. My dad stared ahead, eyes alight. No more than thirty yards before me, an adult black bear and cub foraged along the edge of the trail, noses to the ground. They were oblivious to us. We stared in amazement as another cub came into view from the gently wooded slope arching up to the right—followed by the massive father bear, who had to be pushing 500 pounds.

The bear family foraged for insects and grubs, drifting in and out of our lines of vision. The wind must have shifted, for the mother bear looked up alertly. With no signal recognizable to us, the cubs understood. Mama bear and both cubs trotted downslope away from the trail.

*Hmm . . . where, exactly, is Papa bear?*

We silently went through mental checklists of what to do in case of a bear encounter—realizing at the worst possible moment, as we later shared, just how much of our assumed knowledge was contradictory. Shout loudly or remain quiet? Stand aggressively or withdraw meekly? Avoid eye contact or give it a friendly wink?

The answer appeared in the form of the heaving black shoulders of Papa bear, who lumbered across the trail toward his family. Unlike the others, he was in no hurry. This was his forest. We were only visiting.

During those moments of watching the family of bears, I felt that I could have been in any great American wilderness. And I was. I was in New Jersey.

Years have passed since that black bear encounter, one of my first wild New Jersey experiences. So my dad and I decide to return to the bears of Wawayanda State Park in Sussex County. We awake before the early May dawn can thaw the frost from the grassy tufts peeking out from boulders and slabs of gneiss bedrock. The sun first appears as rays glancing off the cliffs before us on the Appalachian Trail, which stretches 2,178 miles, all the way from Georgia to Maine. First conceived by Benton MacKaye in 1921, the "A.T." was completed sixteen years later. Up to four million people hike some portion of the trail each year, from casual walkers enjoying a brief jaunt in one of the many national and state parks along the path, to the hardy souls who devote months upon months to hiking its entirety.

Wawayanda's twenty-mile stretch of the Appalachian Trail is as dramatic as it gets. Towering above the farmlands and the grassy meadows to our north, Wawayanda Mountain rises so abruptly that it seems to be an eternal symbol of the geologic cataclysms that shot it skyward from deep in the belly of the earth. It seems to say that no matter how much New Jersey changes, it will not. Wawayanda Mountain will always stand above the fray.

We ascend. The initial stroll through a valley floor pine forest gives way to steep switchbacks. The trail practically doubles back on itself time and time again, rising slightly higher along the cliff with each bend. My feet do not touch trail bottom for steps at a time, as we scramble from boulder to boulder. Crevices appear and disappear between massive slabs of rock, mini-caves offering dark respite for wildlife. Lichens, ferns, and moss provide the primordial cover.

If there is a better place than Wawayanda Mountain to launch a year of exploring New Jersey's wildest places, I am not aware of it. Between my deep breaths on this mountain climb, the terrain and vistas bring to mind Yellowstone National Park. Out there, rolling valleys of meadows and forest fill the vast bowl of an ancient volcano, alpine mountains rising around its edges. Here in Wawayanda, the mountain overlook offers a magnificent view of rolling farmlands to the north. The Highlands

**After one of the state's steepest mountain climbs, David Wheeler and Bill Wheeler enjoy the view from atop Wawayanda Mountain near the New York border.**

mountain chain staggers westward, each triangular form backed by another, then another. This being New Jersey ski country in winter, white ski trails wind down the closest peak's wooded face like maple syrup pouring down a stack of flapjacks.

From the mountaintop, the Appalachian Trail clambers up and down the mountains heading east. In the middle of this rugged forest, a thousand feet above civilization, a most unlikely discovery awaits: an antique black mailbox, mounted decades ago, with its red flag up. It's stuffed with a pen and a worn visitor notebook that contains hundreds of entries like these:

20/11/08    Greetings from PERTH AUSTRALIA. Beautiful scenery.
            MANUEL M.

            I wouldn't be here if it wasn't for my cousin, Manuel
            from Australia. I wish I was in my hot tub. God bless!
            Rick, Clark, NJ

10/10       3RD DAY ON THE TRAIL AND I'M IN LOVE, HER NAME'S
            MOTHER NATURE. . . .

3-18-09     Wawayanda Maintenance

That last entry is a crucial one. Six thousand volunteers a year from thirty different trail clubs maintain the length of the Appalachian Trail. In Wawayanda's portion, volunteers from the New York–New Jersey Trail Conference come out every spring and fall to clear fallen trees after the winter storms and cut back overgrown brush at the end of summer. Their handiwork built the stone steps and carved out the switchbacks on some of the trail's trickiest segments.

"Hikers are often surprised about how wild and remote the New Jersey section is versus their impression of the state—especially if they're not from New Jersey," says John Fletcher of the Appalachian Trail Conservancy. "They're often pleasantly surprised at just how much wild land there is—and what a remote feeling they get there."

## Land of the Black Bear

This New Jersey segment of the Appalachian Trail is special for another reason. Just as the grizzly rules Yellowstone, Wawayanda is the land of the black bear. In the decade since we spied that bear family crossing a Wawayanda trail, my dad has never seen another. There would be no shame in that if it were, say, the 1960s.

"Fifty years ago, you probably would have been hard-pressed to encounter a black bear," says Fletcher. "Now New Jersey is one of the most populous areas for black bear on the whole Appalachian Trail."

Black bears were considered to be vermin in New Jersey and across the country until the 1950s. Deforestation had drastically reduced the bear population long before that, and bear expert Kelcey Burguess of the state Division of Fish and Wildlife estimates there were fewer than 100 black bears remaining in New Jersey by 1970.

"In 1970 our Fish and Game Council recognized, as did Pennsylvania and New York, that it needed to be paying better attention to what was going on with the bear population," Burguess told a state fishing group in 2009. "The difference is that Pennsylvania and New York reestablished their hunting season before the end of the 1970s, regulated the number of bears that were harvested during that time, and continue to hunt them and keep a very manageable population even today."

New Jersey, of course, didn't renew bear hunting in the 1970s. Three decades later, 1,660 black bears roamed 580 square miles in the state-surveyed area alone—3 bears per square mile. The bear population exploded at exactly the same time that human sprawl pushed ever westward and northward from the urban centers. New Jersey finally renewed the bear hunt in 2003, but daily headlines and emotional rallies transformed it into a political football. Two years later, the state canceled the hunt.

Long-time New Jersey Fish and Game Council member and Rutgers wildlife ecologist Len Wolgast is concerned, like many, about where the bears' uncontrolled increase will lead.

"There's around 700 cubs born each year, and probably around 100 killed by cars or killed by State Game. There have been six minor attacks," says Wolgast. "We have the highest black bear density in the country, in the same state as the highest human density."

The numbers are startling, and it's hard to deny the potential trouble that might arise from humans and black bears sharing space in northern New Jersey. At the same time, there is something inherently magical about seeing a black bear in the wild. This marvelous creature evokes so many different images, from the fierce protector of its young to the popular icon of the cuddly teddy bear.

## Millipedes and Woodpeckers

On our long-awaited return to Wawayanda, my dad and I hope to encounter New Jersey's largest land mammal once again—from a safe remove, of course. It has been a long time for us, and a long time for the bears. We hike through mountain laurel and rhododendron groves, along mountainside trails with expansive views over ravines and cliffside caves. We pass swamps dotted with witch hazel and black huckleberry, as well as skunk cabbage and berries—some of the black bear's favorite foods. The timing seems right, the foot traffic is sparse, and the weather is comfortable. Everything is in place but the bears. No sightings, not even a pile of scat to give us hope.

Fortunately, Wawayanda is plenty wild even without a black bear in sight. The bounty of other wildlife soon overcomes any disappointment. I turn over a few logs and leaves to uncover large millipedes, their size dwarfing the red-backed salamanders found in the same leaf litter. The moist soil of the mixed pine and oak forest is ideal for many ground-dwelling species like salamanders, shrews, and moles. Near a waterfall on another trail, a pileated woodpecker crosses a clearing not far ahead of me, my first sighting of this gorgeous, large bird, which displays a thick tuft of red feathers on its crown. In person, it is far more majestic than its cartoon image, Woody Woodpecker.

We soon cross a trail of stones edging a glacial lake in a remote corner of the park. This lake sits nearly two feet above the water flowing past our walking stones, held back by an expertly engineered dam of beaver-cut sticks. On the far shore, a beaver dam rises up behind some dabbling ducks, serving as headquarters and sentry post for the entire operation of hard-working beavers. There are more glacial lakes here in the Highlands than anywhere else on the eastern seaboard. Glacial lakes like this one, formed by the ice left behind as a glacier retreated northward, offer ideal habitat for migrating waterfowl, river otter, and a wide variety of amphibians and reptiles.

As for the bears, they will have to wait. If we cannot find them again in Wawayanda, surely that perfect encounter awaits elsewhere in New Jersey.

# The Carnivore Corridor of Stokes Forest

# 2

When you encounter a wildcat in a place like New Jersey, it really is a symbol of the wilderness.
—Wildlife biologist MacKenzie Hall

On a warm June night in 2006, Shaun Fitzgerald, a Vernon Township police officer, and his wife awoke to unearthly wails from their Glenwood backyard. They opened the door to find a mountain lion and its cub.

"We went outside to see what was making loud, piercing shrieks in the backyard," Christine Fitzgerald told *ABC News*. "Fifteen feet away from us, we saw a large blond female mountain lion along with a cub that had just killed one mother cat and two stray cats."

The encounter held one especially puzzling detail. Cougars—also called mountain lions, pumas, panthers, and catamounts—were extirpated from New Jersey in the 1800s. In fact, cougars were wiped out of the entire United States east of the Mississippi River. Concerned about the risks to livestock from this powerful predator, New Jersey and other states put a bounty on cougars. Overhunting and deforestation likely eliminated cougars from the Northeast by 1900.

Nonetheless, sporadic reports of cougar sightings in New Jersey persisted throughout the early 2000s, as researcher Chris Spatz from the Eastern Cougar Foundation knew all too well. When he follows up on most reports, the perpetrator nearly always is a misidentified bobcat or housecat. Photographs that appear credible have no reference to show scale or turn out to have been taken in another state entirely.

The Fitzgeralds' sighting was different. This was a prolonged encounter from close range, with a police officer, in the very habitat that would best fit mountain lions in New Jersey. Spatz got in his car and drove to Vernon. He spent the entire summer putting motion cameras around the area, then followed up by keeping cameras active for a full year at High Point State Park in nearby Sussex County. Spatz's study turned up neither cougar photographs nor cougar tracks.

Surely it was an escaped or released pet, an orphan of the illegal exotic pet trade. There is still little evidence that cougars have come back to New Jersey naturally. But it wouldn't be the first time a long-lost predator resurfaced here after a century away, against all odds.

## The Ancient Splendor of Tillman Ravine

Nearly all of New Jersey's *terra firma* has been cleared by human hands at least once and, in most cases, many times. At only a handful of spots can you enjoy the feel of an old-growth, primordial forest. Tillman Ravine in Stokes State Forest, in New Jersey's far northwest corner, is just such a place, where things are as they were for centuries past. Primal. Here, I feel as if I could be in the forests of Alaska's jagged mountain coast or the vast Canadian taiga.

In Tillman Ravine, a rushing mountain stream has carved out an ancient river canyon. Clear water surges around sharp bends, plummeting down one waterfall after another. Steep banks rise on either side, with towering hemlocks and oaks and maples that seem to reach the very sky. Standing well over 100 feet tall, some hemlocks are nearly two centuries years old. These trees were never felled for farms or civilization. Tillman Ravine was never the home of man. It belongs to the bobcats, to the porcupine, to the fishers, to the coyotes of the night.

On a frosty winter morning, I join a fellow adventurer for a sunrise hike into the ravine. This cold is the kind that takes your breath away, the kind that attacks you from all sides, the kind that makes it hard to notice anything else—until I descend into the ravine. The mountain stream twists and turns, crashing over jagged boulders and toppled trees. Patches of ice share the surfaces with moss and lichens. Along the riverside rocks, some icicles grow upward from the waterfall mist. The stream flows higher than normal from heavy recent snows and rains. One trail disappears from time to time beneath the surging water. This is one wild place.

It is easy, here on this early morning, with no sound but the crashing torrent, to imagine the wildlife that lives here. A mother bear warily leading her cubs down the steep mountain slope to the water for a drink. A mink slinking along the boulders in search of its next meal. Scarlet tanagers, Blackburnian warblers, and red-eared vireos flitting between the trees. A river otter family tumbling in the currents downstream. A golden eagle soaring high above the towering hemlock skyline.

One visionary wildlife researcher is doing a lot more than imagining that. Charlie Kontos is seeing it all. Through his motion-detector cameras and wilderness tracking, through his exhaustive historical research and coordination with state and national wildlife geneticists, he is leading the charge to ensure that the species we nearly lost are still welcome here in the wilds of northwestern New Jersey. For Kontos, that safe haven cannot be some isolated pocket of land. We must restore an active wildlife corridor that connects to the Catskills and the Appalachians and the Adirondacks, all the way up into New England and the great boreal forest of Canada.

### Return of a Forest Legend

I meet Kontos on a December afternoon in Stokes State Forest. The park is empty but for the cars of hunters parked intermittently along the forest roads—their gunshots ringing out every so often. In his early thirties, Kontos is friendly and enthusiastic. When he was young, he would spend hours studying maps of North America, letting his imagination whisk him away to the northern haunts of the porcupine and wolverine, the caribou and moose. He would read about wildlife across the world and pioneering researchers like Alan Rabinowitz, who tracked jaguar in the jungles of Belize. Kontos was hooked.

"I wasn't sure I'd be able to get to those places, so I started looking into New Jersey, what was here. We had elk, fisher, martens—maybe some are still here."

After all, the forests had come back to claim much of New Jersey and the Northeast. Beaver, otter, black bear, and bobcat had returned to numbers near their previous levels. We need to reintroduce some of the other species we removed so long ago, Kontos thought. Cougars were fascinating—yet the public probably wasn't ready to reintroduce such a top predator. But fishers? His academic advisors told him it could never happen. Like nature's Don Quixote, Kontos was tilting at wildlife windmills.

But something told Kontos differently. The fisher—a tree-climbing, wolverine-like predator larger than a woodchuck—is most commonly found in the Adirondacks and Canada. Kontos felt certain it was already back in New Jersey. People just didn't realize it yet.

David Wheeler

**Wildlife researcher Charlie Kontos uploads images from a remote motion camera at Stokes State Forest.**

Kontos set up his first motion-trigger cameras in the remote wilds of northwestern New Jersey. The first six months produced not a single image of a fisher. Kontos was nearly ready to give up the dream when he uploaded a motion camera's photo stills onto his laptop one morning. There it was—a clear, unambiguous photo. The fisher was back in New Jersey.

### Hair Samples and Gusto!

We hike into the rugged Stokes backcountry. Hemlocks tower overhead, and boulders litter the ground, each rock uniquely spattered with its own pattern of lichens and moss. Forest ferns shoot up between the rocks. We reach one of Kontos's cameras, strategically positioned low to the ground to trigger at the slightest sign of movement. A few feet away, a wire hair snare extends out to snag a hair off passing wildlife. How does he know an animal will pass by this very location? For starters, it's a worn trail, an obvious travel route. But Kontos realizes he needs to game the odds a bit. He opens a bottle of Gusto.

"What's Gusto?" I ask.

"It's a special lure of ground-up skunk's anus soaked in garlic. My landlord called me and said I had a delivery. It was Gusto and cougar urine," he says, with a grin. "Let's just say it was an odiferous package."

I take a whiff. To call it pungent would be a vast understatement. "What does your girlfriend think of it?" I ask while holding back tears from the acrid scent. "I had a girlfriend," laughs Kontos, "but not since I got the Gusto!"

Whatever the reason, Kontos's camera traps are producing serious results. Over the last four years, he has captured twenty different images of fishers, plus countless snaps of other species—coyote, bobcat, bear, and wild turkey—in their most remote habitat. His hair snares snagged 200 samples in a single recent summer, and even though most are from common species like the Virginia opossum and raccoon, the few predator catches make it all worthwhile.

### The Carnivore Corridor

The fisher was deliberately reintroduced to upstate New York and western Pennsylvania, but New Jersey never took that step. The fisher made it here on its own. Despite intense development in the northeastern United States, a largely intact band of rugged habitat stretches down from the Adirondacks to the Shawangunks and Catskills in New York, and from there to New Jersey's Kittatinny Ridge and Highlands, and on to the Poconos of Pennsylvania. For Kontos, this tri-state carnivore corridor is just a start. He envisions a continental-scale corridor connecting America's wild areas along mountain ranges like the Alleghenies and the Appalachians.

The functionality of this wildlife corridor was aptly demonstrated in the late 1980s and early 1990s. After New York State released 80 lynx in the Adirondack Mountains, one made it all the way to New Jersey—200 miles south—even though logic dictated its best habitat would be in the opposite direction. Another lynx was found 485 miles away eight months after its release. Highways and development may present significant obstacles, but good-sized mammals can clearly cover great distances.

Although the lynx in New Jersey was something of a fluke, another wildcat is here to stay. Through the 1970s, New Jersey Fish and Wildlife researchers thought the bobcat was extirpated—or completely removed—from the state. So they released 24 bobcats, originally caught in the Maine interior wilderness, in undeveloped areas of Warren and Passaic counties. Each cat was tagged and outfitted with a radio collar. Soon after the release, a bobcat was found as roadkill, but it had no tag or collar. Bobcats, it turned out, had been hanging on in New Jersey after all.

Biologist Mick Valent has worked with endangered species like the bobcat for New Jersey Fish and Wildlife for more than twenty-five years. During the past decade, he has live-trapped bobcats to monitor their health and fit them with tracking collars. Reports of bobcats began increasing in the 1990s, says Valent, but tracking radio-collared individuals proved difficult with such a far-ranging animal, which typically prefers to travel far from roads. Once satellite tracking became technologically feasible, Valent had an easier way to follow bobcat movements.

"Bobcats have such large home ranges, males ranging twenty-five miles, and females less," says Valent. "Highways act as barriers, but just based on the number of roadkills, it seems clear that their population is increasing. Their best habitat is a line from Route 80 north—though mainly in the more rural habitat until you get east around Fairfield."

In addition to satellite tracking, Fish and Wildlife researchers now use dogs trained to detect and locate bobcat scat. They also plan to conduct a genetic study with other states to better understand the bobcats that launched this recent expansion. Were they the reintroduced cats from Maine? Or did cats from New York and Pennsylvania move back into New Jersey on their own?

## Feline Phantom

Valent wants to study the Pine Barrens as well, where reports of bobcats continue despite a much weaker prey base. Such sightings, though not always reliable, still generate a thrill. After all, bobcats are typically as wild and secretive as they come. A bobcat could be just off the trail, and you would never know it. Even the biologists who actually track and satellite-collar bobcats consider them out of reach.

"I see bobcats in a trap or other captures, but I tell people I still have never seen a bobcat in the wild," says Valent. "One guy was hiking the Appalachian Trail, looked to the left and there was a bobcat on a fallen log, stretching its back like a housecat. He stood there taking photos from thirty feet away, and it happened to be one of the animals we collared. I think they're really magnificent animals."

Every so often, a biologist can get lucky.

MacKenzie Hall of the Conserve Wildlife Foundation of New Jersey does fieldwork on endangered species from bats to grassland birds. Though she started out tracking bobcats, her most memorable experience came while looking for something completely unrelated.

"I was tracking rattlesnakes, poised up on a knoll covered in mountain laurel, when I saw something in the distance," says Hall. "All of a sudden it became clear it was a bobcat, and when it got fifty, forty, thirty feet away I saw it had a fresh kill in its mouth—a rabbit. It just looked at me and changed its course ever so slightly. It didn't stop suddenly or run away. When you encounter a wildcat in a place like New Jersey, it really is a symbol of the wilderness."

# High Point's Call of the Wild

# 3

There was about him a suggestion of lurking ferocity, as though the Wild still lingered in him and the wolf in him merely slept.

—Jack London, *White Fang*

For the thrill of riding a dogsled through a winter wonderland, you can read a Jack London novel like *White Fang* or *The Call of the Wild*. In those pages, you can let your imagination carry you to the far-off wilderness tundra and taiga of Alaska and the Yukon Territory.

Another option awaits much closer to home. You need freshly fallen snow, at just the right depth and snowpack, on the trails at New Jersey's tallest peak. Under the right conditions, you, too, can trek into the backcountry area of High Point State Park. There you will find the New Jersey Sled Dog Club.

Stunning wolflike huskies and malamutes, with their thick winter coats of silver and white and their piercing eyes—one might be gray, the other translucent blue or yellow—yelp and bound in anticipation. Each step resounds with the crisp crunch of snow. The sled dogs are ready to hit the trails.

Yes, there is dogsledding in New Jersey.

"Mush!"

New Jersey is not the Arctic by any stretch of the imagination. Nevertheless, we once shared one of that region's apex predators: the wolf. At least we did until the arrival of European settlers started the clock ticking on wolves in New Jersey.

"New Jersey has a long history of exterminating predators dating back to 1675, when the first wildlife regulation in the colony allowed for the payment of 20 shillings for a wolf's head," says carnivore expert Charlie Kontos. "As forests were cleared for agriculture and as hunting and trapping occurred without restriction, many top predators such as cougars, wolves, bobcats, and fishers were extirpated."

Over time, wolves were wiped out from all but a handful of states, allowing settlers to feel safe from the feared nursery rhyme villain. Once the wolf was gone, though, its sinister reputation began to yield to a more romantic totem of wilderness lost. Generations of Americans would now have to live with no memory of the wild howls of wolf packs.

Surprisingly, New Jerseyans today can still hear that wild symphony—at the Lakota Wolf Preserve in Columbia, near the Delaware Water Gap. Four different wolf packs run free, each within its own fenced territory. Their stunning howls greet visitors like a timeless echo of primal life on earth. Years after my last visit, I can still hear those howls in my mind. Lakota Wolf, relocated to New Jersey from Colorado, is home to three different subspecies of gray wolves. Timber wolves, which are mostly brown and black, once roamed New Jersey's forests; the gray tundra wolves and pure white arctic wolves are found only in the far north. If the howls are the wolves' insignia, their behavior also opens eyes for Jim Stein, one of the co-owners of Lakota Wolf.

"They have a really close family unit, they get along well and take care of each other. We've raised them since they were puppies, and we're accepted as part of the pack. They'll come up like they do with higher-ranking members and lick at your face. We can pet some of them, but we don't roughhouse with them like you do with dogs.

"They're still wolves."

### High Point Iditarod

The wolf's descendents live on in the German shepherd barking in your neighbor's backyard, the bulldog drooling on your living room floor, and the chihuahua in a purse on Rodeo Drive in Beverly Hills. Much more fittingly, its living wild spirit still haunts the packed trails of High Point State Park.

On a bone-chilling January afternoon, I join Kathy Murarik of the New Jersey Sled Dog Club and three teams of dogsledders as they launch purebred Siberian huskies, Alaskan malamutes, and mixed-breed Alaskan huskies into the snowy powder of High Point. Within seconds of being hitched to the sled, the dogs take off down the white-packed trails in a timeless scene out of Eskimo dreams. The howls of the huskies echo through the frozen forest like a true call of the wild. The native Inuits of Alaska, northern Canada, and Greenland have relied on sled dogs to travel across the frozen north for more than a thousand years—and many still do to this day.

"The dogs are bred for this—the instinct is in their blood," says Patty Bryce, who is here with her team of Alaskan malamutes.

I went dogsledding once before, in the winter wonderland of Mont St. Laurent northeast of Quebec City. That trip ranked among the most magical experiences of my life, guiding sled dogs along a winding forest trail on a thick layer of snow beneath white-capped mountains. My sled spilled at one curve, tossing me—thankfully—into the natural cushion of a soft snowbank, averting the blunt impact of the countless spruce trees all around. Years later, I am pleasantly surprised that the trails of High Point State Park in New Jersey provide a comparable experience.

For some of the racers, this is no time for a winter daydream. Murarik is out on the trails with her husband and son two or three days a week when the conditions are right. Their Alaskan huskies are well trained and built for speed.

"Alaskan huskies are a mix of Siberian huskies bred with any of the faster dogs, such as German shorthaired pointers, English pointers, greyhounds, or any hound dog," says Murarik. "Their top speed is twenty-two miles per hour, whereas Siberian huskies can run up to fourteen or fifteen miles per hour."

The Iditarod, of course, is the gold standard for dogsledding. That 1,150-mile, two-week Alaskan trek takes its mushers from Anchorage to the frozen arctic tundra of the Yukon River.

"It would actually be like hooking up our dog team here and driving to Orlando and going to Disney World," says Murarik.

Only with dogsledding, the rides are real. Still, the sport requires patience in a place as far south as New Jersey. A mother-daughter team is out here on this frigid winter day for the first time in six years. It is an outdoor love that is passed down through the generations—not only for the sled drivers, but for the dogs as well.

"We started when we got our first Siberian, named Kapuga. Now her granddaughter's on the team," says Cindy Geertsema, whose daughter Jeanette is riding the sled today. "We've been in love with the breed since she was a child."

"Mush!"

David Wheeler

**Dogsledder Jeanette Lamphere readies her huskies for a run along a snow-packed High Point State Park trail.**

## The Ice Storm

Unfortunately, the years that can pass between sled rides are a testament to the warming climate over the past few decades, which has brought less and less snow to New Jersey. This winter is shaping up as a healthy exception, with plenty of big snowfalls to keep the runs active. Although some professional racers use wheeled dogsleds to practice without the snow— the flat sand roads of the Pine Barrens make for ideal racing runs—recreational dogsledders often wait for the real thing. I can understand why.

Freshly fallen snow has transformed the High Point backcountry into an enchanted land that seems nothing like New Jersey. Snowmobilers, cross-country skiers, snowshoers, and winter hikers are all out enjoying the untouched winter snows. Living up to its name by rising up more than 1,600 feet above sea level, High Point is the tallest peak in our coastal state. This mountain also receives more snow than anywhere else in the New York metropolitan area.

I experience this bounty firsthand on another winter visit. Nearby areas received only a cold rain, but I arrive at the park to find an other-worldly crystal ice forest. Walking along the Appalachian Trail on this day

Bill Wheeler

**David Wheeler explores the Appalachian Trail through High Point State Park after an ice storm encases it in a tomb of ice.**

is like entering an enchanted Norse Valhalla, with everything from entire trees to the smallest red berries enclosed in a clear tomb of ice. I carefully step across an alpine bog, my boots denting the ice layer atop the water. Home to the northernmost bog in New Jersey, High Point holds many plant species more typically found in the northerly climes of New England. With ice covering all of the mountain ridge today, it feels more like Maine than New Jersey. I can only imagine what the wildlife make of it. Judging from the songbirds already moving from tree to tree, they will be just fine.

### Blood of the Wolf

Stepping along the ice, I recall an anecdote about an incident in New England. Coyotes had tried to force a white-tailed deer out onto a frozen lake, where other coyotes were waiting. If that sounds a lot like a pack of wolves, there is good reason. Beyond the dogsled runs of High Point and the enclosures of Lakota, the wolf—at least its genes and its untamed spirit—is alive in the wilds of the Northeast. After the wolf was eradicated from eastern forests, the coyote stepped in to fill the niche. Coyotes have remarkably expanded their range from their stronghold in the American West to occupy every state in the continental United States. In New Jersey, coyotes have reached all twenty-one counties, largely over the past two decades. The eastern coyote, however, is significantly larger than its western counterpart and more likely to form packs.

Massachusetts-based researcher Jon Way has studied the eastern coyote for more than a decade, and he now calls this special animal a coywolf. As they expanded eastward, coyotes moved through the Great Lakes states and southeastern Canada, where they bred with wolves.

"Their rate of colonization is indeed incredible, because their habitat is basically everywhere. They can survive like a coyote does or eat deer like a wolf. That hybridization is really a perfect fit for this environment over the last fifty years," says Way.

Without predation from wolves and cougars for the past century, the populations of white-tailed deer and cottontail rabbits exploded across the forests and suburbs of the Northeast. For a large animal like the eastern coyote—which can eat anything from berries and mice up to white-tailed deer—the wilder places of New Jersey and the Northeast offer a virtual smorgasbord of prey options, with little competition in sight.

Charlie Kontos finds eastern coyotes showing up more often in the images taken from his motion cameras in northwestern New Jersey.

"Much of their success stems from coyotes being better suited for edge habitats and more tolerant of human disturbance than wolves, which were eliminated from New Jersey over 100 years ago. Coyotes may now be serving a crucial role in our ecosystem once performed by wolves by preying upon sick or injured deer and reducing the number of detrimental rodents."

Of course, predators must overcome those sinister reputations rooted in folklore that crossed the Atlantic Ocean with the colonial settlers. Ranchers and settlers shot, trapped, and poisoned the coyotes— denigrated as dangerous vermin—for centuries. Even today, the coyote is certainly capable of snacking on a small pet left outside overnight. Clearly, families living next to undeveloped areas shouldn't let young children play outside unattended. Still, rather than villainizing the opportunistic coyote, Jon Way urges a little perspective and common sense.

"We should just do our part to avoid interactions, like keeping dogs leashed and cats inside. If you're scared of a coyote in an outdoors area, then you should be petrified of your drive home—it's hundreds of thousands of times more dangerous. The level of danger is statistically laughably low, if it wasn't for those fears."

Those fears, associated with many New Jersey carnivores, are diffi-cult to shake. Prior to European settlers, the coyote enjoyed a quite dif-ferent reputation in North America.

"Their howls have echoed throughout the hills since time immemo-rial," says Kontos. "Native Americans referred to them as 'the trickster' and believed that if all other animals were eliminated, coyotes would be the last ones left."

It wouldn't be the first time Native Americans proved more adept than the European settlers at reading the tarot cards of nature.

# The Mountain Kingdom 4
# of Rattlesnakes

There was painted a Rattle-Snake, with this modest motto under it, "Don't tread on me." . . . [The rattlesnake] never begins an attack, nor, when once engaged, ever surrenders: She is therefore an emblem of magnanimity and true courage.          —Benjamin Franklin

Deep in the forest, miles from the nearest home or store, I am lying belly to the ground like a serpent. A forked tongue flickers in my direc-tion just a few feet away. Two eyes—vertical slits as exotic as a sphinx—peer out at me from the darkness. The forked tongue flickers again. The snake's rattle is not visible, but its body's rough, ridged scales are un-mistakable. Snapping one last photo, I figure there's no need to press my luck any longer. The venom in one bite from this timber rattlesnake—or either of the other two rattlesnakes under this boulder slab—would be enough to put me in the hospital. Maybe worse.

Kris Schantz, who is tracking these rattlesnakes for New Jersey Fish and Wildlife, confirms it is time to move on and leave the snakes alone. Such caution is not for our own protection. It's for the snakes' sake.

Unlike the cougar and the wolf, one reviled carnivore managed to sur-vive the era of hunting, trapping, and forest clearing. This predator does not endear itself to humans with the seeming cuddliness of the black bear and its cubs or the majestic grace of our top avian carnivores, such as the peregrine falcon. This creature, moreover, has a bad reputation to contend with: it must overcome its association with Satan in mankind's fall from grace in the Garden of Eden. And if the sinister reputation of the snake isn't enough, the timber rattlesnake and the copperhead are feared as the only venomous snakes in the most densely populated state in the Union. No matter how much they try to lie low, they still carry a poisonous bite that can serious hurt or potentially even kill the poacher or overly aggressive collector. Such dark myths and stigmas are a lot to overcome, particularly for the rattlesnake, whose menacing rattle is unique in the animal world.

"Unfortunately, Hollywood movies have done rattlesnakes—all snakes—an injustice," says Schantz. "It's a combination of movies, old wives' tales, myths. But snakes don't chase you down. They don't fly out of trees at you."

Fellow state biologist Dave Golden has seen similar reactions from people in his work with timber rattlesnakes in the Pinelands. "Snakes have been vilified through history. It's hard to get a sympathetic ear for a venomous snake, as you would for, say, a bald eagle."

The rattlesnake and the bald eagle do share one commonality, and it's a luxury that the cougar and the wolf never received. Those predators once had state and federal bounties placed on their heads, but the government now is working to protect the timber rattlesnake. The State of New Jersey issues habitat protections against development wherever the snake is found to be nesting in our most inhospitable terrain, the rocky slopes of our northern mountains.

Such protections are clearly needed, and they show our progress as a society in understanding each animal's role in the greater ecosystem. But bad reputations persist. I have always been fascinated by snakes, although I recognize the paralyzing fear they can instill in others. One popular New Jersey nature blog even declines to run photographs of snakes on its home page, so as not to freak out ophidiophobics, that is, people afraid of snakes.

So how did the timber rattlesnake come to be protected in a state where most people would react with bemusement or outright mockery if you told them rattlesnakes even live here? I wanted to find out how exactly we formed the union of the snake and the state.

## Trail of the Rattlesnake

My hike up a Highlands mountain with Schantz and with Gretchen Fowles of Conserve Wildlife Foundation has scarcely begun when we encounter beguiling wildlife. Before Schantz can even hold aloft a radio

State wildlife biologist Kris Schantz radio-tracks a timber rattlesnake through a rugged Highlands mountain forest.

David Wheeler

transmitter, we see three red-spotted newts in their eft stage, a juvenile phase in which they live on land prior to becoming aquatic adults. These newts practically glow bright orange, their red spots bordered in black, as they crawl over the mossy green tussocks along the trail. They are new to me, but seeing a few newts on a trail is no big deal for Schantz.

"After a rain, the forest floor is crawling with them. You really have to watch your step."

The trail ascends higher. Then Schantz and Fowles stop short and silently point to our left. An adult black bear and a younger one scramble across a mountain ridge clearing. I get just a brief glimpse through the trees. I can already picture my dad's excitement at hearing about my sighting and can imagine a renewed urgency for his own bear encounter. But today we're not climbing a mountain for bears or red-spotted newts. We're hot on the trail of a timber rattlesnake.

And It can be quite a trail. Timber rattlesnakes can travel up to five miles in their meandering journeys over the course of a year, which is more impressive when you realize they often end up back in the very same den as the previous year. As a result, a new condominium development in the wrong place can force a rattlesnake to waste its resources unnecessarily. Schantz notes that the snakes form such strong attachments to foraging grounds, shedding sites, and dens that they can become disoriented if those areas are destroyed. And a disoriented rattler is quite often the snake that enters a new backyard freshly carved out of the rugged terrain of north Jersey. Teams of state volunteers are on call to help with such encounters. The Venomous Snake Response Team gets hundreds of calls each year, but, Schantz says, "99.999 percent of all calls are for snakes that aren't venomous."

At times like that, it would be revealing for the public to get a glimpse of the real animals, which can reach six feet in length and can be either tan-and-black banded or an especially fearsome silver-and-black—like old Oakland Raiders of the reptile world. Not long after she started tracking rattlesnakes, Schantz had a particular snake—Male #5—that would casually slither over her boots and explore the contents of her backpack lying on the ground. Once satisfied, he would meander back to the forest to continue hunting.

On another instance, Schantz was tracking rattlesnakes with MacKenzie Hall of Conserve Wildlife. Hall was tracking a snake when Schantz asked why she was getting so close. Hall, still a healthy distance away from her tracking snake, was puzzled by Schantz's question. Then she realized Schantz was looking in a different direction—at Hall's feet.

"I didn't even notice there was another coiled snake right next to my boot, looking in the direction of my ankle, two inches from me," says Hall. "It still didn't strike at me. They're very docile, reclusive animals, whose only cares in the world are getting an occasional meal and catching some sun."

## Chasing a Specter

Not too far from Wawayanda Mountain, on a previous hike, I climbed up a steep, rocky slope to a peak from which I could see the trail's entire descent down to the stream—and on the other side of the stream, the trail's full ascent to the next peak. The habitat was perfect for snakes, offering boulders at each step, jagged slivers of rock etched into ridges, and overhanging rock slabs with each boulder. Huge rectangular outcroppings ran in parallel rows across the mountaintop. I climbed and jumped from one slab to the next, going hundreds of yards along the mountain ridge without touching the ground, all the while looking eye-level at vultures riding the wind thermals. Stunted pines and gnarled black cherry trees grew uncertainly out of the gaps between the boulders, and mosses and lichens spattered each slab like a postmodern canvas.

With each step, I expected to see the flicker of a tail or a movement in the brush from a snake seeking cover. More than once, I could hear leaves or scrub branches rustling in a thicket below my feet. I checked closely for the source, thinking it had to be a timber rattlesnake. But I never did see one.

I have far better odds on this day, however, because Schantz and Fowles are using radio telemetry to follow a male rattlesnake. Even so, as they warn me at the hike's outset, it might be a long day. And you are never certain to find the snake. It could be too far from a road, or the signal could turn intermittent because the surrounding mountains disrupt it. Rattlesnake tracking offers no guarantees.

As we hike, we talk about copperheads, New Jersey's only other venomous snake. Found primarily in northern New Jersey, reaching as far south as Bridgewater, copperheads use the same habitat as rattlesnakes and even share denning and basking areas. Though many experts believe their numbers are declining, the copperhead is listed only as a "Special Concern" species in New Jersey, unlike the endangered timber rattlesnake. We simply do not have enough data to know for sure.

The copperhead is strikingly attractive: the chestnut color of its head gives way to alternating red and dark hourglass-shaped bands. Like the rattlesnake, the copperhead is a pit viper, named for the heat-sensing pits on its face. Hall, for one, always had the copperhead high on her wish list of encounters. She had no luck—until one summer day while tracking rattlesnakes in a limestone forest near Johnsonsburg.

"I always wanted to see a copperhead. They seemed so much more secretive, spending more time underground and hidden in logs. Finally, a couple summers ago, I encountered one basking. In mid-step I looked down and saw it. I had tears in my eyes for like three minutes, just staring at it like it was the Holy Grail."

### An Aesop's Fable

As Schantz, Fowles, and I continue through verdant slopes of blueberry and huckleberry, the radio beeps come more frequently. We have reached the source of the sounds: a large flat boulder. Schantz lies down and peers under it from one side, exploring nearby boulders to ascertain the source.

"There he is." I am just making out the snake's outline, six inches from the edge of the boulder, when Schantz notices something else.

"There's two. There's three!"

Three timber rattlesnakes—wow! The snakes are within striking distance when I lie down to snap some photos. The front snake has a bad left eye—and Schantz's guess as to the cause is startling.

"Perhaps a mouse nibbled on it while the snake was hibernating," she surmises. A fearsome rattlesnake mocked by a little mouse? It sounds like an Aesop's fable.

Otherwise, the snakes appear healthy. This big shelter rock offers perfect habitat by creating a microclimate—absorbing the sunlight, then giving off heat underneath into the night. Snakes particularly benefit from a crevice that extends deeply into the ground; they can spend the evening further removed from the mountain chill of the open air.

The rattlesnake peeks out a bit once we give him some space, but retreats rather quickly. After awhile it becomes clear that the rattlers are not going to leave the shelter this afternoon—the clouds keep the temperature too cool to make a foray worthwhile. The snakes go back under the rock they crawled out from, so to speak.

"When people ask why snakes need to be protected, I always resort to the old-fashioned food pyramid, with snakes near the bottom," says Schantz. "They eat things, and many more animals eat them. If you start pulling out pieces, the pyramid might stay intact for some time, but then it can start to crumble. Our children and grandchildren will see the impacts, because we're all interconnected in the natural system."

# Part Two

## The Urban Northeast

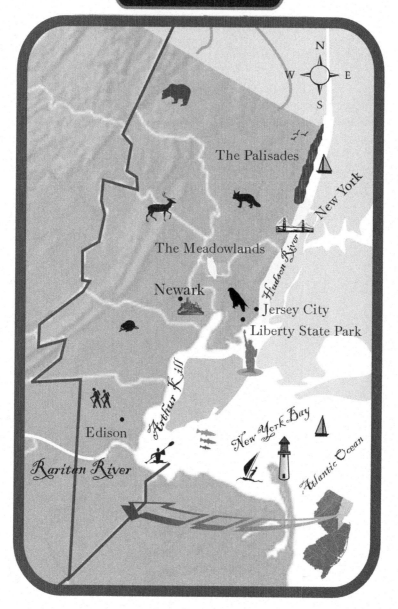

# Volcanic Cliffs over the Big Apple

# 5

This is a very rugged area, with steep climbs and nor'easters coming right off the river. It's not for the faint of heart.

—Nancy Slowik, Greenbrook Sanctuary

Imagine a place where towering columns of volcanic rock drop sheer into a mighty river and where a 200-pound, sharklike prehistoric fish migrates past.

A place where you climb amid moss-covered stone ruins, careful to avoid reaching into a crevice that is shelter to a poisonous snake.

A place where waterfalls cascade past mountain switchback roads and where a rockslide occasionally carries off an entire section of the roadway.

A place where a hike can entail stepping across chasms from boulder to boulder, with nothing to guard you from a tumbling plummet to the rocky coast below.

Now suppose I told you that this fantastic place is located just across the Hudson River from New York City and its 8.3 million residents. The Palisades are all you can imagine, and then some.

As the most dramatic wilderness in the metropolitan area, Palisades Interstate Park encompasses more than 100,000 acres of cliffs and forest and rocky riverfront shore. More than 300,000 cars each day cross the park over the George Washington Bridge—the busiest bridge in the world—yet many drivers and passengers miss the Palisades' forty-plus miles of Yosemite-like jagged cliff line.

"So many people tell me, 'I've lived here for thirty years and I never knew this was here,'" says Christina Fehre, the Palisades trail crew supervisor.

For Fehre, such awareness was never an issue. She grew up hiking the Palisades with her dad and was volunteering here by age fourteen. Now Fehre works here full-time and leads public nature tours.

"It sometimes feels like the Palisades are New Jersey's saving grace, with its seeming remoteness in the city atmosphere," says Fehre. "Just across the river is the city, and next to here, towns are turning into cities—but in the Palisades, we have this huge natural area."

Wildlife certainly appreciates it. Fehre sees foxes regularly with their cubs in tow and sometimes encounters coyotes near her office early in the morning. Bobcat and bear are reported every few years, although at only a half mile across at its widest point, the park lacks enough territory to maintain such predators on a regular basis. Atop the cliffs, raptors can be seen riding the thermals over the Hudson. State Line—the border between New Jersey and New York—is a popular birding hotspot for hawk watches.

Down along the Palisades coast, a harbor seal spent a recent winter at Ross Dock, enjoying the shelter provided by a public boat basin. Striped bass, blue crabs, and mussels are more frequent visitors. And the aforementioned Atlantic sturgeon—a primitive, toothless behemoth that evolved during the reign of the dinosaurs—grows up to eight feet long. When this armor-plated fish visits, however, it is not always in the best of shape.

"Sturgeon wash up, and they stink to high heaven," says Fehre. "They're almost Jurassic."

### Magma Rising Outside Manhattan

I arrive on a late autumn morning after a moonless night. The tide is responding with fervor. The Hudson River has risen up over the sea wall of the Shore Trail, leaving a jagged hopscotch wall of rocks jutting out of the river. There is typically a six-foot tidal difference at this point on the Hudson, a gentle reminder that the Palisades operate according to long-established natural laws easy to forget in the hustle and bustle of the metropolis.

The Palisades are the result of that strangest of New Jersey events— a massive volcano. Molten rock, or magma, was released from deep in the earth as a fiery underground river. The magma never reached the surface, which was then a vast seabed. Instead, it cooled over thousands of years to become diabase, the rock of the Palisades cliffs.

"The softer rock of sandstone and shale washed away, leaving the edge of the Palisades sill, a row of upright cliffs," says Eric Nelsen, the park's history interpreter for more than a decade. "It looked to those in the seventeenth century like a palisades fence, a kind of fort stockade." Hence the name.

The results of that long-ago volcanic activity can still be seen when beachcombing. Visitors on Fehre's beach tours often find volcanic rock and volcanic ash in the sand along the shorefront boulders. On the eastern North American coastline, you would have to go as far north as Maine to find such a rocky coast along a tidal waterway.

The history of the Palisades has always been intertwined with the Hudson River. The Hudson provided a major trading route for Algonquin Indians, fur traders, and settlers, yet the sheer physical barrier posed by the Palisades sheltered the inland area that is now Bergen County.

"It left the area a generation behind—settled not from the Hudson but through the back door of the Hackensack and Passaic rivers," says Nelsen.

## Victorian Views

A century after European settlement, quarries along the Palisades loaded boats with talus—rock naturally dislodged from the cliffs and piled up at the bottom—to build seaports in Manhattan and Brooklyn. When the talus ran out, the quarry owners began blasting the cliffs with dynamite. Concerned citizens on both sides of the Hudson, wishing to preserve the perfect postcard views, banded together to close the quarries. One such campaign, by the New Jersey State Federation of Women's Clubs, helped launch the women's suffragist movement.

New York and New Jersey created a joint commission in 1900, with the New York signing done by then-governor Theodore Roosevelt. One year before he became president of the United States, his conservation-minded activism on the Palisades presaged the remarkable leadership he would show as the founder of the National Park system.

"New Yorkers got the ball rolling, but New Jersey women got the ball and ran with it," says Nelsen. "There was no real precedent for how to preserve it. I can't find anything else like it in 1900—a local movement acquiring big tracts of land to preserve scenery in a crowded, already urban area."

The states, with donations by J. P. Morgan and other wealthy industrialists seeking to preserve their glorious riverfront views, formed Palisades Interstate Park. Another leading philanthropist, John D. Rockefeller Jr., extended the park to its current reach three decades later. When the George Washington Bridge was completed in 1931, Rockefeller grew concerned about the easy access and newfound demand for development across the Hudson from New York City. He purchased the Victorian-era cliff-top mansions along the New Jersey side and donated the land to the park.

There were two conditions: no visible manmade structures (Rockefeller tore down the existing mansions once he purchased them) and the construction of a scenic north-south parkway, with limited access to ensure no further development of the area. Separated from the maze of traffic and stoplights that characterizes the rest of Bergen County and metropolitan New York roadways, the Palisades Interstate Parkway offers a winding, wooded drive for miles on end. Thanks to Rockefeller, that view is still jaw-dropping nearly a century later.

### The Ruins of History

History lives at your fingertips throughout the Palisades, and nowhere more dramatically than at the Undercliff. Fehre brings me to this remote section of the park that feels far removed from everywhere. Terraces of sparse oak forest and rocky clearings are broken up by countless stone walls. From the towering trees atop the cliffs, a raven's jarring call echoes down the mountain slope. This spellbinding, intelligent bird seems more at home in the Rocky Mountains or high in the Adirondacks. Thanks to a certain Edgar Allan Poe story, the raven conjures a sense of the sinister in many people.

Along the Hudson River shore below, I notice the impressive ruin of an old stone building. During the Great Depression, President Franklin Delano Roosevelt created the Works Progress Administration and Civilian Conservation Corps, putting people to work across America. Workers constructed new park roads and trails in the Palisades, along with bathhouses for the thousands who enjoyed the manmade bathing beaches. All that remains of one of those bathhouses is this stone foundation—its walls still intact, a stately stone stairway leading to the ghost of a second floor that must have crumbled decades ago. These ruins and the departed raven have me expecting Vincent Price to appear at any moment, costumed in gothic splendor.

The nimble Fehre climbs down the talus slope to a flimsy plywood board connecting the cliff with the top of the stone foundation walls. I haltingly follow. As I stand atop a foot-wide moss-covered wall, she pulls herself through a foundation window and jumps a few feet down. I place my hiking boots in footholds to pull myself down. Then Fehre reminds me about the copperheads that bask on the rocks and shelter in the gaps between boulders.

The stonework holds up remarkably well after nearly a century. Exploring this foundation, I feel as if I've been transported to medieval ruins in the Scottish countryside—only with a view of the Hudson River under the mighty archway and through the stone windows. The scene is contradictory, especially with the towering mountainside behind us. It's another uniquely Palisades moment.

Sixty years past its heyday, the old bathhouse is visited by only a few curious hikers, though Fehre mentions a more recent use: a group prac-

ticing tai chi within the foundation walls. The ruins offer the perfect setting for such a spiritual and physical exploration.

Up on the cliffs, another kind of study is taking place.

## The Living Lab of Greenbrook Sanctuary

Most nature destinations hold little hard data about all of the species
actually living and breeding there, their numbers, and their historical
trends. Rare bird sightings might draw attention to a single species, but
otherwise visitors have little more than a vague idea of what lives there.
In the Palisades, however, anecdotes give way to very real knowledge.

"Greenbrook Sanctuary is probably the most studied 165-acre parcel
of land in northern New Jersey over the last sixty years," says Nancy
Slowik, the sanctuary's director and chief naturalist.

Stretching a mile long by a half mile wide, Greenbrook is the jewel
of the Palisades. Five streams course through Greenbrook's rugged
forests, and waterfalls plummet down its sheer slopes to the Hudson
below. A sphagnum bog offers a nursery for amphibians, with species
like spotted salamanders and wood frogs breeding here. Eels, freshwater
sponges, frogs, and snakes thrive along a stream twisting through skunk
cabbage wetlands, boulders, and moss-covered tree roots. Greenbrook
Sanctuary is a living, breathing museum of natural history. In fact, the
American Museum of Natural History—you know, the world-famous
museum near Manhattan's Central Park with the whale hanging above
the reception desk and Ben Stiller patrolling the halls at night—is one of
the research centers that has been studying Greenbrook for the past sixty
years.

Slowik, who previously worked for New York City Parks, began
working at Greenbrook twenty years ago. It has been a nonstop learning
experience. Mammal studies every decade. Birds on a seasonal basis. Butterflies. Fungi and mushrooms. Macroinvertebrates and benthic studies.
Trees and shrubs. Biomonitoring. Dragonflies. Reptiles and amphibians.
Ferns.

"You're constantly learning new things, and I love the challenge—it
keeps you fresh," says Slowik. "I started with botany, but I had to learn
birds, then I had to learn reptiles, then amphibians, and so on. You can
never know everything, so you're always adding new knowledge."

The ceaseless learning serves a practical purpose as well. A previous
naturalist discovered the Allegheny woodrat in the Palisades. This endangered rodent once scurried along the Appalachian Mountains from Ten-
nessee to New York. Now the Palisades Park hosts one of the few isolated

populations remaining. For sure, the Allegheny woodrat is the only "rat" we want to protect in the metropolitan area. Fish and Wildlife's Mick Valent studies charismatic wildlife like bobcats, rattlesnakes, and peregrine falcons; but for him, the Allegheny woodrat is equally fascinating. This mammal actually can walk upside down under rocks—a rather necessary adaptation for a species that, in New Jersey, lives only in the Palisades.

"A person who glimpsed one quickly might think it's just a Norway rat," says Valent. "But they have a hairy tail, not a naked tail, and their ears are different as well. I think it's one of the coolest animals I work with."

Most wildlife preserves focus their field surveys on more easily quantifiable classes, such as birds or reptiles. Not so at Greenbrook. Slowik works with the American Museum of Natural History on mammal surveys. Small mammals such as woodrats, field mice, and voles are notoriously difficult to find, count, and study because they spend much of their time underground. Slowik learned one such difficulty firsthand. Opening a trap during one of the studies, she found what appeared to be a dead mouse. While she jotted down a note, the mouse—obviously playing dead—jumped up and leaped out of the cage.

"That was the one that got away," says Slowik. "I'm sure it was a jumping mouse, which hasn't been otherwise documented here. But it got away before I could see for sure."

Other places have fish tales. Greenbrook Sanctuary has "jumping mouse" tales.

### Lost Brook Falls

On a December hike, Slowik leads me along the trails closest to the visitor center. We pass a quartet of playful deer and trees identified with plaques, such as black huckleberry and sugar maple. Then we reach the cliffs. Land ends, suddenly, as if geological time takes over. The cliff drops off, sheer and straight away, to a talus slope below on the edge of the Hudson. Tankers and barges power down the river, one after another in an orderly assembly line from as far upstream as the Tappan Zee Bridge.

Lost Brook Falls, the southernmost waterfall in the Palisades—so named because it "gets lost" in the rocks before entering the river—plummets through the ravine beneath us. The Green Brook drains the sanctuary and sends torrents of water tumbling down the cliffs to connect with the Hudson below. Green Brook Falls is one of three significant waterfalls in the Palisades, though I count dozens of smaller ones. You rarely go more than a few minutes without another waterfall trickling or gushing down the cliffs.

**The bald eagle is one of many raptors that can be found soaring above the Hudson River along the Palisades.**

Tam Stuart

"Here we are at treetop level, 375 feet above the river," Slowik says. "It's like a canopy walk in the rainforest, where you can see everything at eye level. An osprey carrying a fish, the bald eagle stealing it away. Peregrine falcons nesting, ravens tumbling around in courtship. If you're lucky, under the right conditions, you can even see the fish migration— an amoeba-like shape moving along the Hudson in this unique area of land, sea, and sky."

Hiking further on my own, I hear rustling atop the wooded slope. A herd of inquisitive deer approaches. The leader takes a keen interest in me, walking in my direction with heightened curiosity. The doe stamps the ground with her right front hoof, then with her left. I'm about ready to take the hint—*I get it, this is your territory, I'll be on my way*—when I hear a fainter rustling to my right. I have been still for a while, a part of the scenery. That faint rustling now takes the orangish-red form of a red fox trotting through the forest no more than seventy-five feet away.

The fox nears the trail I just hiked, crosses it, then trots on toward the cliff tops. Its thick coat is all the more gorgeous for its contrast with the dull browns of the tree trunks and downed leaves all around. The fox sits alongside a fallen tree near the cliff line and grooms itself. Then it trots out of sight. I try to get up to the nearest peak to scan the nearby ravine, but it has moved on for good. Or it's hiding in plain sight, as red fox do.

The last leg of my hike is a rush. I am so thrilled with the fox that I nearly skip the striking views of New York City across the Hudson. Slowik reacts with wide-eyed enthusiasm as I recount my red fox encounter.

Then I remember that within moments of my arrival at Greenbrook, Slowik had mentioned seeing a gray fox for the first time.

"It was early morning October 25, on Shoreline Trail, and I was leading a small group looking at the ducks and waterfowl . . . ," she had begun.

Though nearly two months had passed, she could recall the exact date. It's a date worth remembering, partly because, unlike the common red fox, the gray fox is seldom encountered anywhere in New Jersey. Hunters can spend decades without ever seeing this widely dispersed but reclusive creature. But the date of the sighting means even more at Greenbrook. Here, deep knowledge of nature's daily routine goes back sixty years. The gray fox is yet another memorable diary entry in the long and fantastic life of Greenbrook Sanctuary. The outdoor nature lab for the American Museum of Natural History is in good hands here in Bergen County.

# Urban Jungle on the Hudson

# 6

We tend to side with the prey, but we should cheer for the predator.

—Coastal activist Dery Bennett

Twenty-five miles south of the Palisades, another wild skyscape boasts even more sensational overlooks of the great New York City metropolis. This windswept locale, full of danger and drama, offers the rare visitor a breathtaking bird's-eye view, literally. If the Palisades are a cliff-top wilderness, then this is the upper canopy of the urban jungle.

I am speaking, of course, of the skyscrapers of downtown Jersey City. For it is here, while accompanying fearless New Jersey Fish and Wildlife researchers, that I am dive-bombed by peregrine falcons, the fastest creatures on earth. From this unlikely perch, peregrine falcons hunt smaller birds by diving from the skies at 185 miles per hour. Their huge talons are sharp enough to tear a good-sized chunk of flesh from the scientist who dares to band their chicks.

Kathy Clark and Mick Valent of New Jersey Fish and Wildlife have the scars to prove it. But they wouldn't trade a minute of their adventures. After all, the nationwide recovery of the peregrine falcon is arguably the prototype for wildlife returning against all odds—and thriving—in a neon wilderness that is the most artificial of humanscapes. New Jersey's biologists have led the charge in making this American comeback tale a reality.

## Reality Show

Let's start at the top. The roof of 101 Hudson Street in Jersey City, to be exact, a modern corporate building overlooking the Manhattan skyline. Peregrine falcons have nested here since the year 2000. I join Clark, Valent, and a few lucky others on the once-a-year banding of the newest brood of chicks. With the gracious approval and involvement of Barbara Deen, the building manager for Mack-Cali Realty, our group begins the expedition. We wind through a maze of cargo elevators, steel storage rooms, and maintenance areas, a twisting backroom tour reminiscent of Martin Scorsese's extended camera shot entering through the back kitchen of the fancy Stork Club in *Goodfellas*.

Our glamorous wildlife destination is a storage room near the roof, bordered with huge steam pipes and a janitorial sink glowing under industrial lighting. One device, however, separates 101 Hudson from the dozens of other skyscrapers across the Jersey City corporate skyline: a computer and monitor dedicated to the nesting peregrine falcons. This portal allows thousands of everyday people to watch mom, dad, and three youngsters born just three weeks ago. Launched in 2001, the roof-top camera just on the other side of the thick external walls records the family's daily life—grooming, feeding the chicks, fussing for space in the nestbox—and transmits it live via webcam to viewers worldwide on the state Department of Environmental Protection Web site.

Paul Tarlowe is the man behind the camera. After entering the pass-words, he shows us what is airing right now on computer screens distant and near.

"In May, we get over 500 visitors a day on the live webcam, and over 1,000 visitors a day for the still images. In June, it's nearly 2,000 hits a day, plus stills," says Tarlowe. "I enjoy the birds, don't get me wrong, but I'm not one of those people we refer to as falcoholics."

Falcoholics contribute their own observations about the webcam images on a page called "Nestbox News." A sampling shows how per-sonally involved they become:

At 11:05 AM Mom appeared on ledge near Dad.

I have to admit, my heart jumped into my throat whenever
I saw one of them approach the windows of the tower.
Each time though, they pulled up and flew alongside the
windows/building beautifully.

Some of the falcohol abuse—I couldn't resist—might be taking place in this very building. A large flatscreen monitor airs the webcam reality show downstairs in the 101 Hudson lobby, but that isn't enough for at least one company working here.

"We had a new tenant set up plasma screens throughout their office to watch the stock market," Deen recounts with a smile. "I went in there once and they had the falcon webcam up on the big screen."

From Jersey City, reporting live, it's "Real World Jersey City"—all peregrine nestbox news, all the time.

### Attacked!

On the other side of the wall, like guests in a television green room, three young peregrine falcons sit in anticipation of their next meal of pigeon or sparrow. Business comes first. Like all great wildlife explorers, we first drop to our hands and knees to crawl along the industrial floor under a three-foot wide steam pipe. I feel a weird flashback to cave exploring until the bright flash of open sky greets us. Mick Valent opens the door to a rooftop view of the Hudson River and the Manhattan skyline close enough to touch. Even in the light fog of this June morning, the view is awe-inspiring. The natural light crashes like a wave through the roof door.

Once we're outside, the moment to savor that penthouse view never arrives. An angry peregrine falcon parent immediately swoops in just a few feet above our heads. The falcon shrieks its sharp warning calls, demanding that we leave the area right now. It arcs upward in a graceful figure eight, ascending like a roller coaster going up the incline before its accelerating freefall back down toward our scalps. The other parent stalks the stone parapets like a living, breathing gargoyle, its fearsome-looking beak highlighted against the buildings in the distance. Hunched forward, marching along menacingly with his wings at his side, the father falcon seems like a raptor version of a villainous general in some World War II movie.

Here it comes again—duck!

"Umbrella!"

A volunteer passes it forward as Mick and Kathy break for the nest-box across the roof from the door. Valent, tall and slender with short gray hair and an earring, told the group a few minutes earlier about his past experiences in his quiet, understated way: a scar on his hand, a gash in the side of his face near his eye, both courtesy of peregrine talons. Now I can picture it all too vividly as the next attack comes from above—duck!

For Valent, the air raids are nothing new. He and Clark installed a nestbox on the roof of the Union County Courthouse in Elizabeth. The nestbox had to be located next to the same hatch door from which they access the roof. The fiercely protective mother, "Elizabeth," is legendary among the researchers.

"She could hear us coming up the ladder, and as I opened the hatch, she was waiting," he says. "She came from behind and nailed me right on the hand with her talons. Then she's in the nest with her talons raised. That's the most aggressive bird I've ever seen. We started wearing hard hats, and we even tied ourselves in with some ropes."

I'm starting to feel that I've got the hang of this. Just watch the bird, then duck and cover your head when it starts its next dive-bomb. Simple enough, really. Except suddenly, from the other direction, the other parent attacks. Peregrine falcons share the responsibilities of raising their young, and that includes dive-bombing the rare rooftop intruder. The double-barreled attack from opposing, ever-changing directions is straight out of Sun Tsu's *The Art of War*. It is unnerving to say the least—duck!

Duck *again!*

Soon Mick and Kathy have the three peregrine chicks securely in tow in a covered container and usher us back inside. Industrial lighting and steam pipes never felt so comforting.

## Puff the Magic Falcon

Safely inside, we see another side of this apex predator—the warm and cuddly side. The three peregrine nestlings, three weeks old and the size of robins, are little more than fuzzy white puffs of feathery down, certain to be any child's favorite stuffed animal. Volunteers take turns holding the puffballs, and Clark measures each bird's beak, checks its health, and bands its leg with an identifiable, non-intrusive band. She feeds the birds medicine to prevent trichomoniasis, a disease that affects predators of urban pigeons. Clark wraps the tiny white pill in a morsel of raw chicken, like a parent tricking a toddler into eating vegetables.

Though it kills birds each year, trichomoniasis is child's play compared with the threat that nearly wiped the peregrine falcon off the face of the planet. Forty years ago there were no peregrines east of the Mississippi River. The effects of the insecticide DDT, used for mosquito control, pushed the bird to the edge of extinction. Environmentalist Rachel Carson revealed DDT's effects on America's environment in her seminal 1962 book, *Silent Spring*.

"DDT was so detrimental to birds—not just the bald eagle, but the peregrine falcon, brown pelican, and many other birds at the top of the food chain," says Dr. Len Soucy, who founded New Jersey's Raptor Trust. "From World War II until the 1960s and 1970s, DDT was heavily used in farming and crop-dusting, and the birds' eggs became so thin that it disrupted breeding."

Influenced by Carson's revelations, the federal Environmental Protection Agency banned the use of DDT in the United States in 1972. After being reintroduced to New Jersey later that decade, peregrine falcons have rebounded so strongly that even Hudson County—one of the nation's most densely populated areas—is now a peregrine hotspot.

Twenty active nests are now found across the state. Instead of choosing the sheer cliffs they inhabit elsewhere in the country, New Jersey falcons mostly peer down from bridges and skyscrapers in search of their next meal. Look at a road map of the state's busiest highways and bridges, and it's likely that a peregrine is nesting or perching on one of them at that very moment. The George Washington Bridge and the Route 3 bridge over the Hackensack River in the north. The Newark Bay Bridge and the Bayonne Bridge in the urban centers. The Garden State Parkway's Driscoll Bridge and New Brunswick's Route 1 bridge over the Raritan River. And in the south, two bridges linking New Jersey with Philadelphia: the Betsy Ross, taking Route 90 west from Pennsauken, and the Walt Whitman, carrying Interstate 76 from Gloucester City to meet the Pennsylvania Turnpike. All yield regular sightings of peregrine falcons.

### A Most Civilized Raptor

Some peregrines nest in style in reputable establishments, such as the penthouse of the Atlantic City Hilton. The Hilton nest is a special one for Clark. Another aggressive peregrine matriarch nested here from 1985 until she finally succumbed to old age in 2001. Like a good casino gambler, the falcon didn't like unwarranted attention. And like any major celebrity, she fought off the paparazzi to protect her kids; when the casino owner invited media to her annual banding, she attacked a photographer. After she died, Clark could finally read her full leg band and learn her story.

"She came from the nest tower at Forsythe refuge, and she was one of the first to fledge from New Jersey nests. She lived in Atlantic City her whole life," says Clark. "She was there through all the changes. It started as the Golden Nugget, then became Bally's Grand, then the Grand, and then the Atlantic City Hilton. She was there for all of it. She had quite a life."

It's no surprise that falcons are partial to the Atlantic City skyline. A buffet of pigeons and coastal birds along the boardwalk and beach is complemented by huge flocks of shorebirds and migrating birds in the vast salt marshes of nearby Edwin B. Forsythe National Wildlife Refuge.

"Peregrines use the taller vantage points to look out over the creeks, wetlands, and marshes," says Scott Barnes, a senior naturalist with the New Jersey Audubon Society. "Peregrines are such strong flyers that they'll actually wear out their prey to the point of exhaustion."

The late naturalist Dery Bennett saw this firsthand. Bennett was walking the beach at Sandy Hook when he saw a pair of peregrine falcons chasing a shorebird over the water.

"One peregrine hit the shorebird at full speed, knocking it down, then a black-backed gull flew out and swallowed the shorebird in one gulp. That's the only time I've actually seen a raptor make a kill. I've seen ospreys dive for fish—but that was the real McCoy. You watch and say, 'That poor bird.' But then you realize the skill it takes. We tend to side with the prey, but we should cheer for the predator."

## A Warrior in Training

Back inside the forty-first floor of 101 Hudson Street in Jersey City, I get a chance to hold a peregrine falcon nestling. Firmly but gently, I cradle the soft and cuddly puffball, amazed to hold an endangered bird of prey that couldn't even be found in New Jersey thirty years ago. But at three weeks old, it already has immense talons, like long yellow scythes that might as well be sheathed in a scabbard. The falcon chick is a mighty warrior in training, like an awkward young teen whose agility hasn't filled out his angular frame. I hold one of these natural miracles for just a few minutes. Soon that same fledgling will be out on the hunt, keeping the Jersey City pigeon population in check with aerial maneuvering unparalleled in the animal world.

For now, the young birds are powerless in the wild. Knowing their vulnerability, Valent and Clark move the nestbox to a safer location. The previous spot was ideal for surveying the water and land below, but bore the brunt of nor'easters and winter storms. Tarlowe holds the umbrella while Valent installs webcam wires for the new rooftop nestbox. Then Valent and Clark return the young chicks to the nestbox, relying on that flimsy umbrella for protection from the air raids of the fastest wild predator on earth. For a few moments, it is raining peregrine falcons. After a twenty-year drought, that's a forecast to treasure.

**David Wheeler holds a young peregrine falcon that will soon grow into the fastest predator on earth.**

Ezra Tarlowe

"That thing hit the umbrella three times. If it had hit Mick's head, it would've been ugly," says Tarlowe.

With the chicks back in their nest, thousands of watchful viewers—in New Jersey and far beyond—cheer at their work stations and home computers.

"What impresses me the most is the widespread appeal. We've gotten e-mails from England, Australia, the Netherlands, California, Florida—people across the country and overseas," says Tarlowe with a laugh. "You just know these people are supposed to be doing work, and they're watching the falcons at their office cubicles."

Cheer for the predator!

# Snowy Owls in the Shadow of Liberty

**7**

The fact that you can provide a Beastie Boys concert and offer these functioning ecosystems in the same place—that's pretty unique in the entire country.

—Naturalist Frank Gallagher

**X** marks the spot. To locate famed pirate hideaway, me hearties, follow ye the treasure map:

> Ye drive around endless jughandles, across concrete overpasses, and through many a stoplight.
>
> Ye enter one of the most crowded, traffic-packed megamalls in northern New Jersey, filled with shoppers, chain restaurants, and high-rise hotels.
>
> Ye pass idling tractor trailers unloading cargo and fool's gold, and ye park along the chain-link fence.
>
> Prepare ye to walk the plank—literally!

No, really, it is a regular Treasure Island. Only instead of pirate's booty, there is a ghost-stumped cedar swamp bounded by a mall and millions of drivers. And instead of a parrot on your shoulder, there are egrets, ducks, and raptors o'erhead. Ahrrrgh!

### Buccaneer Archipelago

The Mill Creek Marsh has the drabbest entrance of any nature preserve in all of New Jersey. Besides the mall, the New Jersey Turnpike zooms past a stone's throw to the east, and housing developments sprawl along the west. Yet as I walk these trails on a chilly winter day, I walk through history—and not the history found only in books. This history I can see with my own eyes today, vividly. This history reveals itself with stump after mottled stump of Atlantic white cedar, rising like an archipelago of islands from the icy Meadowlands waters all around. I have never seen anything like this graveyard of tree stumps.

Early settlers deliberately burned down the forest of Atlantic white cedar and tamarack trees—but not to till the land or to build a town.

They leveled the forest to chase away the pirates. Pirates were hiding out in the Hackensack River's tall, marshy cedar woods back in the late 1700s, lying low between raids on the shipping ports around Newark. The Atchensehaky River, or "River of Many Bends," as the Lenape Indians called it, served as the perfect getaway route and shelter for the region's buccaneers. Without the forest, the pirates lost their hideout.

What was left of the cedar forest died out when the Oradell Dam was constructed seven miles upstream on the Hackensack River in 1823. With no steady, free-flowing fresh water from upstream, salt water took over downstream of the dam. Trees could no longer take root in the brackish soils. Freshwater fish like chain pickerel and small-mouthed bass disappeared as tidal species moved in. Freshwater plants yielded almost entirely to the reed known as phragmites.

The Atlantic cedars were not replaced by a new wave of trees. Instead, they remain as a dramatic graveyard to our colonial past. Walk the planks of the Mill Creek Marsh boardwalk trail today and you will see plenty of ducks, gulls, and muskrats taking shelter in the tidal marsh—but not a single new tree taking root.

### Turnpike Tundra

In summer, a young snowy owl scanned Labrador's endless flats in northern Canada from a pingaluk rise in the tundra dotted with pink arctic willow. He was on the lookout for small rodents like voles or arctic birds such as ptarmigan. A herd of caribou grazed on reindeer moss, and an arctic hare foraged among the liverwort. Spying a movement in the alpine milk vetch along the frozen ground, the snowy owl swooped in and snatched a lemming off the tundra with its razor-sharp talons.

Six months later, it is a bitterly cold morning in January, and I am shivering in Lyndhurst near Giants Stadium. The snowy owl stands in an abandoned lot before me. The owl favors these debris piles and steel stacks, along with the high school baseball field behind me. Though not magically gifted like Hedwig in the Harry Potter film series, snowy owls in the real world are just as mysterious, appearing like visitors from another world—all white, with bright yellow eyes and a powerful beak and talons.

I can see why Snowy thinks of this New Jersey landscape as a January substitute for his typical arctic hunting grounds. I mean, he has Giants Stadium behind him. He has the garish, multicolored entertainment complex known as Xanadu in construction to the immediate north, just across Route 3. The New Jersey Nets' Izod Center sits alongside Xanadu, along with two nearby hotel skyscrapers. Directly to the east—

no more than an Eli Manning Hail Mary pass away—thousands of tractor trailers and commuters motor along the New Jersey Turnpike at seventy-five miles an hour. Beyond that, the Manhattan skyline beckons. It is clearly an arctic hunter's paradise.

Yet Snowy has found this area of towering dirt piles and landfills to be ideal for his daily winter occupation: hunting small rodents and birds. The cottontail rabbit is bountiful here, and no one said rats don't serve a purpose. Here in the Meadowlands, the animals that thrive on human development offer a tasty buffet for the snowy owl.

## Like a Ptarmigan

When I arrive, the owl hasn't moved for two hours, as I learn from a dedicated birder who keeps vigil with a generously furred hood over his head and mittens gripping a pair of binoculars. Snowy is just a thick, white oval far away, standing on the ground in front of a curb between two large piles of concrete rubble.

Another birder, Bill Lynch, notes that patience is a requirement for watching snowy owls: "The only movement I saw in three hours was the bird hopping behind the steel beam about 200 yards away, further obstructing the views of a few very cold birders. Despite the weather and the distance between the bird and myself, it really felt magical seeing an arctic specialist like the snowy owl only forty-five minutes north of where I grew up. This perfect hunting machine, accustomed to the frozen tundra of the north, was sitting in the middle of the Meadowlands."

Michael Britt grew up exploring the wildlife of the Hudson County region, observing everything from kestrels to opossum as a kid in Bayonne. It's doubtful anyone knows the wildlife of this urban and industrial area better. Britt first saw a snowy owl in Jersey City a few years back, and since then he has followed their near-annual winter visits to the state. The key factor, according to Britt, is the barren ground that covers much of the Meadowlands.

"We primarily had phragmites in the marshes and mugwort in the upland area until the failed Encap development project cleared out hundreds of acres, leaving just dirt fields," says Britt. "Now it's an ephemeral state of low vegetation, open ground, and piles of rubble. What does that remind snowy owls of? Tundra."

The low growth is perfect for the huge number of cottontail rabbits, as well as meadow voles and the booming population of ring-necked pheasant. And those prey species are just right for snowy owls. As Britt says, "A pheasant is just a ptarmigan to a snowy owl."

## Arctic Meadowlands

Michael Newhouse, the naturalist for the New Jersey Meadowlands Commission, believes the Meadowlands habitat and prey are so ideally suited for this owl that we may be seeing only the tip of the snowy iceberg.

"We had two snowy owls here all winter—they were found the week before Christmas and stayed into winter. There's actually so much open space that I think a lot of snowy owls show up here and we don't see them. And the snowy owls don't see humans as a potential threat because they don't even see humans where they breed in the high Arctic."

Fortunately for enthusiasts like me who happen to visit on the snowy owl's day of rest, the winter skies are filled with raptors. Northern harriers course low over the same plot of land where the snowy owl is hiding near a pile of rubble. The beautiful marsh hawks, as the harriers are known, also survey the baseball field across the street. A red-tailed hawk perches atop the highest rubble pile for a bit, and two pairs of rough-legged hawks make their way across this raptor Grand Central Station, alternating between the field and a nearby pole. An American kestrel leaves an orange traffic cone on the rubble field for a perch atop the same telephone pole occupied by a herring gull. The sight of the massive gull dwarfing the tiny kestrel on this single telephone pole sends the huddling group of birders into a photographing frenzy.

Like the snowy owl, the rough-legged hawk is a winter visitor from the arctic north. Most of the visitors are young male birds, pushed south by competition with the larger females and more mature adult males. Their numbers are all tied to the population booms and busts of the arctic lemmings, which peak and crash over a four-year cycle. The lemming peak causes a strong breeding season among the raptors, and when the lemming numbers then start to dwindle, the younger snowies and rough-legs have to find a new source of food somewhere farther south. Somewhere like the Meadowlands.

Snowy owls are being found with increasing regularity in recent winters up and down the Jersey coast. The expansive flats of Brigantine. The Scottish-themed golf course in Bayonne. The windswept dunes of Sandy Hook. The flat salt marsh of Nummy Island in Cape May. And Liberty State Park in Jersey City.

## Rebirth of Liberty

I hear only the droning hum of crickets as I walk through the untamed meadow. A monarch butterfly alights on a bonset flower, and a tiger swallowtail butterfly flutters across the trail as a black duck flies over-

Melanie Worob

**The Statue of Liberty watches over Liberty State Park, a recovering urban wilderness in the shadow of New York City.**

head. The meadow grasses and wildflowers are an Impressionist painting of serenity. Then the idyll is shattered by the whirring CHOP-CHOP-CHOP of a New York City police helicopter blasting past. I look up and smile at Lady Liberty watching over us in her green robe from just beyond the near shore.

For a moment there, I lost myself. I had forgotten where I was.

A few minutes east of the Meadowlands, another old industrial area is experiencing a renaissance, this one along Jersey City's Hudson riverfront. One of the most popular parks in New Jersey, Liberty State Park is democratically home to families picnicking on its rolling lawns, youths partying to the songs of Radiohead and other bands at the annual All Points West music festivals, and egrets stalking fish in a remnant salt marsh. It all occurs directly under the Statue of Liberty, which rises up over the park's southern end like a guardian. If that is not enough, a look east across the Hudson River brings visitors a picture window view of the lower Manhattan skyline.

The statue has stood since 1886 as a symbol of victory over oppression, and now Liberty has herself an equally symbolic state park. The 1,200-acre Liberty State Park is a living testament to victory over contamination. Known more for its recreation, picnic lawns, and riverfront biking and walking trail, Liberty has grown as a birding destination over the years. More than 300 species of birds have been spotted here. To say that the park is having a natural awakening is almost missing the point. If you're standing nearly anywhere in Liberty State Park, the very earth under your feet didn't even exist a century and a half ago. Most of the ground that makes up the park was brought in as basement fill from New York City construction sites in the mid-1800s, then topped with a layer of cinder and ash.

I join Frank Gallagher, a Division of Parks and Forestry naturalist, along with Greg Remaud of NY/NJ Baykeeper and Melanie Worob of the Edison Wetlands Association, for a tour of this thriving comeback story. Chromium contamination had relegated a six-acre area along the Hudson River—next to the nature center—into an off-limits wasteland. Two million tons of chromium waste from nearby refineries was used as fill for new building construction in Hudson County, leaving nearly 200 chromium sites.

Nothing grew on this Liberty State Park parcel, except for a stand of phragmites emerging from a puddle in the center. Gallagher removed the chromium waste and planted "aggressive" native plants. Two summers later, we can walk through a gorgeous wild meadow ringing a wildlife-filled freshwater pond.

"There was a gigantic snapping turtle in this mud puddle, and we put it into the bay when we started the removal. Two days after the water was coming back in, the snapper was waiting at the silt fencing to get in. He's in there now," says Gallagher. "This is the shining star of ecological restoration. We took what was a human health hazard and biological risk and turned it in to a viable, functional wetland loaded with fish, turtles, five pairs of nesting ducks, and a nesting pair of swans."

The mallards, black ducks, and gadwalls are complemented by a pair of egrets and a skyful of swallows, sparrows, and butterflies. When Gallagher first arrived at Liberty State Park in 1983, he found another sort of wildlife altogether. Getting the lay of the land on his first week on the job, he entered an abandoned tower station, since demolished. Walking up a flight of stairs, he found two wild dogs barking at him on the top landing. The dogs must have been even more spooked than he, because they jumped out a broken second-story window to get away. Through the window, Gallagher watched them run off through a fallow field.

"Now in that same park, I watch a great egret take a fish out of a restored marsh. I've watched red-tailed hawks feed their young in the park interior, and every winter harbor seals are sitting out on the jetty," says Gallagher. "I knew the park as a kid, but even in my professional lifespan here, I see a transformation. The fact that you can provide a Beastie Boys concert and offer these functioning ecosystems in the same place—that's pretty unique in the entire country."

## Butter-and-Eggs

Much of the ongoing recovery has resulted from the work of Gallagher and others. But Liberty State Park also has some singular qualities that amaze even experienced naturalists. Although invasive species thoroughly dominate most damaged sites, Liberty has reached a "dynamic equilibrium," as Gallagher puts it. Both native and invasive plants interact here, offering valuable habitat in a place built on imported fill. One exotic species, the splendidly named butter-and-eggs for its yellow-, orange-, and cream-colored petals, is pollinated by bumblebees and also used by moths and butterflies. Porcelainberry, another exotic plant, offers berries for the birds and mammals—red fox, skunk, opossum, and coyote—found here.

A key mammal missing from Liberty State Park is the white-tailed deer. That is not a bad thing. Trees and plants—native and exotic alike—have a chance to grow without the presence of deer, which would otherwise devour them before they could mature. Liberty State Park may be the one natural area in New Jersey without deer—and it shows in the healthy varieties of vegetation across the park. For a nature photographer like Worob, the opportunity to capture the colorful blooms of a wildflower meadow with a backdrop of the Statue of Liberty is priceless.

As we near the end of the meadow trail, we pass an older gentleman seated on a bench, sketching the wildflowers all around him. On the trails lining either side of this restoration area parents push strollers, men and women speed past on bicycles, and families pose for photographs with Lady Liberty. Gallagher leads us through a gate into the sprawling mid-section of the park, fenced off from the public for the past two decades. Northern harrier have returned to this heart of Liberty, and Gallagher is developing a restored tidal wetlands complex and adjoining public walkway that will connect the inland Liberty Science Center with the Hudson riverfront.

"Yeah—this really feels like downtown Jersey City," says Remaud with a laugh, as we step down into a shaded birch grove, ferns dotting the shady forest floor. Remaud helped lead the public's involvement in insisting that Liberty State Park be naturally restored, rather than just capped over for a golf course, as the original plan dictated.

"The whole Gold Coast and gentrification of Jersey City wouldn't have started without Liberty State Park," says Gallagher. "It wouldn't have been half as much as it is today."

Remaud smiles. "You know, from Jersey City you can walk across and you can see freshwater wetlands. You can see salt marsh. You can see open meadow. You can see woodlands. You can see all that in a highly urban area with hundreds of thousands of people."

Liberty's rebirth started with a simple boat ride back in the 1970s. Morris Pesin, a councilman from Jersey City—and, by all accounts, one of the few honest politicians in an era of rampant corruption—took the media on a canoe trip to bring some attention to the Jersey City waterfront. At the time, it was highly contaminated and rarely visited. A visit to the Statue of Liberty took nearly two hours by train, bus, and subway into New York, but there was a far quicker option—if only we could reclaim New Jersey's Hudson riverfront. Pesin's canoe trip from Jersey City to the statue took seven minutes. The seeds for Liberty were planted.

My final park stop today is the ferry terminal for the Statue of Liberty. Those ferry rides were not possible forty years ago, when this building served an entirely different purpose. Constructed in 1889, it was once a bustling train terminal for shipping traffic and trade in the metropolitan area. Now the dozens of old train platforms sit frozen in time in the open air, iron gates separating them from the ferry's modern gift shops and snack bars.

It is the strangest scene: huge green trees and plants grow right out of the terminal's foundations behind the wrought-iron gates, reaching up through breaks in the ceiling as pigeons and sparrows nest amid the crumbling ruins. Sunlight pours through the open portions of the roof. It is a scene from a post-apocalyptic movie like 12 Monkeys or a book like The World Without Us. It is also Liberty State Park in a microcosm: the past and the future side by side, public recreation sharing a canvas with wild nature.

### The Tiger and the Owl

Part natural experiment in recovery, part work in progress, Liberty State Park has much in common with the nearby Meadowlands—including snowy owls. At Liberty, Norway rats thrive under the docks by the boat basin. On one unsuccessful visit in search of my first snowy owl, I parked in the dimming twilight at the boat launch. My eyes caught a movement along the water's edge, and I flashed through the possibilities. Muskrat? Raccoon? Instead, I queasily realized that there were dozens of rats under a single dock overhang. Owls feast on these abundant rats, as well as Liberty's rabbits, pheasants, and waterfowl. And with its vast lawns and fields, Liberty State Park offers snowies plenty of low-growing vegetation.

Michael Britt's first sighting at Liberty was a memorable one.

"There was a wicked wind blowing through, and believe it or not, the owl was sitting on a park bench getting dive-bombed by crows for an hour. This was a bench where joggers would be taking a rest, where 100,000 people have watched Fourth of July fireworks. I was blown away."

Best of all, Britt has enjoyed the privilege of watching the owl doing what snowies were born to do—hunt.

"The head is bobbing and swiveling around, up and down, zeroing in on that sound source. All of a sudden, the owl takes off into the reeds—and it has itself a cottontail."

The snowy owls appear to appreciate New Jersey's hospitality more with each passing year. In August 2009 Britt was shocked to receive a photograph from a friend who had been on his way to the Barclays Golf Tournament in Jersey City, just south of Liberty State Park. Tiger Woods struggled and missed the final cut, and underdog Heath Slocum ultimately prevailed with a twenty-one-foot par on the final hole. But the real shot of the day belonged to Britt's friend. Looking out at the Liberty State Park beach along Caven Point, he found a snowy owl peering back at him—in summer, in New Jersey.

Now *that* is a birdie. Under the watchful eyes of Lady Liberty, the snowy owl invasion is under way.

# The Meadowlands 8

## NATURE REBORN

It's unique to find all of this special habitat so close to an urban center—and you can't get any more urban than having New York City four-and-a-half miles away.

—Michael Newhouse,
New Jersey Meadowlands Commission

**W**ith the June tide going out, Captain Bill Sheehan steers his pontoon boat down the Hackensack River. To get here, I had driven our group— Sara Imperiale, Dana Patterson, and Melanie Worob—through a monsoon-like downpour that filled Meadowland Parkway with water two feet deep in the span of an hour. When we met Sheehan and Greg Remaud at a private dock behind the Red Roof Inn, where Sheehan keeps this boat, our dusk cruise was doubtful. Then the sun shined in.

Sheehan, the Hackensack Riverkeeper, spins tales of the old Wild West days of the Meadowlands. Stories of landfills spontaneously erupting into flames, of Giants Stadium built atop a landfill that had burned daily for years on end. Suddenly he puts the boat into neutral as we approach the Norfolk Southern railroad swing bridge between Kearny and Secaucus.

"I'm not sure we can make this," he says, pondering his options aloud. Sheehan wears a ballcap over his red-brown hair and sports a mustache and a small hoop in his ear. "But if we call for the bridge to open, we're gonna be waiting for a while. There's only so much daylight left."

It looks far too close to call. The other passengers and I prepare for a brief delay in our trip. Then Sheehan shifts the boat forward.

"You guys might wanna sit down for this."

We grab hold of the railings tightly, all eyes dead ahead on the bridge's underside. Sheehan guides his boat under the bridge with zero room to spare. The roof rattles against the bridge's undercarriage, sending a few ornamental plastic scallop shells tied on a ceiling line tumbling to the floor. I exchange open-mouthed, wide-eyed glances with my fellow passengers as Sheehan resumes his story.

No one but an experienced captain who knows his boat like he knows himself would have tried—and made—that pass. Clearly, with his bravado and casually expert seamanship, Sheehan belongs on this boat, in this place. Perhaps the pirates never really left the Meadowlands. Only instead of pillaging and raiding, this one is preserving and restoring.

### From Hoffa to Herons

In the years before Sheehan, and two centuries after pirates were chased out of Mill Creek, another wave of prototypical outlaws ruled these forsaken grounds: the mob. Organized crime's legacy in the Meadowlands is apparent today in the landfills rising like a mountain range throughout the thirty-two-square-mile region. In this swampy underworld, legends and reality were so entwined that distinction became irrelevant. Sure, Jimmy Hoffa is buried in the end zone of Giants Stadium. Yes, the Meadowlands is the eternal resting place for more dead bodies than a cemetery. Of course, the Soprano family really did control waste disposal in North Jersey.

By the 1970s, between organized crime and the legendarily corrupt Hudson County political machine, the Meadowlands had become a noxious no-man's land, an infamous wasteland that helped cement-shoe New Jersey's notorious reputation as the Turnpike & Trash Capitol of the eastern seaboard. The Garbage State was fit for nothing except burying the past—granite Doric columns from New York's original Penn Station along with rubble shipped over from the Nazis' air raids on London in World War II. The Meadowlands—and by extension, New Jersey as a whole—was consigned forever to be known as the open trash can at the foot of the great Big Apple. The only way to redeem the place, it seemed, was to pave over thousands of acres of wetlands and wastelands to build new malls and condominiums.

A former taxi driver viewed the Meadowlands in a different light. After volunteering weekends for NY/NJ Baykeeper, Bill Sheehan devoted himself to the Meadowlands as his full-time passion. He founded Hackensack Riverkeeper in 1997, recruited by Waterkeeper Alliance president Robert F. Kennedy Jr. Sheehan's maverick approach occasionally crashed headlong into the Meadowlands government arm—then known as the Hackensack Meadowlands Development Commission and now called the New Jersey Meadowlands Commission—colorfully captured by Robert Sullivan in his book The Meadowlands. Yet the end result was a sea change in the Meadowlands and the start of a long recuperation from the bygone days of open landfills and frightening pollution. The public perception followed suit. Once a foreboding wasteland, the Meadowlands is now a beloved urban wilderness.

### Getting Off Life Support

Just a few decades ago, fish populations and recreational fishing had all but disappeared from the Meadowlands. Maybe 100 species of birds were found there, few of which built their nests in the area. Phragmites—the omnipresent, feathery-plumed marsh reeds that tower alongside Meadowlands roads and waterways alike—seemed to be the only living plant. The Meadowlands were on ecological life support. Now, thanks to the Clean Water Act of 1972 and the work of Sheehan and others, more than 275 species of birds can be spotted in the Meadowlands.

"Fifty or sixty years ago on the Hackensack River you would not see double-crested cormorants, you would not see hooded merganser, you would not see osprey, because there were so few fish since it was so polluted," says Meadowlands Commission naturalist Michael Newhouse. "Now you see cormorants up and down the river, and you see nesting osprey on the Hackensack due to our work restoring habitat and improving water quality."

A double-crested cormorant dries off above the Hackensack River, with the Pulaski Skyway in the distance.

Melanie Worob

The presence of so many birds is a good sign, but it hardly gives the water a clean bill of health. Some waterways, such as Berrys Creek, continue to harbor seriously high levels of mercury, PCBs, and other toxins. The Meadowlands is still a work in progress—but that progress has been extraordinary.

Sheehan guides our boat down a channel and approaches the New Jersey Turnpike, a monumental exit sign looming overhead: "Exit 16E for Lincoln Tunnel/Secaucus, 2 miles." A yellow-crowned night-heron, threatened in New Jersey, perches atop a tree along our channel, just a few feet away from the overpass. The steady calls of marsh wrens gurgle around us. The Meadowlands offers both nesting and migrating birds a tremendous oasis of habitat in an otherwise heavily developed region. Many herons and egrets that nest in New York feed here. Rare birds are also spotted in the Meadowlands, such as the white ibis, a subtropical wader with a bright red bill, and the black-necked stilt, a salt-and-pepper shorebird with a needle-like beak and long legs as thin as drinking straws.

Patterson notices the blurring movement of a muskrat dropping into the water from the marsh bank. In an open area behind the wall of reeds,

I see a sturdy muskrat lodge. Among the most adaptable of creatures in the Meadowlands, the muskrat increased dramatically in numbers after generations of muskrat hunters abandoned the trade. Resembling a small beaver, except with a narrow tail more akin to a rat's, the muskrat builds its lodge with sticks, twigs, cattails, and bulrushes, reinforcing it with the mud of the marsh. Each lodge has an underwater entrance, which can be problematic for the ecosystem as a whole, according to Newhouse.

"We see quite a few muskrats, and their lodges are actually a negative for habitat. They dig tunnels, which can weaken a berm. Also, their dens make great breeding habitat for unwanted species like Canada geese and mute swan."

### Kayaking Past Terrapin Station

Our pontoon tour with Sheehan ends with a dusk close-up of a peregrine falcon nesting under the Route 3 bridge. Like the peregrine, the Meadowlands continues to overcome staggering odds in its resurgence. Having whetted my seagoing appetite, I am eager to experience the Meadowlands from the water itself. A group of us—regular paddlers and novices alike—

David Wheeler

**Hackensack Riverkeeper Bill Sheehan and Greg Remaud of the NY/NJ Baykeeper lead an ecocruise through the Meadowlands and Saw Mill Creek Wildlife Management Area.**

join Nick Vos-Wein of the Hackensack Riverkeeper paddling center for a summer kayak tour leaving from the Laurel Hill boat launch. On my first visit a decade earlier, just a handful of lonely canoes rested along the riverfront. Now Hackensack Riverkeeper has a quaint office, gift shop, visitor tables, two dozen and more kayaks and canoes, and a floating dual kayak launch—plus the two pontoon boats and six boat trailers. All told, Hackensack Riverkeeper brings 10,000 people out to the river every year.

As we paddle leisurely up the Hackensack, it isn't long before we see an osprey on a transmission tower. A turn into Kingsland Creek brings a black skimmer speeding past our heads. The skimmer's lower beak protrudes far outward, enabling the bird to scoop fish from the surface as it flies along. The next channel crossing yields a pair of gorgeous ruddy ducks—pastel-blue beak on a black-and-white head over a chestnut body—hiding in the reeds ahead.

Vos-Wein points out two diamondback terrapins resting on a rock jutting out of the low-tide shallows of the Saw Mill Creek Wildlife Management Area. Testament to countless near-misses, these are the first diamondback terrapins I have recognizably seen in my life.

"Diamondback terrapins are very strong here, and we're actually doing a diamondback terrapin trapping study to determine how many terrapins we have," says Newhouse. "We have no idea how many. They are somewhat of a sensitive species, an indicator species for the health of the marsh."

The tour through Saw Mill Creek offers our group everything a great kayaking tour could promise. Wildlife at every turn. The twisting green reeds of a brackish salt marsh. The splash wars of our rowdy crew cooling us off in the hot July sun. It has something far more impressive as well—the one-of-a-kind context of "only here, only now." The railroad bridge to our north. Both sun-basking terrapins and zooming tractor trailers on the New Jersey Turnpike's western spur in the same view from binoculars. The towering, curving eastern spur of the Turnpike arching over us and the Hackensack River before disappearing into the brown cliffs of Laurel Hill. Even that classic Meadowlands smell—part briny salt marsh, part landfill gases from the old mounds across the Turnpike. All of it unmistakably Meadowlands.

It is not pristine by any stretch—but it may be more memorable.

### "Get a Piece of the Rock"

We paddle our kayaks through the Saw Mill Creek marsh, and a bend brings us to Laurel Hill—a real live mountain rising high above us. One made of rock, not rotting trash. A geological marvel, not a manmade Meadowlands landfill. This jagged rocky outcropping, which the Turnpike uses as a stepping stone over the Meadowlands waterworld, is the only natural break from the flat lowlands for miles. Like the Palisades, this ancient volcanic rock pushed up from the earth's core an estimated 180 million years ago.

From the highway, Laurel Hill's graffiti-sloganed sides and tree-topped plateau make a memorable reference point for drivers. Yet, in the shadow of the nation's busiest thoroughfare on a gorgeous afternoon, Laurel Hill is a completely different place, looming overhead like the Rock of Gibraltar. In fact, back in 1896 an advertising executive traveling to New York City thought the same thing. He was so inspired by this natural landmark that he believed his insurance company could demonstrate its rock-solid reliability by urging consumers to "get a piece of the rock." Thus was the famous Prudential Insurance logo born in the much-maligned swamps of the Meadowlands.

This Meadowlands mountain always caught my eye, too, both from the Turnpike and from the New Jersey Transit commuter line rumbling below on the way to Penn Station. Living in New York City and spending nearly all my time in the concrete jungle of Manhattan, I always felt that my trips through the Meadowlands were like visits to the wilderness next door. From the train window, wildlife abounded—whether a muskrat paddling across a drainage channel, or a snowy egret in the marsh, or a hawk perched on a barren tree in falling snow. When I moved back to New Jersey, the Meadowlands offered quick and convenient outdoor hikes. My first walk up Laurel Hill brought a chance encounter with garter snakes—not surprising, considering that the mountain was long called Snake Hill. And the first bald eagle sighting of my life came while walking the boardwalk trails at Richard W. DeKorte Park in Lyndhurst.

Years earlier, however, "The Rock" of Laurel Hill was nearly eradicated for good. Before 1960 it survived decades as the site of a prison, mental asylum, poorhouse, hospital, and graffiti canvas. Then Hudson County leased Laurel Hill to a traprock quarry, which proceeded to demolish three-quarters of it within five years, lowering its height by fifty feet in the process. The remainder would have soon followed if the Turnpike hadn't started to vibrate when the blasting got too close. Acting as nature's guardian was certainly a new role for the New Jersey Turnpike.

A five-minute hike up a path carved into boulders brings a view shared by Continental Army soldiers on their Revolutionary War lookout post. To stand high above the Turnpike on an ancient rock overlooking miles of marshland, surrounded by blooming trees and colorful butter-flies, is to treasure an oasis of nature in the heart of the great metropolis. Miles of wide-open flatlands below give way to urban skylines and suburban sprawl on all sides. The greens of windswept reeds and phragmites are intersected by the twisting, interlocking Hackensack and Passaic rivers, canal drainages, railroad lines, and the Pulaski Skyway and other raised highways.

On the last leg of our kayak tour, the Saw Mill Creek funnels us into the Hackensack River. I coast along with the incoming tide. Laurel Hill's slope yields to a clear view of Midtown Manhattan, the Empire State Building watching over us incongruously as I dip the paddle. I peer back one last time at Laurel Hill as we disembark, and I remember the ravens nesting there for the third straight year and the howls of coyotes echoing from that rocky outcrop in the night. What was once nevermore has returned to life. The wild has reclaimed a wasteland.

Nature is staking its claim wholeheartedly and defiantly in the Meadowlands, like an American flag being raised in Moscow's Red Square during the height of the cold war. Here—on a giant rock over the New Jersey Turnpike, with a bird's-eye view of the New York skyline and millions of people commuting past, surrounded by landfills and old mob landmarks and the gasping breaths of industrial decadence—the life-blood of New Jersey flows again.

# Commuting by Wing in New York Harbor 9

The challenge of nature in an urban setting is that we can't just let it be. There are just too many human threats.
—Glenn Phillips, New York City Audubon Society

The northern half of the New Jersey Turnpike may be the most widely traveled road in America. It is certainly among the most notorious. The fuming smokestacks, industrial wastelands, abandoned factories, and former landfills that pass for scenery have ensured that the smirking question—"Which exit are you from?"—never gets old for out-of-staters. The 650,000 drivers each year seldom forget the stretch between Exits 11 and 14.

Oil tank farms line the Turnpike at milepost 96. In the opening montage of *The Sopranos*, Tony Soprano drives along the Turnpike past one white cylindrical tank painted with the message "DRIVE SAFELY." This is an android metropolis. Its smokestacks are skyscrapers, its sprawling tank farms and towering industrial cranes and distant smog-shrouded bridges compose a postindustrial sci-fi skyline. It's a bizarre collage, with the wastelands of the region's infamous "America's Armpit" moniker sharing the new public image of Hollywood glorification.

For years, you could call this stretch a lot of things, few of them repeatable in a family-friendly setting. Now you can also call it something good. The Turnpike corridor is living, breathing proof that, given time, nature can rebound from just about anything. With a little help. Here, the Rahway River drains into the Arthur Kill, one of the most industrial waterways in the world. Yet just off the Turnpike shoulder, with the Manhattan skyline visible in the distance, glossy ibis can be found stalking the reeds in the shallows. The tall bird's scythe-shaped, downward-curving beak calls to mind its revered Egyptian relative haunting the reeds of the ancient Nile. The Arthur Kill is lined on both sides with refineries and factories, but the ibis has risen like a phoenix from a desecrated burial site. The dichotomy is stunning.

### "Baptized in Oil"

On our thirty-foot wooden skiff, we pass a sailboat cruising north through the narrow tidal strait. A double-crested cormorant flies above, its sleek black form unmistakable against the powder blue sky. A grassy mountain of meadows looms behind the sailboat, stretching for miles. In a few hours, low tide will bring great egrets, glossy ibis, and great blue herons by the score. That mountain is Fresh Kills Landfill, the largest landfill on earth, so massive it is among the few manmade structures that can be seen from space. And the water under the boat is the Arthur Kill, connecting Newark Bay with Raritan Bay.

Thousands of tankers carry billions of gallons of oil through this strait each year, making the Arthur Kill America's busiest industrial waterway, even more heavily used than the Panama Canal. One byproduct is an extra layer of security in this post-9/11 era. On an Arthur Kill trip with Captain Rick Jacks of the NY/NJ Baykeeper, he warns me and the other passengers not to photograph the oil tanks and bridges as we pass them.

"They are watching us, and they are watching us closely," he says.

After Jacks notifies the Coast Guard that our destination is the Arthur

Kill, we are actually shadowed by a state police boat for most of the way there—coincidentally or not.

Another feared downside to that industrial traffic reared its ugly head on New Years Day 1990, when an Exxon tanker spilled 567,000 gallons of oil into the Arthur Kill, which separates New Jersey from Staten Island.

"We had just started monitoring the Kill in 1989, and you talk about being 'baptized in oil,'" said Andy Willner, founder and former executive director of NY/NJ Baykeeper, as his boat passes marshes growing out of abandoned barges and ospreys nesting on crumbling bulkheads. "It was awful, but it led to the restoration and awareness of how important these wetlands are. These smaller parcels are like the last little Gardens of Eden in this vast gray industrial area."

After the oil spill, humans took a more hands-on role in helping nature recuperate. Plastic bottles and other floatables lining the 3,000-acre Fresh Kills Landfill were finally brought under control, and the world's largest landfill closed in 2001. Even that progress couldn't please every bird. The landfill's closure coincided with a drop in the population of cattle egrets, small land birds that thrived on the savannah-like vegetation of Fresh Kills. Cattle egret numbers dropped from 500 to just two pairs after Fresh Kills closed. And because many of the "harbor herons," as they're known, are colonial nesters—dependent for their safety on nesting with hundreds of other birds—the cattle egrets' departure hurt island colonies such as the Isle of Meadows.

### The Harbor Herons

Putting aside the picky tastes of cattle egrets, the habitat finally had a chance to recover. It just needed some help. Ecologists are replanting native spartina, a marsh grass, to re-create many salt marshes destroyed by industry and oil spills. The U.S. Army Corps of Engineers is leading a $3 million ecological restoration of a wetlands complex between a residential cul-de-sac and the New Jersey Turnpike's Thomas Edison Rest Area.

"It's the corniest line, but it really is true with tidal wetlands: If you build it, they will come," says Mark Gallagher, an ecological consultant who has worked on wetlands restoration projects on the Arthur Kill for two decades. "The very first day you let the tide come in, the fish and crabs come in with the tide. Soon after that you see birds like kingfisher and terns and wading birds there to eat the fish."

More than 4,000 herons, egrets, and ibis nest in the greater estuary, many feeding in the Arthur Kill. Such abundance would have seemed far-

The great blue heron is found along waterways throughout the state, including highly urban rivers and wetlands.

Tam Stuart

fetched 100 years ago, when many wading birds were on the verge of extinction due to overhunting. Their attractive feathers added gaudy ornaments to fashionable hats. The Migratory Bird Treaty Act of 1914 put an end to the hunts, and the herons and egrets recovered around the nation over the ensuing decades.

The New York City chapter of the Audubon Society began monitoring the estuary's birds in 1979 and, for many years, found the Arthur Kill's islands to be favored nesting areas. More recent Audubon surveys, though, found no nesting herons here. Human disturbances, such as boaters coming ashore near the nests, disrupted the colonies, as did overgrazing by deer that swim to the islands. But nothing matched the infestation of the Asian longhorned beetle. The beetle's relentless tunneling causes so much damage to hardwood forests that the New York City Parks Department had to clear all trees at risk—in this case, the trees of Pralls Island, which provided nest locations for hundreds of colonial nesting birds like herons, egrets, cormorants, gulls, and terns.

Now relocated to the other side of Manhattan, the harbor herons share a common element of life in the big city. Like many tristate residents, the birds commute to work.

"The birds from Hoffman Island are mostly foraging in the Arthur Kill and Sandy Hook as far south as the Navesink River," says Glenn Phillips, executive director of New York City Audubon. "The birds from South Brother Island next to Rikers and Mill Rock tend to forage in the Meadowlands. That's around six miles flying over Manhattan, which is a fair haul."

Using the archipelago of small islands lying in Kill Van Kull and the East River, the harbor herons build nests that keep eggs and chicks safe from mainland predators like raccoons, opossums, and feral cats. No nesting spot could have helped the birds forty years ago, however. The Arthur Kill was so polluted that living creatures such as crabs or clams would die within an hour if submerged in its waters. The 1972 Clean Water Act forced the construction of modern sewage treatment facilities for the metropolitan area, dramatically improving the water quality of waterways like the Arthur Kill. Though far from pristine, these wetlands and mudflats again feed the harbor herons and an abundance of other wildlife.

"There was a point when our waterways were really polluted, and we seem to forget how much the whole estuary has improved over the last thirty years," says Mark Gallagher.

### Some Birds

Gallagher is one of the people giving nature a little help. On a late summer tour along an industrial Port Reading waterfront, he leads me through a twelve-acre Arthur Kill restoration project. Within an hour, we watch a northern harrier gliding low above a twisting tidal channel and a merlin—a dark blue raptor resembling a small peregrine falcon—speeding overhead. Great and snowy egrets and a black-crowned night-heron forage on killifish, mud snails, hardshell clams, and fiddler crabs in the tide pools of the restoration area.

The buffet lasts all year, as the Arthur Kill remains ice-free even during the fiercest winters. When ice seals off the Raritan River and other nearby rivers and lakes, thousands of ducks, such as buffleheads and mergansers, flock to the Arthur Kill at the mouth of its largest tributary, the Rahway River. The Rahway delta serves as perhaps the most important regional foraging area for glossy ibis. And even though the endangered red-headed woodpecker had disappeared over much of the state by the 1970s, a pair has wintered in suburban Rahway River Park for many years. They seem to prefer the towering oak, sycamore, and beech trees, while enjoying the view of the municipal swimming pool—and public restroom building—below. In real estate, location is everything.

Some birds have adapted, but others struggle as the push of development continues along the region's urban waterways. Fred Virrazzi of National Biodiversity Parks has birded the Rahway River area for years and is also studying the region's declining population of diamondback terrapins.

"Yellow-crowned night-heron are nesting in Roselle right in the middle of a neighborhood, and you get glossy ibis at Ashbrook Reservation, feeding and dispersing," says Virrazzi. "But we're losing American bittern, we're losing pied-billed grebes. With diamondback terrapins we're possibly seeing the slow lead into local extirpation. If we can't have a small animal with small needs survive, it's a real warning."

To better understand the overall ecological health of the greater New York Harbor estuary, Susan Elbin of New York City Audubon is studying the birds that make these waters home.

"We're using double-crested cormorants as a biological indicator for the harbor and wading birds as a biological indicator of the health of the wetlands," says Elbin. "Cormorants are diving birds in the open waters, and herons feed in the shallow water, so we really are able to cover the harbor between them."

## From Glaciers to Patriots

Across from Perth Amboy, on the southwestern corner of Staten Island—once a part of New Jersey in the colonial era—Tottenville Beach offers a scenic park along outcrops of terminal moraine, where the Wisconsin Glacier reached its end around 75,000 years ago. The Arthur Kill was initially an abandoned outlet to the sea, carved out by the Hudson River when its main channel was blocked by glaciers or moraine east of Staten Island. Those remnants of the last ice age remained visible on Tottenville's old roads, which were paved with millions of oyster shells in the early 1900s.

On September 11, 1776, Benjamin Franklin and John Adams rowed across the Arthur Kill from New Jersey to Staten Island for a peace conference with Lord Admiral Richard Howe. Their journey was a final bid for reconciliation between the American colonists and representatives of King George III.

Franklin and Adams failed to reach an agreement, but the patriots left a tangible legacy here. That same stately manor, known as the Conference House Museum, still impresses boaters today. For New York City Audubon's Glenn Phillips, the Arthur Kill's ecological legacy is no less apparent.

"The challenge of nature in an urban setting is that we can't just let it be. There are just too many human threats."

# The Raritan's Industrial Wilderness

**10**

Behold the "Valley of the Dumps."

—Bob Spiegel, Edison Wetlands Association

**A** typical encounter with a loggerhead sea turtle might go something like this:

Boater asks self, "What's that debris floating in the water?"

Turtle gulps its fresh air, then vanishes into the depths.

Boater realizes he had been looking at a nearly four-foot-long, 800-pound reptile that spent years adrift at sea as a young hatchling, floating on rafts of sargassum and vegetation. Loggerhead turtles have swum the seas since the time of the dinosaurs.

In his decade as Raritan Riverkeeper, Bill Schultz has encountered sea turtles fairly often. One Raritan Bay experience might be more aptly called a terrapin hijacking. Schultz was boating past the staked enclosure of a fisherman's pound net off of Keansburg and Union Beach when he saw what looked like multiple loggerhead turtles in the net. He contacted the fisherman and arranged to bring the turtles down to the Marine Mammal Stranding Center in Brigantine to check on their health.

"I met the fisherman at some ungodly early hour," says Schultz. "Next thing I knew, there were twenty-three loggerhead turtles walking around the deck of my boat. Twenty-three loggerheads!"

## A River in Recovery

The longest river solely in New Jersey, the Raritan is among the most historically industrial waterways in the nation. Through the 1990s, any positive attention the Raritan River received from wildlife enthusiasts was the ecological equivalent of a backhanded compliment. The river hosted one of the state's largest gull populations. Why? Because gulls liked feeding on its open landfills.

On my first Raritan tour nearly a decade ago, I expected to see little beyond belching smokestacks and abandoned factoryscapes devoid of life. I couldn't have been more wrong. I walked along the Raritan riverbank mudflats on a cool fall morning—all the landfills were by then either closed or better contained—and peered up through my binoculars at a bald eagle soaring high overhead. Within a few minutes, a second bald eagle appeared, trying to catch a fish just above eye level fifty yards downstream. This gorgeous white-headed adult flapped its mighty wings in place as it sought the right angle for its attack. Thousands of sea gulls steered clear from the raptor, staying near East Brunswick's Edgeboro Landfill across the river. Fifteen minutes later, a third eagle—this one a brown-headed juvenile—checked out that same spot before flying toward its regular perch on a landfill transmission tower. A salty old fisherman at the nearby Edison Boat Basin shook his head in disbelief.

Raritan Bay flows within the Marine Gateway to New York Harbor, for nearly a century the entry point for millions of immigrants who came to America to start a new life. Here you find a view unlike any other. Careful, though—it comes atop the towering twin spans of the Garden State Parkway and Route 9 as you're driving sixty-five miles per hour and avoiding those going eighty-five. The seascape stretches from Perth Amboy, Sandy Hook, and Staten Island to the far-off Rockaways and Coney Island at the southwestern tip of Brooklyn, Queens, and Long Island.

With the exception of fishermen and crabbers, metropolitan residents overlook this coast in favor of the beautiful beaches and traffic jams of a sweltering summer day at the Jersey Shore or the Hamptons. Our longtime dependence on waterways for commerce and transportation yielded to sprawling automobile traffic corridors within the Hudson-Raritan Estuary. The New Jersey Turnpike, the Garden State Parkway, Interstate 287, and Routes 1 and 9 flow like mighty asphalt rivers, their confluence transforming central New Jersey into a vast, paved delta of interchanges, exit ramps, and cloverleafs. Rush hours ebb and flow like modern-life tides, occasionally spilling over their banks to bring the whole region to a halt.

The hectic, 24-7 atmosphere of auto exhaust and bumper-to-bumper traffic and road rage would be unbearable if not for a watershed discovery in recent years. From sea turtles to bald eagles, wildlife is regaining its own natural corridors—the skies over the cities, the water under the bridges, and the wooded buffers along rail lines and waterways. And not just white-tailed deer and Canada geese, either. Birders have spotted the American white pelican and the wood stork, far more common in the Everglades, in Cranbury and Sayreville, respectively. Flocks of the greater scaup, a black sea duck, gather each winter in Raritan Bay in numbers rivaling the world's greatest wildlife migrations, with up to 50,000 in a single mass migration. The haunting barn owl and bobolink frequent Raritan Center, an industrial business park on the sprawling grounds of the former Raritan Arsenal, the U.S. Army home of millions of World War II weapons.

Winter brings harbor and harp seals, and summer lures the sea turtles. Loggerheads are the most common, and green turtles, Kemp's ridley turtles, and leatherbacks are also spotted. The world's heaviest reptile, reaching nearly eight feet long and weighing up to a ton, the leatherback carries a deeply ridged carapace resembling a horsehide football helmet from a century ago. In June 2006 a bottlenose dolphin swam fourteen miles up the Raritan, past downtown New Brunswick, before retreating to its ocean home.

Wildlife has overcome lottery-type odds to survive here. For most of the twentieth century the Lower Raritan was off-limits for all but the most adaptable species—and only the hardiest human visitors. The stretch from East Brunswick and Edison down to the Raritan's mouth at Sayreville and Perth Amboy was dubbed the "Chemical Belt" for its preponderance of heavy industry and chemical manufacturers. Wildlife also faces the challenge of dwindling habitat. After all, the Lower Raritan Watershed is one of the most densely populated areas in the United States. More than 2,400 people live in every square mile—compared with 80 for America as a whole. That's a whole lot of people for a very small place.

## Landfill Safari

Many of the Raritan's largest industrial plants have moved on, allowing the river to settle into natural revitalization after a century of industrial abuse. The Raritan also benefited from having a protector who has devoted the last twenty years to cleaning up its worst toxic sites. Bob Spiegel, founder of the nonprofit Edison Wetlands Association, never shied away from a fight in his campaign to restore the Raritan. Contrary to what you might assume about a former Grateful Deadhead-turned-environmentalist, Spiegel relied then on confrontation rather than the cooperation practiced by most conservationists. In an overdeveloped place like the Raritan estuary, he had little choice if he wanted to succeed.

In the early 1990s Spiegel rented out the Forum Theatre in Metuchen to spread the word about the uncontrolled hazards of a local toxic site. The U.S. Environmental Protection Agency, in turn, felt pressured into holding its own meeting soon after. When the case manager declared the site safe, Spiegel pulled out a jar filled with the bright green ooze that festered along the site's creek next to a row of homes.

"If the water's fine, then drink this!" shouted Spiegel, slamming the jar down as the official recoiled. "This is what our kids are playing in— so go ahead and drink it!"

I join Spiegel and two interns for the most unlikely New Jersey wildlife tour I can imagine: a landfill safari. Spiegel guns his truck engine and we speed up a dirt trail to the top of the Edison Landfill. The Grateful Dead's "Hell in a Bucket" blasts from the speakers, and the interns shriek with laughter from the backseat as reeds bounce off the truck windows. On the way, we pass a ring-necked pheasant, its turkey-like body shape subverted by a long, straight tail and colorful blue-and-red head. The omnipresent phragmites abruptly open up to an expansive view that would be stunning from anywhere, let alone the top of a landfill. We survey an oxbow bend in the Raritan that creates a scene worthy of the Everglades' river of grass. At our feet, a killdeer nest holds four speckled, oblong eggs in a small indentation in the gravel. Common yellowthroats, with their black masks, sing "wichety-wichety-wichety" from the scrub, and a northern flicker flies to one of the landfill trees. Far below, a herd of deer trots off into the riverfront forest as a motorboat trailing a jet-skier powers up the sun-speckled river.

It is a gorgeous view, especially welcome in the largely flat terrain of Middlesex County. There's a reason for the special view from Edison Landfill, however. The marshland in three directions is broken up only by three other "mountains"—Edgeboro Landfill, Kin-Buc Landfill Superfund Site, and the Industrial Land Reclaiming Landfill. This is the Raritan, after all.

"Behold the 'Valley of the Dumps,'" says Spiegel. "This is as beautiful a place as there is anywhere, especially knowing the progress we've made on the Raritan."

In a comeback worthy of New Jersey's own history, some of those long-forsaken landfills are being transformed into ecologically valuable habitat. On Edgeboro Landfill in East Brunswick, a legal action taken by Spiegel resulted in the cleanup of a mile-long stretch of riverfront where trash once washed out with each outgoing tide. In its place, ecologists planted native vegetation and fruit-bearing trees to attract migrating birds and butterflies.

Our tour of Edgeboro Landfill, guided by Jack Whitman of Edgeboro Disposal, finds cedar waxwings dining on berries, swallows criss-crossing over the surface near an abandoned ferry, and Baltimore orioles zipping from one side of the river to the other. Spiegel calls it "turning brownfields into greenfields, a model garbage-to-gardens project." Across the

Raritan, another of Spiegel's landfill projects is complete: a public walkway with a footbridge, kiosks, and native butterfly gardens along the Edison Landfill riverfront. The initial set of trails opened in early 2010—the first extended public access ever on Edison's seven miles of Raritan riverfront. Before our landfill safari is complete, we find a box turtle, spy a northern harrier, and hear a bobolink—a grassland-dependent bird with very little habitat remaining in the region.

Environmental consultant Mark Gallagher advised on the Edgeboro restoration and views the Raritan's legacy in synchronicity with the dramatic changes occurring in public perception of our wetlands and waterfronts over the last sixty years.

"In the 1940s and 1950s, we kind of looked at placing landfills in wetlands as a desirable way to utilize land. There was an old kids' book, *Mr. Garbageman*, that went through pictures of what happens to your garbage, dumping it in a nasty swamp. The last photo was a shiny new shopping mall where the wetlands once were. That was the goal forty years ago, but now landfill restoration puts a habitat value on what was essentially lost land."

### Wildlife Reclaims the Raritan

New Jersey Audubon's Nellie Tsipoura surveyed the river's birdlife in 2009 and came away impressed—not only with the birds, but also with the remaining habitat.

"These deserted industrial areas provide the broken-down docks needed for ospreys to nest securely in the middle of the river. The habitat has been neglected, but it is functioning more than one would think," she says. "Just past the Route 35 bridge, we pulled the boat into a marshy area, and for a second there it could've been Cape May. We had clapper rails, quite a few marsh wrens, herons and egrets. I was shocked—I could hardly believe what I was seeing."

The Raritan gets cleaner as the contaminated sites left behind by industry are remediated and native vegetation replaces exposed trash along landfill riverfronts. First to benefit from the improved water quality are the fish and crustaceans. Downstream, where the river enters Raritan Bay, the water teems with striped bass, bluefish, and eels. Oysters, quahog clams, lobsters, and blue crabs claim the bay floor below.

The bountiful fish population helps birds to expand. Birders spot American oystercatcher, black skimmer, yellow-crowned night-heron, northern gannet, and bald eagle regularly in the bay and river. Double-crested cormorants nest on each of the channel markers, with large

Melanie Worob

**Kayakers and canoers enjoy a trip down the Raritan River, the longest river solely in New Jersey.**

groups gathering on the different tiers like contestants on *Hollywood Squares*. And no fewer than eleven osprey nests sit jaggedly atop pilings and bulkheads along the river from New Brunswick to Raritan Bay— without a single piling going nestless.

"As long as you have a strong fish population and nesting over water, safe from ground predators, you can have high densities of ospreys," says Kathy Clark, the state raptor expert. "It certainly says that the Raritan River is improving in terms of fisheries and water clarity. The classic osprey fish is menhaden, or bunker, which is a fairly large, robust fish that tends to be in large schools near the surface."

Birds enjoy the healthier populations of bluefish, winter flounder, and striped bass, and so do recreational fishermen and crabbers.

"The Raritan is a world-class fishery for striped bass and sport fishing," says Riverkeeper Schultz. "Fishermen are pulling in bass up around fifty pounds plus. A couple seasons ago, a police officer was called down to the river in Highland Park for a report of a man pulling a dead dog out of the river. It was a fifty-eight-pound striper taken off the mudflats."

Just as the Meadowlands was transformed into an ecotourism and recreational destination seemingly overnight, fishermen are rediscovering the Raritan River in recent years. The apparent contradictions—nature returning as habitat is lost, stunning wildlife vistas set to a backdrop of landfills and industry—are vital to what's driving people back to the water.

### Wreckdiving the Hudson-Raritan Estuary

Schultz, a former Perth Amboy fireman, began wreckdiving in the estuary "about twenty-some-odd years ago." He's been back to the sunken wrecks north of the Outerbridge Crossing at least thirty times since. From a seventeen-foot outboard, Schultz and other ex-firemen drop down into the deep one by one, armed with full-body hooded wetsuits, scuba tanks, regulators, masks, fins, and flashlights.

"We started in the open Raritan Bay, but there it's like the ocean—the bottom's like a desert, ripples in the sand bottom and nothing there," says Schultz. "But wherever there's something on the bottom, it becomes habitat. Glass shrimp attract the small fish, and they attract the bigger fish."

Schultz has seen schools of fish swarming like a single organism, but one moment proved most breathtaking of all. Literally.

"I saw a sand shark one time. For the fraction of a second before the depth registers, I don't know if I'm looking at a two-foot shark right in front of me or a ten-foot shark ten feet away from me. I inhaled about 1,000 pounds of air right then."

Schultz's blue eyes twinkle as he smiles and adds, "Of course, as firemen, we can control our breath, so we can get one and a half hours down there exploring when most people can get only forty-five minutes."

After the first hurricane of the season each fall, especially following a hotter-than-usual summer, the warm currents of the Gulf Stream sweep semi-tropical and tropical fish up into Raritan Bay. From late August to November each year, depending on the weather conditions, Schultz watches a phenomenon unfold.

"The top fifteen feet of the water explodes with color, bright yellows and bright oranges and blues," he says. "We're used to seeing gray fish and black fish and silver fish. But during that time you'll see blue tangs, spotfin butterflies, bright orange squirrelfish, different varieties of triggerfish."

Tropical Raritan Bay? Go figure.

# Part Three

## The Jersey Shore

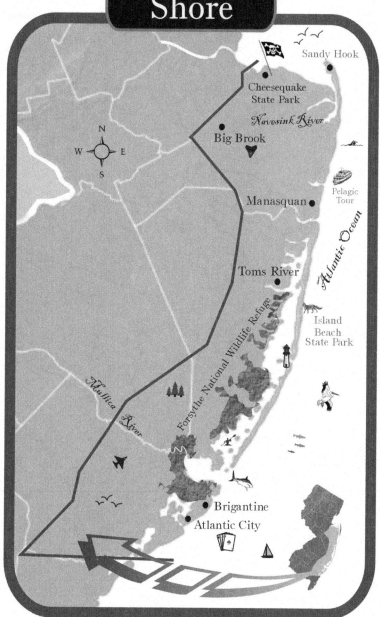

# Captain Morgan and the Sargasso Sea Voyagers

Jim Faczak is the
world's most intense
naturalist.
—Greg Remaud,
NY/NJ Baykeeper

On June 30, 2007, a Western reef-heron was seen wading in the mouth
of Morgan Creek on the outskirts of Cheesequake State Park. Normally
found in Africa, India, and the Red Sea, the statuesque, dark blue reef-
heron—with its long bill, hanging blue plume, and white throat—
remained in South Amboy for a day. The bird then flew over Staten Island
to spend two weeks in an even more industrial Brooklyn harbor. Prior to
its New Jersey sighting, the Western reef-heron had been spotted only
once in all of North America before 2006.

Even without a miracle sighting, a visitor is seldom bored at Cheesequake State Park in Old Bridge. That's because Jim Faczak makes darn sure
of it.

"There's another osprey—he's diving! He's diving!"

The osprey, also known as the fish hawk, pulls its bent wings to its sides
and freefalls into Cheesequake Creek with a splash, just a few hundred feet
from Faczak and his fellow kayakers. Faczak—a wiry, bald-domed former
photographer bursting with enthusiasm—began leading kayak ecotours at
Cheesequake in the summer of 2007, and they soon sold out for the season. With a long waiting list, Faczak expanded the public tours and added
another ten kayaks to his fleet, thanks to a grant from the Conserve Wildlife
Foundation of New Jersey and the Edison Wetlands Association.

"Did he get the fish?" I ask.

Raising binoculars to his eyes, Faczak steadies his kayak with his
other hand.

"They usually do—they have a pretty good success rate."

Before 1997, the osprey was seldom seen in Cheesequake, but now
this threatened species is hard to miss soaring overhead or feeding chicks
on platforms throughout the park. At the annual osprey banding in 2009,
a dozen conservationists gathered around Faczak and Jeanne Heuser of
the National Park Service as they banded a bird that migrates here from

Costa Rica. Sara Imperiale of Edison Wetlands was one of the observers that day and was struck by the helplessness of the young osprey.

"The osprey's talons are strong, and the beak looks like it could bite your finger off—but its wings don't work," says Imperiale. "The wings are these behemoth things just weighing down the body like dead weight. They haven't learned how to fly yet."

At seven weeks old, young ospreys finally learn to use those wings, which will ultimately span six feet across from tip to tip. These raptors have plenty of company in the skies and waterways around Cheesequake. More than 200 birds, from American bittern to fish crows, thrive here in the largest estuary marsh in central New Jersey. Kayakers also see diamondback terrapins popping their heads out of the water or basking in the sunshine on the tidal stream banks.

## Paddling Cheesequake

Guides Jim and April Faczak are clearly at ease on the water on our kayaking tour, maneuvering with expertise and paddling backward as Jim recounts tales of Cheesequake to a dozen fellow kayakers. Under a near-cloudless sky stretching over the undulating marsh grasses, kayakers paddle down Cheesequake Creek against the incoming tide. The creek winds for more than a mile from the park, flowing under the Garden State Parkway and emptying into Raritan Bay.

The marsh's sky-blue serenity is interrupted every few moments by the subtle splashes of tiny grass shrimp breaking the surface to elude hungry bluefish below or by the flapping white wings of a snowy egret lifting off from its foraging grounds. Near the launch, fiddler crabs scurry across the creek's muddy banks. Each male raises a giant claw longer than its body as a warning to any would-be predators. "Giant" in this case means the size of your thumb. The crabs also dig thousands of burrow holes, which keep the salt marsh healthy by aerating the soil and moving nutrients around.

"Cheesequake's the largest open-space tidal salt marsh in northern or central Jersey that's still working correctly—not like the Meadowlands," says Faczak. "And I like the Meadowlands, don't get me wrong. But it doesn't compare with Cheesequake."

As we paddle toward a clearing, our splashes startle a willet—a striking sandpiper with a long beak and flashing black-and-white wings. The mother flies large circles around the area while three young willets amble about the grassy clearing just a few feet away from us. The willets are an exciting find, but participants in a 2008 New Jersey Audubon bird

The osprey has increased in numbers eightfold over the past few decades and can now be found in many coastal estuaries.

Tam Stuart

count were even more fortunate. One birder spotted a golden eagle, rare even in the most likely New Jersey spots, over the Cheesequake salt marsh.

Reaching the mouth of Hooks Creek, we stop for a break. Overhead, at least half a dozen ospreys twist and turn and dive-bomb in an aerial display reminiscent of a Sea World dolphin show. The ospreys, unlike trained animals, behave with utter unpredictability. One hovers above, seemingly locked in on a fish. I am certain it will dive. Instead it circles back up with the wind and looks elsewhere for food. Of course, once I give up on the osprey, it pulls its wings back and plunges straight down with a splash. Fool me, fool the fish.

Our group of kayakers, novices and experts alike from all over New York and New Jersey, paddles around a bend into a narrow tributary. The bottoms of the kayaks scrape against the sand, and we brace our boats against the creek's banks to get out. In hiking boots and sneakers, our crew steps into warm, knee-deep water. The first few steps are jarring. My boots feel squishy as I lumber awkwardly through the creek. Then something changes. Walking in the water feels refreshing, even comfortable. Faczak leads the way and helps himself to an all-natural buffet, passing around dates that he picks right off the creek-side vegetation. They're tasty. It's an unexpected moment in a very unexpected place.

Until 2007, most visitors could enjoy Cheesequake State Park only on foot, walking actual trails, not wading up creeks. Fortunately, its nearly 1,500 acres are impressive enough by land. A transitional zone, Cheesequake holds flora from both northern and southern ecosystems, including "the most northern part of the Pine Barrens in New Jersey," as Faczak notes proudly. The park also encompasses Atlantic white cedar swamp, dry pitch pine woods, mixed northeastern hardwood forest, meadows, bog, freshwater marsh, and, of course, that tranquil salt marsh.

## Trekking Across the Sand Flats

On any mild day, Cheesequake's hiking trails have their share of families, dog walkers, joggers, and serious hikers, as well as birders enjoying the bird's-eye view of the osprey platform nests from the wooded streamside cliffs. Less crowded is the 234-acre Somers Woods, just across the marsh. On a brutally hot August day, Greg Remaud and his German shepherd, Duke, lead me through Somers.

In the span of two hours, we walk through a dense, ridged pine forest that seems transplanted from South Jersey's Pine Barrens. Old sand-mining operations once ravaged these bright white, scorchingly hot sand flats. Unmarked trails lead us over sandy pine ridges until we stumble upon a serene lily pad–covered lake as hidden and welcoming as any desert oasis. We search for endangered orchids in bogs, hike through rare Atlantic white cedar groves, and find an abandoned nest of turtle eggs atop a towering dirt mound far from the water. Somers Woods feels as diverse as any state park; yet, for now, it is merely a forgotten outlier of Cheesequake.

By the time we get back to the car, Remaud and I are beaten down by the heat. But we could not be more impressed by this hidden gem that doesn't even formally exist except as a blank space on the map. That is what Remaud is working to correct.

"The critical part is the buffers," he says. "Cheesequake Park is shaped like a bowl, and with erosion and runoff from developments around the park, buffers are vital not only for the aesthetics, but also to slow the encroachment on Cheesequake. Since 1999, we've worked with the state Green Acres program and Cheesequake State Park to permanently preserve approximately 100 acres on five different projects, and we're now pursuing another 300 acres."

Encroachment poses an immediate threat. Already the northeastern cliffs of Cheesequake have been condo-ized: a wall of oversized, cookie-cutter homes looms over the marsh, eroding the cliffs. Millions of people live within an hour's drive of Cheesequake. Yet, even as most of central Jersey is built out, Cheesequake and its thriving tidal wetlands stand apart, thanks largely to advocates like Remaud and Faczak.

For Remaud, protecting Cheesequake has a deep personal meaning. His first wildlife memory as a boy growing up on the Raritan Bayshore was encountering a box turtle on a trail in Cheesequake while playing with his neighborhood friends. Finding and holding the box turtle, with its domed yellow-and-green shell, proved far more memorable than seeing a bird in a tree. For Remaud and, hopefully, for the kayakers and hikers today who enjoy Cheesequake, an encounter with nature—up close and personal—made a lasting impression.

Now one of New Jersey's most visited state parks, Cheesequake was a popular destination long before it was formally preserved. Mule-pulled trains and steamships imported textiles from New York City to Cheesequake's steamboat landing around the turn of the century and hauled out salt-glazed pottery made from the clay mines that drove the local economy. Before that, Native Americans enjoyed its ideal fishing and shell-fishing opportunities for hundreds of years.

"Just as we do, Native Americans would travel down the shore in summer, catching fish and shellfish at Cheesequake," says Faczak. "And sailors and old-time pirates also used the Old Spye Inn right on Cheesequake Creek. It was all called Morgan Creek then—for Captain Morgan, the pirate now known for rum."

## From Sargasso to Cheesequake

Cheesequake's kayakers may not encounter pirates nowadays, but another improbable visitor seems just as exotic. I join Faczak and Melanie Worob on a seasonal April morning to see the spectacle up close. From a grassy walkway along the side of Hooks Creek Lake—which will be packed with families and splashing summer campers in just a few months—Faczak abruptly careens down the other side of the bank, practically disappearing into the tall reeds along a tiny stream.

Faczak dips his net, sifting with Worob through wet leaves and mud for our trophy. Tiny killifish squirm through the first two catches. The third time's a charm. We behold three inches of wriggling glass eel. Fully transparent, the eel resembles a slender ghost. Two large eyes and a thin bloodline extending the length of its body are the eel's only visible features.

Glass eels, the juvenile stage of the American eel, swim here all the way from the Sargasso Sea, between Bermuda and the Bahamas. All along the East Coast, glass eels seek out narrow streams that funnel into calm, clean lakes with few predators. Cheesequake's Hooks Creek Lake offers the main attraction in this part of the state. Thousands of glass eels use this spillway to reach the lake each spring. Though our timing this year is a bit early for those big migration numbers, we happily examine the eels we find before setting them free.

"Eventually, this glassy eel is going to grow to an elver, into a green eel, an adult eel, up to four feet long," says Faczak. "After sexually maturing, it will turn into a yellow eel, then a silver eel, and eventually a black eel, when it's on its way back down to the Sargasso Sea."

Once fully grown, these eels become aggressive and opportunistic predators, eating crabs and small fish during a lifespan that can reach twenty years. That seems like a long way away. The eel's life cycle recalls a human's stages from newborn to senior citizen—growing up, moving out, traveling. Yes, the tiny glass eels of the Sargasso Sea swim all the way to Cheesequake Creek just to grow up. They return to the open seas as four-foot long, ferocious predators—an amazing journey complete.

# The Lost World of Jurassic Jersey     12

The fossil hunter does not kill; he resurrects. —American paleontologist George Gaylord Simpson

I park my car on a quiet, upscale suburban street in Marlboro. My six-year-old daughter, Kayla—a fearless and inquisitive explorer—and I walk with another family to the end of the block. To an outside observer, we could be walking anywhere on this warm, late spring morning—a neighbor's built-in pool, a backyard barbeque, the playground at the neighborhood park.

But we're not. We're going fossil hunting. And on this day in the Big Brook, we won't come back empty-handed. We will be joined by a goblin shark, a Cretaceous porbeagle, and an ancient squid. Just another day in the suburbs of Monmouth County.

## Portal to the Dinosaur Era

New Jersey is not often thought of as a hotspot for paleontology, but the Garden State has an incredibly rich history of prehistoric finds. In some places, like the Big Brook, the discoveries continue each day. At many other sites across the state, explored in detail in William B. Gallagher's book *When Dinosaurs Roamed New Jersey*, key findings have helped further the study of dinosaurs on a global scale.

In 1856 the marl pits of Haddonfield in Camden County produced the first American fossil ever found. The forty-nine bones and teeth of a duck-billed hadrosaurus represented the most complete dinosaur skeleton in the world. The nation's leading scientists traveled from afar to examine the spectacular twenty-foot-long discovery. Today, a monument depicting the hadrosaurus, constructed in downtown Haddonfield by a local Eagle Scout troop, marks the spot where this prized dinosaur fossil was discovered. The nine-foot metallic statue portrays the dinosaur in its primordial setting, with rocks, a small waterfall, and foliage.

From there, the findings came fast and furious. The lost world of New Jersey was revealed, one clue at a time. It was a world that could put the film *Jurassic Park* to shame. In New Jersey, findings from the Jurassic period are joined by the fossils and footprints of creatures from the Triassic and Cretaceous periods. The first steps to *Jurassic Park*, in fact, took place in New Jersey. Footprints from the meat-eating dilophosaurus—tracks one foot long for a dinosaur that reached the length of three automobiles—were discovered in Paterson and Clifton.

"That's actually one of the famous dinosaurs from *Jurassic Park*. Only in *Jurassic Park*, they made it small enough that it crawled into a car and killed somebody—plus they had it spitting poison," says David Parris, curator of the New Jersey State Museum in Trenton. "We joke that it's the one dinosaur they made smaller—they make most of them bigger. This was actually a whopping big dinosaur."

Seemingly everywhere someone put a spade into the ground, new fossils were unearthed. An armored nodosaur in Monmouth. A gliding dinosaur dug up at Granton Quarry in Passaic County. An armadillo-like reptile in Hillsborough. A long-necked plesiosaur—similar to the famed Loch Ness monster—in Middlesex County. And a pterodactyl in Atlantic Highlands.

There were fierce predators. A tyrannosaurus ancestor found in a Burlington County clay pit along the Delaware River. The nightmarish eight-inch hand claw of a dryptosaurus, originally called an eagle-clawed leaper, unearthed both in Gloucester County and in Upper Freehold. A prehistoric fifty-two-foot giant great white shark known as a megalodon.

The earth also yielded long lost creatures of a more modest stature. The oldest known fossil bees, preserved in amber in Burlington County. A Triassic fossil fish called the coelacanth found in locations as diverse as Princeton, Montclair State University, and along Tonnelle Avenue in North Bergen. Footprints everywhere from Newark to Frenchtown. One of those locations, Roseland's Riker Hill Dinosaur Footprint Quarry, offers hikes through an excavation area where more than a thousand dinosaur footprints and tracks from the Jurassic era have been unearthed.

### Panning for Fossils

New Jersey has proven to be exceptionally fertile for fossil collecting, as it encompasses four primary geological regions within its boundaries. The Monmouth County creek known as Big Brook may be the most productive spot in the state. The Big Brook flows through the sands, silts, marls, and clays that were deposited along the Continental Shelf during the Cretaceous and Tertiary periods. On this spring morning, we reach Big Brook by inching along a fallen oak to cross a deep ravine. We hike through a fen of skunk cabbage tall enough to dwarf the kids. Then we descend a slope to a gravel sandbar carved out by the brook from the steep banks rising up on either side.

Here along the Big Brook I find it easy to picture the days of the dinosaurs. The trees rise up high above, their moss-covered, twisting roots protruding from the riverside. The different layers of dirt and sediment are apparent in the eroded banks. To Ray Lewis, our guide today, they evoke the layers of the Grand Canyon. It certainly feels like we're in a lost world. Lewis lives just down the block from this paleontologist's canvas and comes out with his wife and son, Noah, about four or five times each spring.

"I heard about this from my neighbor, and I went out and bought plastic sieves and dug for a while, but the only thing we found were squid tubes. I found out you don't dig it up—you walk around and look. Once you know the shapes, they're easy to find."

It takes Kayla and me a little while to get the hang of it. Once we do, the findings come steadily through the clear, slowly moving water. We find squid pens—cylindrical shells that fossilized in place as hollow columns—and a few porbeagle shark teeth. Mostly we find goblin shark teeth. The goblin shark teeth are fearsome enough, but the porbeagle shark teeth are the stuff of nightmares—jagged, upturned triangles on either side of each tooth. A shark can have upward of 20,000 teeth in its lifetime, with a back row constantly coming in like an assembly line to replace teeth that fall out. Big Brook certainly has its share.

With the little ones in tow, Lewis has planned ahead. He covertly carries a stash of shark teeth and other fossils he found previously, to make sure the kids have the joy of finding something. Halfway through the fossil hunt, Kayla and Noah don't think twice when they happen upon a stretch of a dozen healthy-sized fossils within a few feet of gravel. The young paleontologists are hooked.

"The Big Brook is concentrated, eroded from a number of formations, with sharks as old as dinosaurs, millions of years old, mixed with

David Wheeler

**Fossil hunter Ray Lewis holds a goblin shark tooth found in the gravel bars of the Big Brook in Monmouth County.**

Ice Age swamp deposits from 10,000 to 12,000 years ago," says Parris. "I took our museum summer academy there for a trip, and a girl found a dinosaur bone the size of a fist."

Howie Cohn of the New Jersey Paleontological Society explains the joy of fossil panning by pointing me to a favorite quotation from the legendary paleontologist George Gaylord Simpson: "The fossil hunter does not kill; he resurrects."

Now retired, Cohn began collecting fossils as a child when he unearthed Devonian brachiopod shells and a glacier-scarred rock near his home. Like Simpson, Cohn takes pride in that unique role of the prehistoric treasure explorer.

"Hunting fossils is the one form of hunting where one finds dead prey and returns it to life—instead of the other way around."

### Jersey's Ice Age
The mixed-era bounties of the Big Brook were never more evident than when a fossil hunter discovered an exposed Ice Age mammoth vertebrae in the side of the stream bank. More than a hundred specimens of another elephant relative, the mastodon, also have been found in New

Jersey, including a nearly complete skeleton excavated by a Swedish immigrant couple as they were enlarging their rural pond in Vernon Township. The pond is now officially known as Mastodon Lake.

Another Big Brook hunter unearthed a tooth from an Ice Age giant beaver, which dwelled in swamps around the edges of glaciers and grew as large as a black bear. Big Brook also yielded a giant claw of a ground sloth. This prehistoric mammal came north from South America during the Ice Age and grew as large as an elephant. As Parris points out, the first "scientist" to describe the giant ground sloth was Thomas Jefferson, our third president. The sloth's Latin name, *Megalonyx jeffersoni*, honors Jefferson, who sent Meriwether Lewis and William Clark westward, believing that one of expedition's byproducts would be the discoveries of living ground sloth and other massive creatures.

"He was a pretty good scientist, too," jokes Parris.

News of finds of prehistoric mammals, birds, and reptiles rippled throughout New Jersey like a wave over the last century. A mammoth found in Camden County, and a mammoth tooth in Holgate. A mastodon found in the peat bogs of Sussex County, and a mastodon tooth at Island Beach State Park. Deerlike camels, peccaries, water rhinos, and giant meat-eating warthogs in the Manasquan and Shark rivers. Giant, flightless birds built to attack, boa constrictor–like snakes, and crocodiles found in the Shark River formation. And the only two skeletons in the world of the giant elk-moose were both unearthed in Warren County.

The most accessible prehistoric site is found along the beaches of our very own Jersey Shore. During the dinosaur eras, much of New Jersey was covered by vast oceans. The Ice Age brought about the opposite scenario: so much seawater was tied up in the world's then vast glaciers that our coastline extended far out into what is now the Atlantic Ocean. Storms or current shifts occasionally dredge up old sediment from the Continental Shelf and, with it, the odd fossil or prehistoric bone. New Jersey's ocean wash-ups read like a visit to a Bronx Zoo of prehistoric America: musk ox, bison, walrus, tapir, manatee, elk-moose, and giant ground sloth.

"I was giving a lecture when a woman brought in a ground sloth vertebrae that probably got washed up in a storm," says Parris. "She found it while she was strolling on a beach in Ocean County."

### Never-Ending Extinctions

Extinctions, though a bit depressing for humans to contemplate, are *fait accompli* in the lengthy process of geological time, in which a thousand years is a blink of the eye. Many of the fossil wash-ups come from animals that went extinct or were extirpated from New Jersey thousands of years ago. But species extinctions hardly disappeared with the last Ice Age. They lasted well into modern times—and continue today.

Though not extinct, the cougar and wolf were hunted and trapped out of existence here over a century ago. The bison, marten, and elk—though never large in number—were chased out as well. The heath hen was common in New Jersey's brushy meadows before being hunted to extinction by 1932. Passenger pigeons once darkened America's skies because they were so large in number, but overhunting killed off this species by 1914. Picture the Canada goose going extinct in 2040—doesn't seem possible, does it?

The queen snake might be next in New Jersey. Slender and brown, this endangered crayfish-eating snake lives in small streams with an abundance of tasty freshwater crustaceans. There hasn't been a documented New Jersey occurrence of the queen snake for a decade in its former habitat along the Delaware River from Hunterdon to Gloucester County, though it was recently found across the river in Delaware. Biologists hesitate to remove the queen snake officially from the state species list until they fully study its suitable habitat on the New Jersey side.

Although a formal determination awaits for the queen snake in New Jersey, the sand tiger beetle was officially gone from the Jersey Shore's sand dunes by 1990. Barry Knisley, a Virginia researcher, led the project to translocate this tiny beach insect back to Sandy Hook.

"Around 1900, any sandy beach on Long Island, New Jersey, Connecticut, and Rhode Island had these beetles, but through human activity, they were all exterminated," says Knisley. "Chesapeake Bay now has 90-plus percent of the existing populations, with the only population north of Virginia being on the Jackie Onassis estate at Squibnocket Beach on the south shore of Martha's Vineyard—double-gated and one of the most protected beaches in New England."

As the dominant insect predator on its few remaining beaches, the sand tiger beetle feeds on other insects, such as flies, making it a welcome returnee in New Jersey. Knisley reintroduced the beetle to Sandy Hook's Coast Guard Station beach, transplanting their larvae from Virginia. After 50 emerged as adults, the population peaked at over 700 beetles. They have since declined, however, and their status remains uncertain.

One species that won't be reintroduced anytime soon in New Jersey is the goblin shark. Lewis caps our day at the Big Brook by finding our largest fossil tooth of the day: an enormous, jagged goblin shark tooth that is classic for its sheer menace. This fifteen-foot prehistoric beast once inhabited these waters and left countless teeth to be unearthed. A goblin shark descendent still swims the earth today, a pink freak of nature with a beaked snout, muscled tongue, and thresher-like tail. Found most often in the Sea of Japan, the goblin shark was named after the "tengu" of Japanese folklore: a beak-snouted demon thought to be a harbinger of war.

Thankfully, goblin sharks are long gone from the waters of the Big Brook. Fresh water in New Jersey is no place for a shark nowadays.

Is it?

# Great White Hunter 13

Sharks are not good business. They don't want you to go into Atlantic City and see ten bull sharks hauled off the Boardwalk.

—Howard Sefton, shop owner

In July 2009 Howard Sefton, a bait-and-tackle shop owner in Atlantic County's Egg Harbor City, hand-wrote a warning for his customers on the shop's chalkboard, a message board that typically displays the times for each day's high and low tides:

> At Lower Bank a
> 7-Ft Bull Shark was caught
> in the Mullica River. Along
> with 4-Ft & 5-Ft Bull Shark.
> Swimmers Beware.

Bull sharks are aggressive, barrel-shaped predators that grow more than seven feet long and weigh nearly 300 pounds. Called "the champion of freshwater sharks," the bull shark's unique glands and kidneys allow it to survive outside of saltwater for lengthy periods of time. They have been found as far up the Mississippi River as Illinois, 1,800 miles from the Gulf of Mexico. They travel 3,000 miles up the Peruvian Amazon and swim upstream in rivers in South Africa and Australia. In Central America they even inhabit a freshwater inland lake, Lake Nicaragua. And in Bangladesh they are suspected of attacking Hindu pilgrims in the holy Ganges River.

Sefton was hearing a growing number of local reports of this creature. A Northfield police officer saw a four-foot bull shark caught off Lower Bank Bridge. One shop visitor was kayaking in the Mullica—wide and brackish, with salt marsh on all sides—when a big fish nearly the length of her kayak swam up alongside and looked her over. And another customer told Sefton he saw bull sharks "playing" in a big fishing hole just fifty yards from the riverbank near the same bridge.

These sightings could be interpreted as just another reminder that people need to exercise caution around wild animals. Bull sharks, though, have a track record that warrants a second look. They are past offenders, if you will. Bull sharks were fully or partially responsible for the worst shark attacks in American history, a blitzkrieg of five attacks that left four people dead in less than two weeks.

The horrors took place not in California or Florida.

They occurred in Matawan Creek, New Jersey.

## Massacre in Matawan

In the summer of 1916, five people were attacked by either one or two large sharks along the New Jersey coast. Three of those attacks occurred in a single day, eleven miles upstream from the ocean in Matawan Creek, a meandering brook that enters Raritan Bay in Keyport. Twelve-year-old Lester Stillwell was splashing in the creek with his friends when a shark dragged him under in a pool of blood. Lester's friends ran out and told the townsfolk, who assembled an armed war party to hunt down the murderous beast.

Watson Stanley Fisher courageously stretched a net across the creek to keep Lester's body from being carried downstream—in the process, securing his own death. Fisher was yanked down with a scream. He put up a fight and was carried to the hospital, but he died from a massive blood loss before doctors could save him. Another group of boys encountered the shark while swimming farther downstream. The shark bit a boy named Joseph Dunn on his legs, but his older brother heroically pulled him out of the shark's death grip.

In his book on the events of 1916, Richard Fernicola describes them as a "perfect storm" of attacks unrivaled in modern times.

"You essentially have five very serious attacks within a twelve-day period, and three in one day in a creek. Both events are fairly monumental anywhere in the world from multiple geographical and statistical standpoints, not just in New Jersey and the United States. Add to that the fact that New Jersey attacks are very uncommon, and you can see the exponential rarity of the sequence of events."

### Scene of the Crime

Matawan Creek flows under the Garden State Parkway at mile marker 119.4. Two tributaries of a winding tidal creek converge here, with woods on one side and tidal mudflats on the other. As I drive past on the Parkway on an August afternoon, I see great egrets and cormorants in the marsh. This marks the tragic spot where Lester Stillwell was attacked nearly a century ago.

I drive through a tightly packed housing complex and park in a dirt lot down an unmarked dead end. From this dismal trailhead, sandy paths lead through a thick birch forest that abuts both Matawan Creek and the Garden State Parkway. A thick wall of reeds prevents easy access to the creek itself, but I can see a semblance of the habitat that the Matawan townsfolk rushed through on that terrifying afternoon in 1916.

During that Good Samaritan response, the second attack—on Watson Stanley Fisher—occurred at a location very close to the Matawan train station.

"Heading northbound, when you hit the creek, this is the exact location where the townspeople went down—you even can find the path along the creek," says Fernicola. "In summer it's really overgrown, but the dimensions of the creek are similar, and the bends in the creek are pretty much the same. Depth probably has suffered from sediment, but that's about it."

I walk the area today and find a world that has changed dramatically in some ways and not at all in others. This stretch of Matawan Creek is almost entirely off-limits now. One of the few public spots is a Green Acres–preserved area along Aberdeen Road. A picturesque waterworld lines both sides of the road, and the railroad trestle towers fifty feet above a culvert that connects the creek to its downstream segment. Two double-crested cormorants take off from the surface of the creek upstream, a snowy egret sits atop the culvert, and two belted kingfishers circle down noisily from the wooded slopes of the railroad line.

The two most scenic vistas of Matawan Creek are from the top of that rail trestle and from the Parkway's southbound lanes. Neither, obviously, is recommended for pedestrians, but to a passenger looking from the safety of an automobile or train, the creek offers a glimpse of our wild past, when a shark took the lives of New Jerseyans who happened to be in the wrong place at the wrong time.

The other two 1916 incidents occurred farther south, off the beaches of Beach Haven and Spring Lake—both fatal attacks on healthy ocean swimmers in their mid-twenties. As in the Matawan incidents, authorities attributed those attacks to a great white shark, the usual suspect. When a great white was caught by a fisherman with a human bone in its stomach, New Jersey waters were declared safe.

### The Hollywood Monster

A decade after that fateful year, in August 1926, a shark killed a swimmer in Seaside Heights. Since then, nearly a century has passed without a person being fatally attacked by a shark in New Jersey. The events of 1916, however, lingered long afterward in popular imagination, with the great white shark getting most of the blame as the monster responsible. If the story seems a bit familiar, there is good reason. In 1975 a little-known director named Steven Spielberg made a film based on Peter Benchley's novel—which itself was based loosely on the 1916 New Jersey attacks.

*Jaws* became the first Hollywood summer blockbuster, grossing more than $100 million in box-office receipts. Millions of people watched, and *Time* magazine ran a cover story titled "Super Shark." Thanks to three sequels—and the availability of the original on video, DVD, movie channels, and pay-per-view—*Jaws* is an American rite of passage. I remember from my youngest days the movie's images flashing through my head while swimming in the ocean. On a childhood visit to Martha's Vineyard, I was awed to visit the Edgartown hardware store and Chappaquiddick cabana-lined swimming beach where key scenes of *Jaws* were filmed. Later, in high school, I had a fleeting glimpse of a fin while paddling on a surfboard—and to this day, I have no idea whether that sighting was overactive imagination or actual shark. Now, three decades after the film, I still make the ominous tuba sounds of the John Williams Oscar-winning score—duh-deh duh-deh duh-deh—as I play shark with my kids in a swimming pool.

"Basically, *Jaws* is a fiction, the making of a Hollywood monster like Godzilla or King Kong," says Dr. Leonard Compagno, director of the Shark Research Institute in Princeton. "The great white shark simply doesn't do all that, but among the older generation, no one can evade the *Jaws* reputation of the great white as monster. Peter Benchley became a shark conservationist before he died, and now kids really love sharks, too—not just we shark crazies and fanatics."

The Shark Research Institute maintains the Global Shark Attack File, a detailed online listing of all suspected shark attacks in history. New

Jersey's first suspected attack occurred in August 1884, off the coast of Bayonne, when a boater's hand was bitten. That was just a precursor to the horrible summer of 1916. In the case of Matawan—the spectacle of *Jaws* to the contrary—it turns out the great white is getting the rap for a crime it didn't commit. The only records of a great white swimming up a river occur in Canada's St. Lawrence River, which is extremely wide and marine. Great whites are not physically suited for hunting in brackish water or freshwater.

"Unlike the white shark, which is a visible hunter, bull sharks are prominent in turbid waters," says Compagno. "They have tiny eyes, and their vision is not as important. It's easy to tell from the bites. The teeth are smaller on bull sharks. You get a white shark bite—you know it."

The great white shark is, however, a bona fide cold-blooded killer in New Jersey—of seals. Many of New Jersey's stranded seals are victims of shark bites. In 2009 at least five seals were mauled by the same shark, which was caught off the Sea Girt Reef.

"Shark-bit seals are quite common, and we sometimes get a lot of them," says Maurice Tremblay, a Marine Mammal Stranding Center volunteer. "We even had one with a bite from an orca."

### Seals in Winter

Pick a sunny but frigid day in the heart of winter. Find a remote, windswept location along the Jersey Shore. Bring a high-powered spotting scope or binoculars, extra layers of winter clothes, and a healthy supply of patience.

Voila! That might be enough to get you a sighting of a seal—or fifty—in the Garden State.

Incredibly enough, seals are becoming more and more common along the coast each winter, eating a daily ration of up to twenty pounds of flounder, other fish, shellfish, crustaceans, and mollusks. Four species visit New Jersey's coastal waters in a given winter. Spotted most frequently are harbor seals hauling out onto exposed sandbars or dredge spoils off the coast. Gray and hooded seals from as far as the Norwegian island of Svalbard visit less often. Each has a unique look. The gray seal's large snout earned it the nickname "horsehead seal." The male hooded seal inflates its nose to attract female seals—and looks like a veritable Bozo the Seal.

The harp seal, on the other hand, is the equivalent of a seal supermodel. You may have seen them many times before. In the 1980s the harp seal's puppy-eyed white pups served as the adorable public face of

Bill Bonner

**Harbor seals are the most common of four species of seals to winter along New Jersey's coast.**

the anti–seal-hunting movement. Far less common in estuaries than harbor seals, the harp seal usually sticks to the North Atlantic and Arctic oceans. Nonetheless, young harp seals are found regularly on New Jersey's coast each winter.

Sandy Hook is a great place for seeing a seal in the wild. Seals often hunt at night and spend their days resting onshore—an ideal schedule for wildlife enthusiasts. That is, for those willing to walk the most windswept waterfront locations in the coldest months of the year. Joe Reynolds, of the Bayshore Regional Watershed Council, is just such an adventurer.

"When it's low tide on a really sunny day, you have the potential to see thirty to fifty seals out basking together on Skeleton Island," says Reynolds.

**The Rescuers**

Reynolds is also one of about a hundred active volunteers with the Marine Mammal Stranding Center. These volunteers up and down the coast serve as the eyes and ears of the unique Brigantine-based center, which was started in 1978 to rescue and rehabilitate injured or stranded seals, whales, dolphins, and sea turtles. Sheila Dean, the center's co-director, has worked for more than two decades to help such marine mammals.

"We had a little seal—we named her Tak, after the harbor where she was born, Takanassee—that was stranded just after being born," says Dean. "Her mother left the baby on the beach—there was just no way she could keep people away. We raised it, but she was just too imprinted on humans. We ended up giving her to the Indianapolis Zoo. I felt really bad, but she would not have survived out there."

Dean wasn't being overprotective. A dolphin in Florida, after being rehabilitated for nine months, was released into the wild. Sharks killed it immediately upon release, with everyone watching in horror. Clearly nature takes its own course.

On the day I visit the Stranding Center, five harp seals are stranded along the New Jersey coast. The center is a whirlwind of activity, with teams of rescuers rushing to the different locations to treat and hopefully release the seals—their release rate is 90 percent. The rescuers and volunteers also have to keep the public away from the seals and their "puppy-dog eyes."

"Seals have a vicious bite—not from malice, but because they're scared," volunteer Maurice Tremblay tells me at the center. "They hang on like a bulldog."

After my tour with Tremblay, I realize I just have to see a seal in New Jersey for myself. I had seen seals off the coast of Northern Ireland and enjoyed the fussy orchestra of the famed sea lions at San Francisco's wharfside, but seals never seemed possible in New Jersey.

I pick the right day: it is absolutely glacial, with a winter storm scheduled to hit within a few hours. My daughter and I head first to Skeleton Island, a long barrier strip on the bay side of Sandy Hook. It is low tide, and the tangy smell of salt marsh fills the air. Many dark, long shapes pepper the distant sandbars beyond the island, and our hopes are high. A closer look through my binoculars reveals no movement. My "seals" turn out to be driftwood logs and rocks.

We watch gulls drop shells against the rocks and plummet after them, and then we head for the northern end of Sandy Hook near Fort Hancock. I drive south along the bay's edge, peering out the passenger window and hoping against hope for a seal. A male red-breasted merganser catches Kayla's eye, its green head feathers tussled in the back like a case of bedhead. I pull off to the right and back up for a closer look. It is then that I see a dark shape that almost immediately goes under. It does not register as a bird, so could it be . . . ?

I turn the car around for a direct view with my binoculars, and there it is! A clear shot of a seal head, dark black with puppy-dog eyes, long face, and whiskers. We watch for a few seconds as it stares back before finally going under. Between the seal and the approaching storm, Sandy Hook might as well be the Arctic.

## Sharks on the Mullica

Many months later, on an early fall morning, I veer off onto a dirt trail off of Clarks Landing Road near the eastern edge of the Pine Barrens. For the next two miles, I pass no cars, no side streets, and virtually no remnants of human habitation. The blackjack oak forest is deep and thick, like an Old South broadleaf forest. The branches above form a solid canopy penetrated by little sunlight. A light at the end of the tunnel beckons, and finally I am out of the forest and into the salt marsh. Now there is nothing but sky and sunlight, save the stark silhouette of an abandoned duck-hunting cabin. Its empty frame rises above the flat marsh like a Dakota Territory abandoned frontier homestead, slowly crumbling into a grassland meadow. This road has brought me to an isolated stretch of the

Bill Wheeler

**David and Kayla Wheeler search for sharks from the safety of a dock along the Mullica River.**

Mullica River. Today the visitors are a low-flying marsh hawk, plenty of noisy marsh wrens, and a sora dabbing at the mudflats near the end of the road.

On another day the visitors might be bull sharks heading upstream. Farther inland, working-class fishermen crowd the railings of the Lower Bank Bridge, which overlooks a wide riverine expanse lined with homes on one side and untrammeled wilderness on the other. The Mullica is prime fishing grounds for catfish, freshwater bass, pickerel, crappy, and yellow perch. For those very reasons, bull sharks may enjoy the area as much as the fishermen.

"My guess is they've been coming for years," says Sefton, who has owned his bait-and-tackle shop for more than a decade. "The bull shark is aggressive, very territorial. You step into the wrong area, you could be in very big trouble. It's the number one killer of humans, contrary to what you think about with the great white and *Jaws*.

"When I go into a bay to get grass shrimp, I've been knocked off my feet in chest waders by a large fish, and it's not funny. It could've been saying, 'Get out of the way.' I'm cautious—I look out for it."

There is a scene in *Jaws* that holds a certain relevance to the Mullica River today. In the film, Mayor Vaughn of the fictional seaside resort town of Amity overrules the police chief's wish to close the beaches:

> I don't think you appreciate the gut reaction people have to these things. . . . It's all psychological. You yell, "Barracuda!" everybody says "Huh? What?" You yell, "Shark!" we've got a panic on our hands on the Fourth of July. I'm only trying to say that Amity is a summer town. We need summer dollars. If people can't swim here, they'll be glad to swim in the beaches of Cape Cod, the Hamptons, Long Island.

On the Mullica River in 2009, life imitates art. According to a story by the *Press of Atlantic City*, a local marina owner reacted strongly to Sefton's warning. "I think it's ridiculous. Bull sharks live in very, very warm water, and I can't see the water being that warm to support them."

That explanation simply doesn't hold any water, pardon the pun. New Jersey's summer inland waters can reach 80 degrees, which is more than comfortable for a bull shark. And although bull sharks are not inherently predisposed to attack humans, the cloudy water in tidal rivers means much less visibility for a hungry shark. Sefton is undeterred in his warning.

"Sharks are not good business. They don't want you to go into Atlantic City and see ten bull sharks hauled off the Boardwalk."

## The Hunter Is the Hunted

The danger of a bull shark attack, though extremely remote, is still possible in murky waters where bull sharks are known to frequent, like the Mullica River. That risk pales in comparison to the fate facing sharks at this moment all around the world. It is the sharks who are on the run from a massive, merciless stalker on the high seas—humans.

"The lack of shark attacks on humans is a double-edged sword," says Fernicola. "It's good, obviously, but is it because we've brought sharks to such low numbers? As an apex predator, it does not reproduce frequently, and we are decimating their numbers."

The worldwide harvest of sharks is close to 100 million a year, according to the late Dery Bennett, who studied our marine ecosystem for more than thirty years with the American Littoral Society.

"Big sharks are down—it used to be the docks were covered with shark carcasses. Nowadays people are smart enough to release them. It's more of a conservation ethic. Most fishermen release most sharks they catch."

The plight of the sharks is best illustrated by the people coming to their defense—the very victims of their rare attacks. In July 2009 nine American shark attack victims testified before the U.S. Congress in support of stronger shark conservation laws, in particular to limit the horrid international practice of finning—already banned in the United States—in which a shark's dorsal fin is sliced off for shark fin soup, with the still breathing shark dumped back in the ocean to die. The Asian market for shark fin soup has made shark fishing in Asia an immensely profitable industry—at least until there are no more sharks to catch. Stronger laws are sorely needed, as the forecast from the Shark Research Institute makes clear.

"Big offshore sharks are in serious trouble from pollution, destruction of habitat, fishing directly, fishing as bycatch for their fins, cutting their jaws out," says Compagno. "They have declined dramatically and they will continue to decline. It's sort of like bailing out a rowboat after a torpedo hits."

One positive note is that the United States has strengthened its shark-fishing laws to limit further declines for shark species, at least at our hands.

"New Jersey captains are not only monitored, but their fishing is effective because a ship captain has a vested interest in abiding by the laws," says Fernicola. "It would destroy his business if sharks were wiped out."

### Chasing Sharks on the High Seas

Shark-fishing captains confirm that both numbers and sizes of catches have gone down over the past decade, but not for all species. Blue sharks tend to be strong, as do threshers—a magnificent-looking shark with a swordlike tail that can reach ten feet in length. The largest shark commonly found close to the coast, threshers swim through schools of fish, whip their tails to stun the fish, and then circle back to eat their catch. This powerful shark dives as deep as 200 feet, sometimes taking a fisherman forty minutes to reel it up from the bottom depths.

"My father got hit by a thresher tail two years ago, and it knocked him right off his feet on the deck," says Captain Darren Volker, who has run shark-fishing trips out of New Jersey for more than fifteen years. "He had a bruise wrapped right around him. They're not mean sharks, though."

In addition to blue and thresher sharks, fishing trips occasionally catch dusky sharks, brown sharks, great white sharks, and hammerheads. Hammerhead sharks—with each eye extending horizontally from the head like a character from *Return of the Jedi*—are fast and strong swimmers, but their finicky tastes make them a less frequent catch than some of the others.

No shark compares to the mako, which Volker calls "the ultimate gamefish for shark fishing." The fastest shark in the North Atlantic, the mako swims in bursts of speed up to forty miles per hour and jumps out of the water up to thirty feet high. To top it off, the mako—which can grow as large as 800 pounds—is legendarily aggressive.

"The thing with shark fishing, you never know what's gonna be there—it could be a 100-pound mako, but it could be a 500-pound mako," says Volker. "They're mean and tough, just a tough fish to beat. When you get them to the boat, there's no making mistakes. You gotta be careful—they're a real challenge."

As for bull sharks, Sefton recently caught one off Brigantine.

"It was only about fifty pounds, but it was like pulling in the *Titanic*. I had a friend tell me they were catching them off the beach. He said, 'Come on down!' He handed me his rod, and I could barely move it. Every time the tide came in a foot, the shark came in a foot. It was just solid muscle."

### Dead or Alive

After my last shark interview, I head to the beach in Bay Head on a sweltering August evening. Tiny fish are jumping out left and right, just inches away from me, and I assume bluefish are attacking below the surface. Hundreds of fish dance on the surface over the course of a few minutes, and the smell is far more fishy than normal. There must be a huge school under here.

I wait for the next good wave, when an eerie feeling suddenly strikes me. Here I am bodysurfing in the ocean, just before sunset and long after the lifeguards have gone home. With so many jumping baitfish, there must be plenty of bluefish, and the blues could, in turn, attract the sharks. That progression grows in my mind with each whitecap in the distance, even if I know the microscopic odds of such an encounter. Yet it is also wonderful to feel the expanse of the ocean and remember that, yes, the sharks are out there. Even if I never see one in New Jersey in the wild—and I'd prefer that sighting from a boat, not from my bathing suit—the sharks symbolize the vastness and enormity of the oceans.

For me, there are fish, and then there are sharks.

And for Captain Darren Volker, there are sharks, and then there are makos.

"Makos have a freaky way of coming back to life. One we caught this year, we shot it in the head, and a half hour later, it came to life and went ballistic. They're tied down but their eyes follow you, and they'll go for you."

I hope that is not the fate of sharks as a whole—watching us from the grave.

# The Final Frontier 14
## BIRDING THE OPEN ATLANTIC

Pelagic birding is the last frontier for bird explorers in North America.

—William J. Boyle Jr., A Guide to Bird Finding in New Jersey

There are many casual birders in New Jersey. Nearly anyone can enjoy watching birds on a feeder through a window. Many of us will even visit a well-known birding hotspot, standing in a bird blind with binoculars and a cup of coffee nearby.

Then there are the adventurers who go on Paul Guris's winter pelagic, or oceanic, trips. The few, the proud—these are New Jersey's extreme birders.

I anxiously join them on a full-day Atlantic Ocean voyage that departs at dawn. A brisk wind sweeps the Shark River waterfront, with a winter storm due to hit this afternoon. On this trip, the *Suzie Girl* is no party boat. High seas alter our itinerary, forcing a detour north. Snow falls intermittently on the ocean all around us. The boat feels like a toy tossed around a wild child's bathtub. A few passengers take turns heaving off the back of the boat and lying miserably in a fetal position along hard benches in the damp cabin. On the top deck, an angry sea transforms the simple act of moving into a challenge of balance—sliding, slipping, and lunging to grip the rails before you tumble headfirst down the open stairwell.

A pelagic tour is clearly not for the casual birder. And yet, after moving past the survival phase of my maiden journey—an hour in which saltines and a dramamine lull help me skirt the edge of nausea—I begin to see why the two dozen adventurers onboard chose to spend this winter day out in the frigid, churning Atlantic. Sightings of sea life from as far away as Antarctica, birds I could have no hope of seeing from shore, get the blood flowing pretty quickly. For wildlife enthusiasts, pelagic birding truly is New Jersey's unexplored horizon.

## A Light-Hearted Obsession

When Paul Guris was a young child, his first love was fishing. As he likes to say, his first trip was prenatal—his mom was out at sea in her third trimester.

"I got saltwater in my veins," he jokes.

On fishing trips Guris furthered his appreciation for the sea life above the water as well as beneath. A birder by age twelve, he soon grew frustrated by the lack of opportunity to go offshore in search of rarities and infrequent visitors from across the globe. No one else was offering the kinds of pelagic birding tours Guris wanted, so he took the helm himself, founding See Life Paulagics (get it—Paul-agics?) in the mid-1980s.

Today, with dedicated participation from birders old and new, Guris leads trips out of Belmar, Cape May, and nearby states every few weeks during the right seasons, namely, winter and summer. In winter, the "short" eight-hour trip stays within thirty miles of the coast, seeking out diving birds like puffin, murres, and dovekies. Summer brings the overnight birding and fishing voyages that look for birds like black skimmers, shearwaters, storm-petrels, jaegers, skuas, and terns over the Hudson Canyon—the largest underwater canyon on the East Coast, extending

The black skimmer, a New Jersey species of concern, uses its extended lower bill to "skim" fish from along the ocean's surface.

Tam Stuart

450 miles southeast across the Continental Shelf from an area east of Monmouth County.

When I arrive at dawn, the voyagers are donning their ski pants and knee-high black rubber boots, double-checking their high-tech binoculars, scopes, and cameras, and tightening their scarves and hats to leave as little exposed skin as possible. Guris stands in the rear of the boat, dressed in jeans, a modest jacket, and a bright orange knit hat over his dark eyebrows and mustache. He's raring to go, giving the passengers a sense of what to expect in a speech that's equal parts enthusiastic and deadpan.

"We use the twelve o'clock"—he points to the head of the boat, then in the other three directions—"the six, nine, and three o'clock. Unless the dyslexia kicks in, then it's three, nine."

A brief pause for the laughs of the voyagers, then he continues in a more serious tone.

"Now watch the center aisle—if a rare bird is seen, you will almost certainly be trampled. Once the birders get their life bird, then they'll come back to help you."

If there is such a thing as light-hearted obsession, Paul Guris, the birder, defines it. He and three fellow trip leaders fan out around the boat as the voyagers take spots along the exposed top deck, the lower deck's open front and back, and the long backless benches of the enclosed cabin. Walking up the steps, I pass the captain's son chopping up bait fish. This casserole, mixed with Purina fish chow, will serve as the chum enticing birds to follow our wake.

### High-Seas Safari

As we head to sea from Belmar along the Shark Inlet, scenic views of the shore accompany an already frantic bird display—cormorants, mergansers, and, of course, incredible numbers of gulls. Then we are out in the open ocean. Rising waves of gunmetal gray fold into scattered whitecaps. The churning water beneath our boat is less noticeable so long as we are moving. Someone spots a razorbill, and the boat slows to get a better angle. We turn slowly, and the waves now crash directly into our side. They are not pouring over our sides—this is far from a perfect storm—but they help us to *feel* the boat's rise and fall quite clearly. One hour into the trip, the waves are enough to make me wonder what is still to come.

Then a call rings out: "Razorbill two o'clock! Just under the Bonies, flying two to three. Just went down. Two o'clock—wait for it to come up." The Bonies are Bonaparte gulls, tiny and sleek and neither rare nor common enough to take for granted. A black-and-white shape materializes behind a passing wave, and I have my first clear sighting of a razorbill. With its jet-black coat and pure white underbelly, the razorbill on land looks like a penguin, though with a thick black bill ringed with a scalloped white line. The next few minutes bring many more razorbills to this fertile stretch of ocean, as well as a black-legged kittiwake and both surf and black scoters. Guris is a blur of spotting, tracking, counting, and helping others find dozens of different species of birds and other sea life in the air, on the churning seas, and diving into the deep.

The northern gannet joins our avian entourage. Mostly white, its head capped with yellow, the gannet boasts a sturdy six-foot wingspan tipped with black at the ends. They remind me of blue-footed boobies, those comically named birds that fill the air during any Galapagos Islands nature program. For the remainder of the trip, ten seconds do not pass without a northern gannet in sight, swooping like a fighter jet in large "figure eight" loops, jockeying for position with the gaggle of gulls following us, and plunging into the water like an Olympic diver who scarcely leaves a ripple on the surface. Meanwhile, gulls fight and snap and dive in groups of three and four and five for each bucket of chum tossed off the boat.

"Dovekie, three o'clock flying over the horizon!" I get a quick glimpse of what looks like a tiny razorbill, catching it for a millisecond before it passes behind the front of the boat; when I look from the other side, it is already lost in the distance.

"Dovekies halfway between us and the horizon!"

I see these two for an entire second. There is an added urgency to these calls. Despite my limited knowledge of seabirds on departure, I am thrilled to see this tiny bird in a vast ocean. We leave the birding paradise and travel north, followed by dozens of gulls and two swooping gannets. A sense of calm settles over the travelers. On the top deck, four of us cram onto a bench facing the back of the boat. I nibble on crackers and a dry sandwich, feeling gradually better after wondering in the early stages just how long I could last. One traveler on the bottom deck is not so lucky. She spends two-thirds of the trip bent over the back rail and the remainder curled up in a fetal position on an indoor cabin bench.

The rest of us settle in, retreating into our frozen bodies. The up-and-down motion, the dramamine, the bitter cold kept out by many, many layers of cozy clothing, all of it brings me to the edge of dozing, eyes shutting and mind going blank for moments at a time and—

"DOVEKIES—two behind the gannet! They're down. They're up! Dovekies are up!"

Wobbly we rise and slide-pull ourselves across the slippery top deck, staggering and lunging for a grip along the side rails. The alarm sounds again. And again. And again. It is no longer just the trip leaders. Each of us sounds the alarm from a different direction.

A pair of dovekies at three!

Dovekie flying away from eight to nine!

Three dovekies at one!

Four, five dovekies, and now we see them up close, sitting atop the ocean as we motor past. It is enthralling. Each bird's tiny head and neck sit atop a round little body floating atop a churning surface, wings beating up and down as if on speed as it flies away to the horizon. One passenger aptly describes them as "black-and-white Nerf footballs with wings," another as "black-and-white rubber duckies." They are both right. In the span of a half hour, we spot scores of dovekies, even if any given person misses half the sightings. We are all experts now in identifying the dovekie.

## Sea Meets Sky

In the midst of the dovekie fever, I see a more familiar shape, and I hear myself shouting "Dolphin!"

The gorgeous gray form knifes through the metallic surface like a sea monster apparition for a lost-at-sea Old World explorer. One dolphin brings other dolphins, including short-beaked common dolphins.

Though they don't follow our wake as we hoped they would, they make an inspiring sight.

Pelagic trips yield many sea life sightings beyond birds, and Guris can identify these creatures just as easily as he can distinguish a Wilson's storm-petrel from a white-faced storm-petrel. (I mean, really, is there anyone who *cannot* tell those two apart?)

Along with inshore and offshore bottlenose dolphins, Guris has seen Risso's dolphin (round shape, very tall fins, found in water over 600 feet deep), common dolphin (slim and petite with an "almost hourglass shape"), Atlantic white-sided dolphin (they throw a spray of water up when they are "porpoising," or breaching the surface), Cuvier's beaked whale (deep-feeding brown whales up to thirty feet long with whitish heads), and harbor porpoises (only four feet long, and visible only when the water is calm and flat). He has seen scalloped hammerhead sharks, manta rays, leatherback sea turtles, and basking sharks. A fishing line set out on longer trips has brought catches of albacore, mahi mahi, marlin, and yellowfin tuna.

One trip brought Guris a sperm whale sighting. "It looked like a telephone pole—it laid there completely flat. It was so big, just fifty yards away. I could hear it breathe, see the wrinkles on its skin."

There has been an equally extraordinary array of bird sightings over the years. The first documented sighting of a Western gull on the North Atlantic in history. The second North American sighting of a Cape Verde shearwater, which breeds in the Cape Verde Islands off northern Africa. The rare white-faced storm-petrel doing a "kangaroo hop" off the water, lifting its tiny body on the strength of the surface breeze alone—and only then snapping open its wings.

A favorite is the clownlike Atlantic puffin. When I traveled through Iceland, the puffin—its huge, sad eyes matched by a bright orange beak that stands out even more next to the black-and-white mask—was omnipresent both along the coast and as a marketing image on product packaging. Yes, Iceland's national bird, found in North America primarily on the coastal islands of Maine, makes appearances off the coast of New Jersey.

To top it off, visitors from Antarctica greet Guris and his passengers. The South Polar skua, a fearsome, dark-coated Antarctic predator the size of a large gull, played a villainous role in the children's penguin movie *Happy Feet*—but was welcomed on a summer pelagic trip.

Of the Wilson's storm-petrel, Guris says, "Some think it may be the most common bird on the face of the earth, just because there is so much ocean, and they are encountered everywhere on the ocean in huge numbers." That storm-petrel is not much bigger than a house sparrow, yet it reaches New Jersey waters all the way from Antarctica.

Finally, we turn away from the Brooklyn and Staten Island and Rockaway coast, the New York City skyline looming in the distance, and we make for home. We pass the long, low stretch of Sandy Hook, the sudden bluff of the Atlantic Highlands, the packed Monmouth County coastline to the south. Guris and the other trip leaders open bottles of beer and swap stories about birds and fish. It's like any great fishing trip, only their eyes never leave the ocean surface and horizon. Guris sums it up in his recap e-mail for the New Jersey birding community: "Birding was generally decent, but without a doubt, the dovekies stole the show." When all was said and done, our trip found seventy-five dovekies—Guris's highest count ever so close to shore.

"On a pelagic trip you've got a better chance of finding something you've never seen before, or hardly ever seen, than anything else you can do with birding or nature. It's the lure of the unexpected," explains Guris. He shifts into his Forrest Gump voice: "Life is like a pelagic trip—you never know what you're gonna get."

You never know when you might see the latest visitor from Antarctica just a few miles off the Asbury Park boardwalk.

## A Million to Avalon

If pelagic birding offers humans a journey into the realm of seabirds, every so often those birds make an unanticipated stopover in our world. Like, say, an albatross—an oceanic wanderer that lives to fifty, flies more than 500 miles in a day, and boasts a seven-foot wingspan. The albatross is rarely found north of the Equator, but May 21, 2000, was one of those lucky days.

"My friend was driving down the Garden State Parkway, and she saw the yellow-nosed albatross in flight," says Guris. "She called it in, and people later saw it on the Delaware Bayshore in Cape May County. I'm surprised she didn't drive off the road!"

Think about that. Rarely north of the Equator means that the West Indies are a real stretch, yet we got one in New Jersey. The lone albatross that shows up on New Jersey's doorstep every few decades is a "one in a million" type of bird. Another count brings a million individual birds within reach in a given year. From September 22 to December 22, in Avalon, you'll find a lone person sitting in a chair at the end of Seventh Street, one eye glued to a spotting scope trained on the great blue beyond. The sight may seem mundane, but the spotter is catching a mass migration of continental significance. At that moment, *he or she is the only person at the only bird seawatch on the entire eastern seaboard of North America.* Other bird watches count migrating birds like raptors and songbirds, but not seabirds. Only in Avalon are migrating seabirds counted, in numbers that must be seen to be believed.

On a cold, sunny late November morning, Sean Fitzgerald tends the scope. A thin, bearded man in his twenties, Fitzgerald is happy to discuss what's in his sights with even the most novice birder. At this moment, a mid-sized seabird rises and falls with the passing waves not far offshore, often disappearing behind a breaker for a few seconds or under the water for seconds longer. My first and second guesses while Fitzgerald gets it in his scope are wrong, and more wrong. A common loon it is.

Fitzgerald is completing his first season as an official counter with New Jersey Audubon's Avalon Seawatch, which has run this count since 1993. He works five days a week, sunrise to sunset. (An alternate counter covers two days each week.) Sixty-plus hours a week spent right here, in this chair, squinting through the sights of a scope at forever undulating waves, rising and falling. Fitzgerald is so dedicated that he doesn't take leaving his post lightly.

Vince Elia, who supervises the Avalon Seawatch for New Jersey Audubon, concurs. "It's an overused term, but our people are a special breed. They need identification skills, the ability to count lots of birds passing through, quite a bit of stamina—they're usually mid- to late twenties—and they need experience with seabirds."

Fitzgerald is no local novice. He once spent six weeks in India to help survey the birds of a mountain lake. But what is it about birding that would make someone like him spend his time glued to this spot in New Jersey counting birds?

"I like migration. I'm fascinated by it," says Fitzgerald. "The birds I see are actively migrating—they're right in the middle of it. I've seen something like 800,000 birds this year!"

On a single day, he has counted more than 60,000 scoters, which look like a bizarre cross between a duck and a penguin, and more than 35,000 double-crested cormorants. Cormorants are one of those birds you can get immune to; they are now commonly found all along the coast and along New Jersey's rivers, even in heavily urban areas. Still, the largest number you might reasonably expect to see elsewhere would be about 35—and Fitzgerald has seen 1,000 times that on a single day here.

## "Cooler by a Mile"

It was not by accident that New Jersey Audubon chose Avalon. The place juts out from the Atlantic coast by about a mile.

"The saying is, 'cooler by a mile,' so species moving down the New Jersey coast have to go through Avalon," says Elia. "Put your binoculars up the coast to the Atlantic City casinos, and it's really an amazing spectacle. There are scoter flocks numbering in the thousands, 30,000-plus black scoters and 30,000-plus surf scoters in a given day, movements of northern gannets over 10,000 in a given day, and thousands of red-throated loons."

Along with the spotting scope, a blue metal-bordered chart sits nearby alongside the streetside barrier. A handwritten column lists around a dozen of the seabird highlights, with their counts for the day and season. The spotters have seen close to ninety different bird species for the year—an astonishing total for an oceanfront location. A number of rarities also pass through: Pacific loon, California gull, wood stork, white-fronted goose, black guillemot, Arctic goose, and even an Atlantic puffin sighting from the shore that Elia calls "totally off the wall."

And, contrary to the activity at the tip of Cape May, hawks and other raptors are the outcasts here.

"Hawks are really hesitant to cross water. The only times they do are with really strong winds. The exception being falcons—merlins and peregrine falcons—which are the only raptors with no qualms about migrating over water," Fitzgerald patiently explains as something catches his attention. "Look—there's a long-tailed duck. See it? Going low just over the water."

I get a clear glimpse through my binoculars. It's beautiful—white with a streak of black wings, obscenely long tail trailing as it powers along as if on a track over the dark blue raceway before it disappears from my view. The long-tailed duck was called an oldsquaw until recent years—a name far more appropriate for a bird that has been following the same paths for millennia. My first oldsquaw.

And my first peek at what migration can mean to a scientist or a dedicated birder. It is not a bird in a tree or at a feeder. It is a part of a timeless global spectacle, an annual event that sets the natural world in motion. Every fall, the capital of that worldwide wonder is New Jersey.

"You can get really good views of northern gannets diving from fifty feet high after a school of moving fish. It's just like watching Animal Planet," says Paul Kerlinger, a birder based in Cape May. "Plus at the

Seawatch, if it gets too cold, you can always just jump in your car to warm up."

That may be the key difference between the Avalon Seawatch and the pelagic boat tours. There is no "warming up" when you are out riding the winter waves on the last frontier of wildlife exploration.

# Wild Summer at the Jersey Shore

## 15

Roll on, deep and dark blue ocean, roll!
Ten thousand fleets sweep over thee in vain.
Man marks the earth with ruin; his control
Stops with the shore.

—Lord Byron, "The Sea"

In summertime, New Jersey's real "wild life" can be found along the famed Jersey Shore. Take Belmar, for example. Group after group come here, sprawl out on the beach and soak in the sun with scarcely any space between them, taking the occasional walk down to the water's edge. They gather all summer and strut their stuff on July Fourth, the very peak of their activity.

Hold on—I'm not referring to the scantily clad sunbathers or the testosterone-fueled revelry of the partiers at Bar A. No, no—clearly my subject is the least tern, the most protected of Belmar's residents. Black-winged and white-bodied, the endangered least tern nests on beaches along the Jersey Shore. Belmar is home to one of the state's largest colonies, with approximately 500 terns tucked into north Belmar between the pier and the jetty.

I spend a sunny June morning with Todd Pover, who leads the beach nesting birds project for the state, on behalf of the Conserve Wildlife Foundation of New Jersey. We get an early start to beat the crowds, but Belmar's Shark River inlet is already a bustle of activity. Boat horns ring out from the jetty, and the drawbridge rises with warning alarms. The least tern colony goes about its business. If not for the temporary fencing that Pover installed to keep dog walkers and beachgoers away from the birds, you might overlook them entirely.

"These inlets are perfect for the birds. They like small fish, and here they have the ocean, the inlet, the back bay. The vegetation—beach grass and sea rocket, some seaside goldenrod—provides some cover for the colony," says Pover.

## New Jersey Is for Plovers

New Jersey generally is compartmentalized: you have the inner cities, the sprawling suburbs, the remaining farms, the Jersey Shore, and the natural areas. "Jersey Shore" and "natural habitat" seem to be contradictory concepts. After all, much of New Jersey's coastline has been built out. Hundreds of thousands of people can visit our beaches on a hot summer day. Yet wildlife dependent on the native habitat of barrier islands and sand dunes still hang on, even in Belmar. The skin-baring and muscled masses sharing the sand with a colony of endangered beach birds?

To ensure it stays that way, Pover partners with a network of volunteers up and down the coast. Belmar volunteer Ed Lippincott, from the Shark River Coalition, greets us early in the morning along the jetty as a gorgeous American oystercatcher—a seventeen-inch-tall species of special concern, with a black head and bright orange dagger of a bill—forages near the tide line.

"I'm out here every morning, and especially on Saturday and Sunday mornings—God knows what went on here last night," says Lippincott. "They're skittish. All it takes is a little dog on a leash, and the birds go ballistic. But they're doing well this year."

Though New Jersey hosts twenty-one least tern colonies, Belmar is one of only three stable ones, along with locations in Cape May County and Atlantic County. These colonies can be home to many species of terns, gulls, and other shorebirds. In fact, more laughing gulls may breed in New Jersey than anywhere else in the world.

Pover is acutely aware of the slim margin for error. The Bible warns of a foolish man building his house on sand—but these shorebirds have no other choice. A 2009 flood at Hereford Inlet in Stone Harbor overwashed Champagne Island entirely, eroding the nesting area for 2,000 endangered black skimmers—85 percent of New Jersey's population. There was still time for those skimmers to find new nesting areas, but as Pover says, "You don't want to have all your eggs in one basket." Pun intended, I think.

Farther north, in Long Branch's Seven Presidents Park, Pover points out a piping plover chick strutting through the dune grass. It looks to me like a tiny head with legs, puttering along under the towering beach grasses. Pover and another volunteer, Eleanor Swanson, discuss the plover chick's latest milestones as the birds call out loudly every few minutes, "*peep-peep-peep*." At another stop, I see the famed "broken-wing dance": a mother plover tries to distract us from her nest full of eggs by calling out frantically and pretending she is injured.

"Aren't they the cutest little critters?" says Swanson, who wears a ballcap adorned with an embroidered plover and the words "Extinct Is Forever." "I just think it's fascinating watching the birds and how they make a living. When I show people the birds, it gets them excited. At the north end, I showed some people the chicks, and the next day they stopped me and asked how the birds were doing."

The unassuming Pover has other stops to make before the morning is out, and it is time to move on. He, too, wears his passions in the open. His bumper sticker: a bird logo with the slogan "New Jersey Is for Plovers."

"If these birds are going to survive in New Jersey, it's not going to be without help. My satisfaction is in being the advocate to provide that help."

## Foxes on the Prowl

Wildlife surviving along New Jersey's beaches is, for me, especially remarkable. I grew up spending every summer and nearly every seasonal weekend day of my childhood and teen years in Ocean Beach on "The Strip," the de facto barrier island separating Barnegat Bay from the Atlantic Ocean, stretching from Point Pleasant to Island Beach. Growing up a beach bum and ocean fanatic, my encounters with nature and wildlife were mostly limited to the chattering squawks of laughing gulls, the occasional jellyfish sting, and the ubiquitous "sand crabs," as we called the mole crabs whose tiny burrow holes were revealed with each retreating wave.

So after I grew up and finally started taking notice, the first red fox I ever saw, in the native dunes of Sea Girt, seemed like an unbelievable mirage that might well have been a grizzly bear. Then I learned about Island Beach's friendly foxes, which walked up to cars in the parking lots looking for handouts. The foxes there have since returned to more typical behavior, but the problems they cause by raiding shorebird nests are no less dramatic.

Rutgers University naturalist Joanna Burger has studied barrier islands and salt marsh islands for years. "The red fox is a problem all along the Jersey Shore. It's not native to barrier islands, and they never got there until we built the bridges. Now they don't have predators, and their population has increased markedly. The birds never had time to adapt to fox predation, so their population has decreased markedly over that same time."

The risk of predators for all beach nesting birds is significant. Species from raccoons and red fox to gulls and crows raid nests when they get the chance. Add in the effects of human recreation and disruption, and the shorebirds' safety is far from assured. Larger preserved areas such as Island Beach and Sandy Hook offer some protection.

## Gateway to Nature

One of the top birding and wildlife areas in the state, the Sandy Hook peninsula extends more than six miles out into New York Harbor. Sandy Hook is part of the Gateway National Recreation Area, which stretches as far east as Jamaica Bay Wildlife Refuge in Queens. Sandy Hook Light, built in 1764, is now the nation's oldest operating lighthouse. During spring migration in the Gateway, wave after wave of birds—hawks, waterfowl, short-distance migrants such as kinglets, and neotropical migrants such as Baltimore orioles—pass through from mid-April to the end of June.

"An easy way to think of it is that April is the peak for hawks, and May is the peak for colorful species like orioles, tanagers, and most warblers," says Scott Barnes of New Jersey Audubon's Sandy Hook Bird Observatory.

Sandy Hook has seen an uptick in the rare visits by two slender raptors known as kites, which are more typically found in the southeastern United States. The Mississippi kite looks much like a gray falcon with a dark eye patch. What distinguishes the swallow-tailed kite is a lengthy tail that extends outward like a giant V as it gracefully soars across the sky.

"You have to be really lucky to be here on the right day. Unfortunately, they tend to be here ten minutes or a half hour, then vanish," says Barnes.

To best experience the spring migration, I join a group of serious birders and novices for the World Series of Birding event run by the Bird Observatory. This annual Sandy Hook count is a public event in which participants pledge a contribution for each species tallied over the course of the single day. As such, it's a friendly day in the field for the participants.

Not so for many other teams across the state. In New Jersey Audubon's World Series of Birding, founded by Pete Dunne in 1984, teams count as many different species as possible on a single day in May. This clever competition has increased our knowledge of more than 450 bird species that visit or live in New Jersey—though some participants might take the competition a little too seriously.

For a satirical news feature on *The Daily Show with Jon Stewart*, comedian Steve Carell followed a New Jersey team around the state from the dark predawn hours to the final scorekeeping decision and ceremony that evening. The piece began with the theme to Monday Night Football, and Carell later announced the winner in breathless, madcap sportscaster fashion: "Do you believe in miracles? Team Nikon has stolen the coveted Urner Stone Cup! What a day for birding!" Like any good birding feature, it concludes with Carell screaming out gibberish—his "calls" of the Virginia rail and worm-eating warbler—as drips of white paint fall onto his suit jacket from supposed birds overhead.

The contest has now caught on around the nation as a Big Year chase, in which some individuals devote thousands and thousands of hours—and dollars—to seeing every species they possibly can on American soil in a given calendar year. Participants have even been known to charter a rickety plane in a winter storm to visit a remote, dangerous Alaskan island in the Aleutian Sea.

Fortunately, we are not worried about any of that today in Sandy Hook. I arrive at the meeting location in the moonlight, out so early that even the Dunkin' Donuts hadn't opened yet. (I knew I should have made my own coffee!) The sixteen-hour count—with participants invited to put in as much or as little time as they please—spans beach dunes, bayside marshes, the wooded North Pond, bayberry thickets, and a locust grove. Our group spots two Mississippi kites, four chuck-wills-widows, pine siskins, and a tri-colored heron. The day's total is 143 species, an excellent tally—and that doesn't count the eastern cottontails spotted along the way or the Fowler's toad we find in the prickly pear cactus clearing. No, this isn't the World Series of Toading.

Thanks to the expert identifications and enthusiasm of Barnes and Linda Mack, our guides, the event proves fruitful for participants who know their basic birds but may not be able to identify instantly, say, each of the two dozen species of sparrows found in New Jersey. The highlight for me is coming around a sand dune just before dawn to find a fog-covered bayfront. As the group walks on, their silhouettes drifting along the mist-shrouded trail away from the gently lapping tide, they might well be apparitions walking off to some strange initiation ceremony. Sandy Hook can be a mysterious place.

### Fifty Miles of Wildlife

Moments like this one highlight why the protection of places like Sandy Hook is so critical for preserving the remaining habitat up and down the New Jersey coast. Edwin B. Forsythe National Wildlife Refuge, established in 1984, is even more extensive, encompassing 47,000 acres of marsh and barrier islands and stretching more than fifty miles from Brick Township in northern Ocean County all the way to Oceanville in Atlantic County. This spectacular back bay habitat in Barnegat Bay, Little Egg Harbor, Great Bay, and Great Egg Harbor is crucial for nesting birds, such as herons and egrets, and as a stopover on the migratory flyways of North American birds.

The centerpiece of Forsythe is the Brigantine Refuge. Just north of Atlantic City, the eight-mile Wildlife Drive takes nature lovers through both saltwater and freshwater marshes, bordered by forest, freshwater swamp, and ocean. Hundreds of diamondback terrapins swim into the channels to find the best spots to lay their eggs. River otters, mink, and weasels ply the waterways. Peregrine falcons have nested for the past few years on the cross dyke.

Fall migration is especially spectacular, with huge concentrations of shorebirds, waterfowl, and wading birds passing through. Just as important for wildlife viewers, the fall migration is less hurried, according to Kevin Holcomb, who manages Forsythe for the U.S. Fish and Wildlife Service. The cooler weather pushes the birds south more gradually, so we have more time to watch them. Forsythe also gets a fair share of rarities.

"It was rare and unusual to see a roseate spoonbill here, and it gives some excitement to birders across the country to see a roseate spoonbill in a different state," says Holcomb. "You can go to Florida and see them in large numbers, but it's unusual to have them occur here. We also have brown pelicans out in the bays."

Roseate spoonbills—a pink flamingo–colored bird with a bill that resembles a shoehorn—and brown pelicans? Since when did the Florida Gulf Coast come to New Jersey? But unusual species of birds are not the only creatures bringing that subtropical experience to the Garden State. The manatee, or sea cow, has visited the New Jersey coastline in three of the four years from 2006 to 2009. This Florida resident rarely swam north of Georgia until recently, but rising water temperatures and artificially warm areas like the nuclear cooling facility at Oyster Creek in Lacey Township are helping the manatee expand its range. A distant relative of the elephant that weighs in at half a ton, the manatee is completely unique in North America.

Tropical species like dolphinfish, flying fish, and the barracuda-like sennet will hitch a ride northward on the Gulf Stream, along with another species best avoided—the dreaded Portuguese man-of-war, with its sixty-foot-long tentacles. This jellyfish floats on the surface and carries one of the most toxic poisons in the sea, capable of killing a human and severely burning someone who even touches a dead, washed-up specimen. Dangerous jellyfish also arrive along the Jersey coast from the north. The lion's mane jellyfish is an Arctic species that grows as large as eight feet wide across its bell, dragging twenty-foot-long tentacles that sting, sometimes fatally. Sherlock Holmes himself pinpointed this killer in one of Sir Arthur Conan Doyle's classic mysteries, "The Adventure of the Lion's Mane." Sea turtles are among the few animals that eat these and other jellyfish, as do the mola mola, or ocean sunfish, one of the oddest-looking fishes on the entire planet.

I will let Captain Jeff Stewart of Cape May Whale Watcher explain: "They look like someone took a handsaw and cut the fish in half. There's no ass end on the fish. On big ones, their eye can be the size of a baseball."

Ladies and gentlemen, it's another day at the beach.

**Anytime, Anywhere**

All along our highly developed Jersey Shore, you can find exciting wildlife—but the time and place are at nature's choosing. In addition to wash-ups of whales or smaller sea life, unforeseen encounters can reveal an animal in its typical behavior. At Barnegat Light on the northern tip of Long Beach Island, visitors regularly see harlequin ducks, which look as if they have been carefully hand-painted by a master craftsman in navy blue and reddish-brown; they are more often found off Nova Scotia or Labrador. A mink family also makes regular appearances at the Barnegat Light jetty.

The more you are out there, the more you see, as I am reminded even on recreational visits to the beach. On the Manasquan beach just before dusk on July Fourth weekend, I find a pod of bottlenose dolphins swimming up the coast a hundred yards out. On Lavallette beach a decade ago, I saw two brown pelicans out fishing—and I had to confirm with my friends that my eyes were not deceiving me that morning after a late night out. And even standard wash-ups, such as razor clams or skate cases—two-inch-long black purses that serve as an egg sac for the babies of this stingray relative, with short, leathery strands extending from each of its four corners—make for entertaining finds to learn more about the natural side of the Jersey Shore.

Children's enthusiasm for the ocean is limitless, as I see on that holiday weekend day in Manasquan. No sun-tanning patch of beach sand is left uncovered, and the tide line is nearly a wall of people. But around a

**David Wheeler searches a Manasquan beach jetty for marine invertebrates and crustaceans.**

Bill Wheeler

jetty, dozens of kids with nets and pails are shouting to their parents and friends, "Look what I found!" The jetties are alive with rock crabs, minnows, mole crabs, coquinas, mussels, clams, oysters, and barnacles, while gulls and terns keep watch from above. The next generation of New Jersey naturalists is in training.

Fortunately, many adults haven't lost that enthusiasm, either. When you get down to the coast for a day at the beach, it's hard not to feel renewed. The late ocean activist Dery Bennett always preferred the off-season to the summer crowds.

"Island Beach State Park in October, when I'm surf fishing for bluefish, you've got waterfowl migrating, hawks migrating, fish migrating, and not a lot of people around. The color of the marshes has changed over to a golden brown—that's the time and the place for me."

Bennett was right—there is something extraordinary about the shore after the tourists have gone home. One place offers that feeling all year long.

### The Road

From the Garden State Parkway, I drive through downtown Tuckerton and take Great Bay Boulevard east toward the coast. A few blocks of residential homes soon yield to a salt marsh safari. Here the vast waters of the Mullica River enter Little Egg Harbor, separated from the Great Bay by this road. Though this road has no homes or businesses for the last four miles, stoplights halt cars from one direction while oncoming traffic uses the single-lane bridges. I wait, prevented from seeing the bridge itself by a bend in the road. Wind whistles through the reeds, and waves kick up against the shoreline to the south. These bridges to nowhere, these stoplights without traffic, give an eerie vibe of the shore sans people. The abandoned factory and ever-expanding salt marsh and mudflat horizon add to the impression. I feel as if I have walked into Cormac McCarthy's *The Road*, were it transplanted to the Jersey Shore. Adding to the post-apocalyptic feel, the only active facility on the entire five-mile stretch is an off-limits U.S. Coast Guard building, lined with warning signs and accessible only by a six-foot-high elevated boardwalk entrance stretching over the marsh.

"Great Bay Boulevard is the most beautiful place—it's so uncrowded, with just incredible habitat on each side," says Margaret O'Gorman, executive director of the Conserve Wildlife Foundation of New Jersey. "There was a very large fish processing factory that went defunct on Crab Island. Now you have terrapins there during the summer and masses of osprey out in the bay."

Though desolate for humans, Great Bay Boulevard is a thriving and expansive habitat for wildlife. Egrets occupy nearly every section of the marsh, and red-winged blackbirds and boat-tailed grackles call along the roadside shrubs. Osprey, bald eagle, and oystercatcher navigate the skies, and shorebirds forage on the tide-gouged mudflats. Muskrat, diamond-back terrapin, and red fox make their way along the shallows and lowlands. Sunset arrives to the west, glowing as white-light, black-light in the tidal islands and archipelagos, turning a sprawling salt marsh into the equivalent of a photograph negative. As I look east, the dwindling sunlight spotlights the grassy tussocks in red while the water channels appear black.

On the Jersey Shore, this is the end of the road. And it is magnificent.

# Part Four

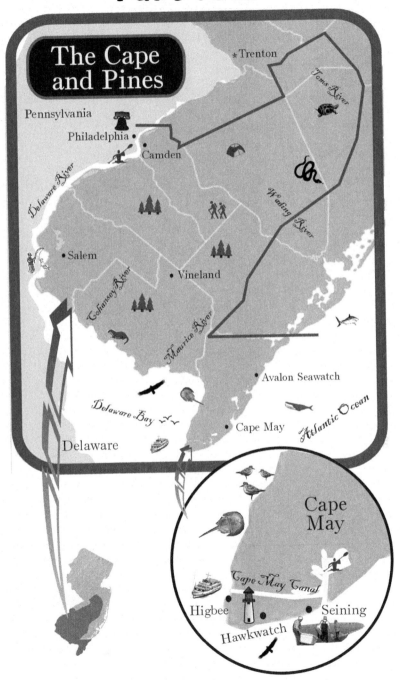

The Cape and Pines

Trenton

Pennsylvania

Philadelphia

Camden

Delaware River

Salem

Vineland

Cohansey River

Maurice River

Toms River

Wading River

Avalon Seawatch

Delaware Bay

Cape May

Atlantic Ocean

Delaware

Cape May

Cape May Canal

Higbee

Hawkwatch

Seining

# Moby-Dick; or, Call Me Cetacean

Towards thee I roll, thou all-
destroying but unconquering
whale; to the last I grapple with
thee. . . . Thus, I give up the spear!
—Herman Melville, *Moby-Dick*

More than thirty whales spent much of the summer of 1992 in the waters off Cape May, New Jersey. That year humpback whales and finback whales moved far south from their feeding grounds in the cool waters of Stellwagen Bank off Cape Cod in Massachusetts, the whale-watching capital of the eastern seaboard. Captain Jeff Stewart of Cape May Whale Watcher had a front row seat for this surprising summertime extravaganza.

"We had five whales breaching out of the water at the same time right in front of Wildwood," says Stewart. "They basically set up housekeeping right off Cape May. It was whale heaven."

Whale watchers from across the Northeast enjoyed the spectacle. A century or two ago, those finbacks and humpbacks would have been cause for another kind of human celebration. Cape May whalers would have had themselves one heck of a hunt.

## Of Harpoons and Baleen

Many of the first colonists came to America, in part, for the opportunities presented by whaling. English whalers emigrated to New England, and some moved south to the Delaware Bayshore, where they hunted right whales from the shore in the 1600s. Cape May itself was partly founded by whalers. After all, it was a lucrative field. Blubber provided lamp oil. Craftsmen worked baleen—the hairlike substance many whales use to filter-feed—into everything from corsets to mattress springs. According to whale expert Joe Roman, the baleen alone from a single bowhead whale could pay for an entire whaling trip.

The land where the City of Cape May now stands was owned by a Delaware Bay whaler named Thomas Hand in 1699. Just half a century later, a local whaler sighted not a single whale in two months of hunting. Overhunting doomed many species of whales, beginning in those times with the right whale—considered the "right" whale to hunt because they were easy to harpoon and floated after dying. Improvements in ship design enabled whaling vessels to render the blubber on board, and as the right whales declined, the hunters' focus shifted to finback, sperm, and humpback whales. That started the clock ticking for those species as well. By the late 1960s, whale hunting was negligible on the East Coast. There simply were not enough whales left to make the trips worthwhile.

The decimation of whales across the world occurred despite the animal's near-mystical significance for many cultures, from the Maoris of the South Sea, to the Barroullie whalers of St. Vincent in the West Indies, to the salty mariners of Melville's Nantucket. Today, limited whaling occurs in a few communities around the world where it has a cultural significance, such as among the Inuit and Eskimos, and a few other nations, such as Japan and Norway, still sanction commercial whaling. The thrill can be just as vivid, however, on another kind of "whale hunt"—one that relies on binoculars, a keen eye, an experienced captain, and a whole lot of patience.

### Cape May Whale Watcher

I board the Cape May Whale Watcher for a marine mammal tour on a clear, comfortable morning in July, taking a seat on the upper level of this 110-foot-long boat that can hold 300 passengers. An osprey nests across the channel from the pier, giving us the day's first good sighting before we even leave the dock. But today we want marine mammals—dolphins and maybe even a whale.

We ride west along the Cape May Canal, which Allied ships used in World War II as a safe passage from the attacks of Nazi U-boats. The canal is part of the Intracoastal Waterway—a 3,000-mile water trail running from New Jersey's own Manasquan Inlet to Brownsville, Texas, offering boats shelter from the perils of the open Atlantic Ocean and Gulf of Mexico. Here on the Cape May Canal, bald eagles can be spotted above the banks, a mix of rural yards, forest, and wetlands. Fishermen sit on bulkheads, and a family walks their golden retriever along the gently lapping waves. Our boat follows in the wake of the enormous Cape May–Lewes Ferry, destined for the state of Delaware on the western coast of Delaware Bay. Gulls flock after the ferry's choppy wake, and I wonder if anyone aboard the ferry is a birder on "the poor man's pelagic tour," as some call the Lewes Ferry.

We are still in Cape May Canal waters when we spot our first bottlenose dolphin, just past the canal mouth on the Delaware Bay. That sighting is followed by groups of two bottlenose dolphins—then three, then four. As the captain circles the boat, dolphins appear on all sides. All told, we see at least seventy-five bottlenose dolphins over the course of the three-hour trip. We circumnavigate Cape May Island and motor as far north as the Wildwoods, but the vast majority of our dolphins appear off the western coast of the cape. Seeing so many dolphins is a revelation—and I later find out that the next few weeks bring far more.

"We're having a phenomenal year, the best dolphin year I can remember in the last ten," Captain Stewart tells me a month later. "In front of West Cape May now, we get 1,000 dolphins—you need a snow plow in front of the boat to make room. I cannot stress the magnitude. Honestly, I don't know anywhere else in the world where you can see that quantity."

What makes the dolphin sightings so memorable is that I am not watching a static animal. They are not perched on a branch, or crossing a road, or basking on a log. I am watching dolphins in action, doing what they love to do. They play with each other. They "porpoise," the dolphin equivalent of a whale breaching the surface. Best of all, they ride the waves.

Dolphins are intriguing animals, and not just because they are mammals that live underwater, or even because they are surfer dudes riding the boat-created swells. Dolphins use sonar to find their food, emitting high-pitched clicks that bounce off other objects in the ocean. As Stewart points out, the echolocation used by dolphins and whales serves as the model for U.S. Navy sonar technology.

It makes sense that humans should be learning from dolphins, because they are very, very smart. Their intelligence is believed to rank them among the top mammals in the world, and researchers are just beginning to understand their advanced language. Dolphins are so smart that they can intuitively read human body language and reward systems, enabling them to thrive in performance shows like Sea World.

"From seeing dolphins doing shows in captivity, I think that humans see human traits in dolphins," says Sheila Dean of the Marine Mammal Stranding Center. "But dolphins learn those human traits from humans. They're smart animals—and they know what will get them food."

## The Ballad of the River Dolphins

That dolphin-human relationship adds an extra element of emotion when things go awry. Valerie Montecalvo, a homeowner along the Shrewsbury River, experienced both the good and the bad of that bond over the course of 2008.

"We were barbecuing down by the bulkhead on Father's Day, when my daughter and her friend started shouting, 'There are sharks in the water—a lot of them!'" recalls Montecalvo. "I saw twelve to fifteen fins popping up, and then came closer and saw they were bottlenose dolphins. What a beautiful sight to see. They were actually just jumping out of the water for hours and hours on end. Every single person who lived along the river came out to see them."

The dolphins stuck around the Shrewsbury and Navesink rivers throughout the summer of 2008. What started with the residents along the river soon became a statewide phenomenon. Spectators lined the streets, boats packed the rivers, and local bayshore towns even charged visitors for boat rides to see the dolphins.

"It was almost as if in a recession and a bad economy, the dolphins brought hope to the communities, because they got everyone out from across the state to the river," says Montecalvo. "They made people see the beauty again in the river, filled with wildlife."

The dolphins enjoyed the Shrewsbury and Navesink rivers so much, they didn't want to leave. Many experts believe they could not tear themselves away from the rich schools of menhaden, or bunker, in the river. A dolphin feasts on up to twenty pounds of this fish in a day.

By the fall, it was becoming obvious that the animals were in distress. Where they once porpoised through the surface every few seconds, they now lacked the energy. Then winter hit—one of the coldest winters in years. The rivers froze over.

Government scientists, researchers, and wildlife advocates discussed many options for rescuing the dolphins or guiding them out to sea. In the end, they let nature take its course, for better or for worse. Unfortunately, the course nature dictated was "for worse."

"I was heartbroken. I felt so helpless, as if I were standing there watching them die," says Montecalvo.

Indeed, most of the Navesink and Shrewsbury dolphins died during the harsh winter. One of the last ones to be found was near rock star Jon Bon Jovi's house along the Navesink River in Middletown. It won't take a celebrity connection for people to pay very close attention in future winters. Something about dolphins and whales makes many people feel a real kinship.

"The dolphins caused great emotion in the region, and the response from the public was extraordinary," says Cindy Zipf of the nonprofit Clean Ocean Action. "Certain mammals attract that personal attachment. There are stories of interactions between dolphins and humans over thousands of years. It's more than just the cute factor—there is something there."

For a generation raised on the television program *Flipper*, dolphins were already part of the family. Roman points to another development that opened eyes to cetacean intelligence: the discovery of whale music. Popularized by the 1970 Roger Payne album, *Songs of the Humpback Whale,* the discoveries that whales make elaborate music and that dolphins use an advanced language led to a sea change in the public perception of these creatures. Once viewed as a target for whalers and a competitor to fishermen, whale and dolphin were now "Gentle Giant" and "Flipper."

### No Line on the Horizon

In our journey around Cape May, we are due south of the cape, in the open Delaware Bay. Captain Stewart tells the group that this area offers perhaps our best chance to spy a whale. Suddenly everyone on our boat—from toddler to senior citizen—is partaking in an ancient ritual. We scan the horizon for the spout of a whale. The trick, Stewart tells us, is in peering far off in the distance. If there is any movement on the surface closer to you, your peripheral vision will catch it. But if you focus on the nearer surface, you will miss any distant breaching.

Captain Jeff Stewart Jr. Cape May Whale Watcher

**Many species of whales can be found on whale watching trips around Cape May.**

As I peer out at the horizon, I ponder some of the sheer numbers associated with whales: 108, as in the length in feet of a blue whale, the largest animal that ever existed—and one that swims past New Jersey's waters far offshore in the Atlantic. Four thousand, as in the pounds of fish eaten by a single whale *each day!* And 70 to 100, as in the number of finback whales out on this very day at Elephant Trunk, a seabed demarcation fifty miles off the Jersey coast—out of range for a whale watching trip.

Humpback and finback whales make up about two-thirds of whale sightings on marine mammal tours over the course of a year. Occasionally a minke whale is spotted, and maybe one right whale a year—a testament to its still shaky status after centuries of overhunting. According to Roman, only 400 right whales remain, even though they have been protected since the 1930s. One glimmer of hope is that right whales recently began birthing twenty to twenty-five offspring each year, a promising rate. Most of the other North Atlantic species are either stable or, in the case of the humpback whale, have been "growing by leaps and bounds for some time," as Roman puts it.

As the overall whale population stabilizes in the North Atlantic, New Jersey is ideally situated to reap the benefits. One government study identified twenty-seven dolphin and whale species in the New York Bight, the gulf that spans out between the Jersey coast and Long Island.

"This region has some of the most diverse marine mammals and sea turtle species in the United States," says Zipf. "We get them migrating, coming and going, north and south. It's extraordinary, the diversity we have here with marine mammals and sea turtles."

### Inky and Beluga

Unfortunately, outside of whale watching tours, our most common encounters with most of these species occur when they wash up on our beaches. In August 2009 a pilot whale washed up in Perth Amboy. Eighteen feet long and weighing nearly a ton, the female pilot whale was spotted swimming up and down the Raritan River with a pod of four to eight whales. Locals helped free the whale after she initially beached on a Staten Island sandbar, but she soon beached for good.

"The bigger the animal, the lesser the chances of survival once it hits the beach," says Dean, who has worked on whale strandings for more than two decades. "The sheer weight alone, without having equal pressure, is like you lying on a beach with several tons of weight on you. It's too traumatic."

David Wheeler

A male black bear forages in a wetlands area of the Delaware Water Gap region.

David Wheeler

A timber rattlesnake seeks warmth under a shelter rock in the Highlands.

David Wheeler tries out a dogsled with the New Jersey Sled Dog Club in High Point State Park.

The Delaware River divides New Jersey and Pennsylvania in the scenic Delaware Water Gap, as seen from the peak of Mount Tammany.

A peregrine falcon stalks an office building's rooftop along the Jersey City skyline.

The Palisades, ancient volcanic cliffs, overlook the Hudson River opposite New York City.

National Park Service rangers
band an osprey at
Cheesequake State Park
in Old Bridge.

Scores of bottlenose dolphins swim alongside whale watch tours
off the Delaware Bay coast of Cape May.

Melanie Worob

Naturalist Johnny Shersick holds a snapping turtle in the Helen Street Wetlands of the Dismal Swamp Conservation Area in South Plainfield.

Herb Segars

A red fox crosses the road in Island Beach State Park, one of many barrier island beaches where the fox is now abundant.

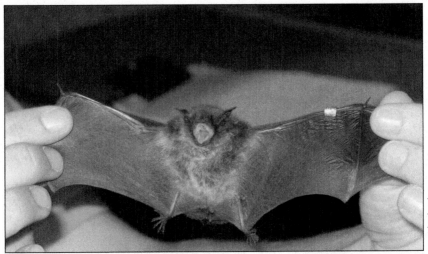

David Wheeler

A little brown bat is banded by state wildlife biologist Mick Valent in a Milford barn.

Michael J. Pazzani

The great horned owl is one of many owl species that can be found around dawn and dusk in New Jersey.

A spotted salamander crosses an East Brunswick road closed to vehicles a few nights each year to protect amphibians migrating into vernal pools.

A Princeton University paddler's path is cut off by a bald eagle carrying a fish across the Millstone Aqueduct of the Delaware and Raritan Canal.

The snapping turtle is one of more than a dozen species of turtles found in New Jersey, which is home to seventy-one species of reptiles and amphibians.

Dana Patterson

Bill Lynch

A belted kingfisher flaunts its disregard for the laws of the land and enjoys a snack in North Brunswick, New Jersey.

One successful whale rescue involved a baby sperm whale that was literally starving to death from the plastic bags he ingested. The Marine Mammal Stranding Center successfully rehabilitated and released the whale back into the wild, but not before it left its mark on the crew.

"Sperm whales have a reserve from the squid they eat, and only sperm whales have this," says volunteer Maurice Tremblay. "They called this whale Inky because every time someone was in the tank with him, he sprayed the person with ink."

A friend of mine once spotted a sperm whale off the Longport jetty south of Margate many years ago. An even more unlikely Garden State sighting took place in April 2005 on the other side of the state. That whale was a twelve-foot beluga—an all-white whale with a melon-shaped head, typically found in Canada's St. Lawrence River and northward. The beluga swam eighty miles up the Delaware River, all the way to Trenton. The unlikelihood of a beluga in Trenton was off the charts. Roman studies whales in the Gulf of Maine, nearly 500 miles north of New Jersey, and he isn't aware of beluga making it even that far south.

The beluga wasn't the first strange whale to swim far up the Delaware River. In 1995 a right whale—nicknamed "Waldo the Wrong-Way Right Whale" in Philadelphia newspapers—beached itself in Pennsauken, just north of Camden, before swimming out to sea.

The simple act of looking for whales makes the whole ocean seem more expansive. New Jersey is no longer a small piece of land, but an immense frontier overlooking a near-endless horizon that belongs to the largest mammals on earth. We see no whales on this tour, yet that role of chance is part of what makes the chase so enjoyable. Besides, you never know what you might find when your eyes are open.

"The other day we're going through the Cape May Canal past the ferry terminal and I look at Higbee Beach and see a coyote walking along the banks of the canal," says Stewart. "I had just finished telling everyone about the bald eagles—and what the hell else is coming! I joked with 'em that I guess we'll see the Jersey Devil next."

# Cape May
## THE NEVER-ENDING
## MIGRATION

**17**

When the weather is right in the fall . . . the number and variety of birds at Cape May can be staggering, and the best thing is that you can just sit in one spot and watch them all pass by like a river.

—Naturalist David Sibley

I can't remember exactly what I was doing on September 30, 1994, but I can tell you this. Five thousand two hundred fifty-seven broad-winged hawks migrated past Cape May that day.

In the previous decade, the year 1984 stands out for a lot of reasons—whether George Orwell or Van Halen comes to mind is a matter of taste. But in Cape May, 1984 was the year that 61,167 sharp-shinned hawks migrated past, from the end of August to early December.

And 298 peregrine falcons passed through Cape May on October 5, 2002. That's nearly 300 birds of a species that couldn't be found at all in New Jersey only thirty years earlier.

If you haven't guessed, Cape May is arguably the best place for birds in the nation and, in turn, for birdwatchers. Once America's first beach resort, Cape May is for birders what Las Vegas is for gamblers. Sure, there are other places you can go, but nowhere else offers the sheer spectacle that overtakes the cape during the fall migration. And while everything that happens in Vegas is meant to stay in Vegas, the birds that pass through Cape May could be a continent away before you know it.

### A Birder's Mecca

The explanation is simple, really, at least on paper. Cape May—a peninsula jutting out between the vast Delaware Bay and the open Atlantic Ocean—acts as a funnel for birds migrating along the coast. The birds invariably wind up at the tip, where they either cross immediately or gather until the proper pieces are in place: numbers, wind strength and direction, and other migratory cues. But that simple explanation overlooks the sense of wonder that leaves even the most veteran birders awed by the cape. In Cape May, the migration never ends.

Don Freiday was the director of a well-known New Jersey Audubon Society nature sanctuary when he was asked to take a similar position with the Cape May Bird Observatory a few years ago. He thought about it "for maybe three seconds" before eagerly accepting. Freiday now leads weekly Audubon birding tours in Cape May, runs the daily BirdCape-May.org blog, and has traveled across the world in search of birds.

"In fall, there's no better place in the country," says Freiday. "On any day, on average, there are more birds in Cape May than elsewhere. There is visible migration concentration in the fall. What separates Cape May is Cape Island, where you're five minutes from all the best spots."

Paul Kerlinger, who writes a birding column for the *Cape May Times*, concurs.

"The lower ten miles of the peninsula have such diversity. There are large numbers of so many rarities and extra-limitals. You can mix it up so that, within ten minutes, you have many species of hawks. Then you look to your right and see seven species of egrets and herons within a half hour. Then you look out over the ocean and you're seeing gannets or loons."

## The Autumn Wind

Now it is October, and I am at Cape May Point State Park, standing before the Hawk Watch platform, where New Jersey Audubon staff and volunteers have recorded each species of migrating raptor every autumn since 1976. It is from this board—equal parts stock exchange big board and Fenway Park "Green Monster" scoreboard—that the numbers begin to tell me the story of those big flight days and years past for broad-winged hawks and peregrine falcons and the other raptors. Or at least part of the story. Nothing compares to seeing it firsthand.

"Peregrines were coming through one day in the late 1980s or early 1990s," says Kerlinger. "I remember I hit it right, about October 2, going over for lunch one day at the Hawk Watch, and there was something like fifty peregrines in an hour. Just beautiful."

Today seems promising, on the surface. The Victorian bed-and-breakfasts color the Cape May streets, birders fill the Hawk Watch platforms, and the sun warms us all, bird and birder alike. Before us, Bunker Pond holds pied-billed grebes, tundra and mute swans, and a gadwall duck. But I have low expectations for the migrating birds. The winds are wrong.

"I often say, learn this phrase—cold front," says Freiday. "If you catch the correct weather pattern—a cold front passing the day before you go

David Wheeler

**In arguably the nation's top birdwatching spot, mute swans float in Bunker Pond by Cape May Lighthouse. Birders line the Hawk Watch viewing platform in the distance.**

birding, the wind pattern out of northwest—you can get a morning flight when migrating birds find themselves over open water at dawn and reverse themselves. You see literally thousands of birds of all stripes. It's a terrific spectacle."

Not today. Winds come from the southeast, meaning most raptors will not attempt to migrate against the wind. The few exceptions are peregrine falcons and the occasional bald eagle and osprey. Otherwise, without a powerful tail wind to push them, birds like Cooper's and sharp-shinned hawks get bottled up when they reach the open expanse of Delaware Bay.

Jessica Donahue, a seasonal staffer, started at the Hawk Watch just six weeks earlier, but she is bursting with energy for the birds passing through. That excitement spreads to many of the visitors watching those birds from this viewing platform. Jessica's enthusiasm could make birding *underwater* sound promising.

"We had one slow migration day—it was rainy, it looked awful. But we had 2,000 tree swallows. The merlins would swoop in and catch them—they have the same body shape, so it's really strange-looking. We had falcons, kestrels, and merlins everywhere! One merlin caught something big and was eating it as it was flying. People couldn't believe it wasn't a bird when we realized it was eating a swamp darner, a large dragonfly."

"Peregrine falcon!" another bird spotter calls. We try to get our binoculars on its distant silhouette before it dips below the tree line. I feel newly confident about today's conditions.

"Peregrines fly sedately, like that guy who's always the best," continues Jessica. "Merlins are like the person who's always second best. They flap hard, and they will attack everything in sight. They go out of their way to attack other birds. There was one merlin that caught another merlin, a kestrel, a swallow, and a butterfly—all in the space of ten minutes!"

So much for the sedate, peaceful birdwatching thing. This is nature as a life-and-death battlefield. Sign me up! After the long drive, my dad and I lack the patience to spend too long at the Hawk Watch platform. We need to get our legs moving. In just a few minutes on the trails, that same magic Jessica Donahue described appears before our very eyes.

## Magical Merlins

As our trail nears Lighthouse Pond, two merlins spiral up and down just beyond a stand of reeds in hot pursuit of a swallow, then reappear on the other side of the pond. They continue their aerial acrobatics within sight for a good ten minutes. We walk along the trails, passing through diverse habitat from cedar swamp to meadows to salt marsh.

Here we once encountered the only sandhill crane of our lives. The statuesque juvenile bird stood silently in a scrubland just twenty-five feet away. At the time, neither my dad nor I realized that sandhill cranes actually visit New Jersey. We couldn't understand why this strange, towering "great heron" stood on the dry ground of a forest clearing. When I later consulted my field book, I was stunned to realize it was a crane, a rare but annual visitor to the state.

Today, we find no sandhill crane. Instead, a colorful and lively array of butterflies flit across our path. Cape May serves as a vital stop-off point for monarch butterflies, with thousands passing through each day. Amazingly, an entire generation of these butterflies does nothing but migrate, living up to nine months rather than the six weeks of a typical monarch. They end up more than 2,000 miles southwest in the mountains of central Mexico, surrounded by millions and millions of their kind in an elaborate tapestry of winged red and orange waves.

At Cape May Point State Park the terrain changes again, and we walk a sandy trail through a forest, passing under a mockernut hickory tree with huge leaves resembling old-fashioned baseball mitts. Four American coots skirt the edge of a marsh, and bright pink flowers dot the greens and tans of marsh reeds. Above, those same two merlins dive-bomb into view again. My dad and I are joking about the merlins' "Napoleon complexes" in comparison with the coolly confident peregrine falcon flyboys, when a mute swan suddenly appears in a channel practically under our feet, as if magically materializing from the very reeds of the marsh.

Finally, the trails bring us to the Atlantic Ocean. We hike over the dunes and onto the beach as a Cape May Whale Watcher boat pushes southward in the distance. The towering Cape May Lighthouse and the historic World War II fortress bunker, pounded by the surf, act as fitting beacons for this wonderland of the unexpected.

### Birding a Nor'easter

Fall—and the world-class Cape May bird migration—will soon come to an end. We are anxious to see another phase in the never-ending migration: songbirds. More than a million songbirds migrate past Cape May each year. That number includes at least seventy-five species of neotropical migrants, or birds that overwinter in Central or South America, such as the American redstart, rose-breasted grosbeak, ovenbird, and Cape May warbler. A few legendary mid-October flights in the past have tallied more than 100,000 birds passing through in a single day.

We book a weekend in mid-October, just before the annual Cape May Autumn Weekend, a popular event that has offered birding field trips, workshops, and lectures for upward of sixty years. Birding is serious business in Cape May. More than 100,000 birders visit each year, spending well over $10 million annually. Birdwatching is so important to the economy that even the Cape May County Chamber of Commerce building offers an elevated boardwalk trail with interpretive signs noting the trees and potential birds of an adjacent marsh.

Lo and behold, not one but two nor'easters immediately precede our visit. I drive us to Cape May through sheeting rain, gusty winds, and weather so nasty that I feel beyond foolish to be traveling five hours round-trip well before dawn to look at birds. That whole concept of "every day is good birding in Cape May"? We are certainly putting it to the test today.

As we approach Higbee Beach, the first hints of daylight break through the gray rain. A great blue heron startles us by rising up from its perch atop a sign for an alpaca farm.

"Maybe there's still hope," my dad says, unreasonably optimistic.

We give it a try. After a few minutes on the windswept, rain-soaked lookout platform, we hike around the edge of the Cape May Canal to the Delaware Bayshore. The waves pound hard against the jetty and narrow beach, more befitting an island outpost surrounded by vast ocean than a supposedly sheltered bayfront. The rain shows signs of weakening, but the bitterly cold winds only get worse. Then something incredible happens—with every soggy step, we see more birds. Flitting between branches, alighting as a flock from a trailside shrub, fighting the winds over the stormy bay. Along the shore, there are scoters and gulls and cormorants. Above, a northern harrier on the prowl toys with two kestrels in the twisting winds. And in the dune brush, savannah and white-crowned sparrows and yellow-rumped, Nashville, and palm warblers take cover from the predators and the gusts.

South Cape May Meadows is great for migrating shorebirds, and Nummy Island is the place for wading birds like herons and egrets. And Higbee Beach Wildlife Management Area is the best place on the continent for autumn migrating songbirds. More than 1.5 million songbirds from over 100 species were recorded from the Higbee platform from 2003 through 2008. Over 267,000 yellow-rumped warblers passed through in a single year alone, and nearly 100,000 American robins migrated past during another year. Higbee gets rave reviews from none other than world-famous birder David Sibley.

"My favorite is Higbee Beach, a spot that is one of the most popular (it would be on lots of birders' 'favorite places' lists)," Sibley told me in a WildNewJersey.tv interview on the eve of his return to Cape May for the Autumn Festival. "In the morning, the warblers and other songbirds reorient and fly northwest, where they pile up along the bayshore at the north end of Higbee Beach. Again, it takes the right weather conditions, but it can be a really exciting spot to sit and watch thousands of these tiny birds, each weighing only a third of an ounce, and dozens of species, in all the urgency of migration."

### Taxi Down the Runway

Once off the bayshore, my dad and I hike through thick, vine-shrouded "rainforest"—or at least it appears that way after three days of heavy downpours. We trek over inland sand dunes surrounded by American holly and pitch pines, where orange mushrooms grow straight out of the sands. We walk barrens-like sand trails lined with the fragrant scents of

Eastern red cedar and pine. And we wade through tall, brushy meadows where sparrows are plentiful and northern flickers call from the adjoining forest.

Today, these meadows serve as airport runways where the high fliers wait out the storm until liftoff. As we hike along the edge of one meadow, a narrow band of forest separating us from the bayfront, great blue herons launch one at a time from their roosts in the upper canopy of the trees. Though individually common, the appearance of a dozen great blues lifting up one by one and circling overhead in different directions is stunning. They seem to be waiting out the storm and the winds. Sibley counts a similar experience—though of far greater magnitude—as among his most prized Cape May encounters.

"One morning in the late fall I went out at first light, and the sky was just filled with great blue herons—thousands of them—in flocks, milling around at all heights from just over the treetops to so high they were barely visible. They dispersed quickly, and within a couple of hours most of them had vanished. But that scene at dawn was very memorable."

Those kinds of encounters can never be forgotten, a theme I hear often among birders.

"For me, spectacle trumps rarity," says Freiday. "Hordes of migrating birds, to me, are more exciting than a rare sighting."

### Winged Globetrotters

For many other birders, the biggest thrill is indeed the chase for a new rarity, a visitor that seldom if ever has been seen in New Jersey. And far more often than anywhere else, those rarities make their appearances in Cape May.

"Every year, I'm looking for something new," says Bill Boyle, the author of perhaps the most comprehensive book about New Jersey birding hotspots. "There's always a chance to find something different."

That something can arrive on the winds of the world, bringing in the most astonishing species.

A South American brown-chested martin spent more than a week at the Rea Farm, or Beanery, a lima bean farm leased for birding to the Cape May Bird Observatory.

Anhingas and magnificent frigatebirds—two heavy-winged tropical birds typically found in South Florida and the Caribbean—have been seen at Higbee Beach.

New Jersey's first white-tailed kite, which rarely makes it north of the Everglades, was spotted at nearby Hidden Valley.

South Cape May Meadows and Lily Lake have had wood stork, fulvous whistling-duck, and white-faced ibis, none of which typically migrate anywhere near New Jersey.

A whiskered tern and a Mongolian plover each spent a day in Cape May in the early 1990s, the tern never before spotted in North America and the plover seen only a few times.

Cape May Point State Park has had rarities like purple gallinules and chestnut-collared longspur, the latter a prairie bird seldom found east of Kansas.

And an ivory gull spent two weeks as a birding celebrity in Cape May Harbor in late 2009, though the species rarely flies farther south than the limits of Arctic pack ice.

Even Cape May parking areas get in on the action.

"We had a Northern wheatear near the parking lot, and everyone was staked out there watching it. Everyone was so excited—it was new to North America," says Jessica Donahue. "Some British birders showed up and were like, 'Oh, we had ten wheatears at the airport before we left.' But those British birders were so excited to see a yellow-rumped warbler, even though it's one of our most common birds with over 200,000 a year!"

With all the visitors who pass through Cape May, the term *rarity* can be a relative one. "I really enjoy that a common bird I've seen a million times before—like the family of Carolina wrens near the Hawk Watch platform every morning—for people from Britain or California, they get so excited," Jessica continues. "I'm seeing it again for the first time through other people's eyes."

Whatever the bird, and whoever the birder, the spectacle of Cape May is all about migration. For former state Division of Fish and Wildlife biologist Larry Niles, that timeless act seemed to reveal its innermost secrets one late afternoon.

"One flock started out low, and they were getting higher and higher, then all of a sudden, a few birds split off. Then others. Then the flock was torn to fragments," says Niles. "They started to circle as if they had lost their nerve, then they came south again. The wind may have been favorable low but turned unfavorable at a higher altitude—I don't really know. But I got to intimately understand the way a flock works."

Niles experienced this firsthand migratory moment on the western coast of—where else?—Cape May, New Jersey.

# Triassic Meets Arctic on the Delaware Bay

18

When you think about it, our waters are really the last wilderness we have around here.

—Naturalist Joe Reynolds

The first catch yields an abundance of squirming, flopping, wriggling sea creatures. Shrimp, fish, calico crabs with leopard-print shells. Clad in chest waders, the eager crew casts the net out again at the captain's command. This time the bounty is even more impressive. An aggressive green crab, claws in the air, pirouetting like a paranoid ballet dancer cornered in a tragicomic opera. A bizarre flat fish, the mottled color of sand, with both eyes on the top side of its head. Spider crabs, razor clams, silverside minnows, horseshoe crabs, and mud snails—as if a primitive undersea scene has been transplanted onto land for the first time.

On this beautiful June morning in the preeminent East Coast fishing and crabbing capital that is Cape May, the charged-up crew trades stories about the morning's catch, lamenting what might have gotten away. An older veteran—all of thirteen years old—helps six-year-old first mate Kayla hold the calico crab. The crew's youngest member, my two-year-old son William—a Quiksilver swimsuit covering his waterproof Huggies #5's—pulls in a grass shrimp and stares at the flounder. The crew has just seined Cape May Harbor. They might as well have landed Moby-Dick.

The crew's captain—otherwise known as associate naturalist Hal Miller—leads the tour from New Jersey Audubon's Nature Center of Cape May, a veritable playground for kids and families. Only on this playground, slides and swings are replaced by Atlantic sea life games, bird books, sea creature touch tanks, and beachcombed treasures. Outside on the harbor beach, as parents look on with the same enthusiasm as the kids, the youngsters touch, hold, and—in the case of the angry eight-inch green crab—admire the wildlife from a safe distance.

Engaging kids and families in the wonders of nature in New Jersey can take many forms, and the many nature centers, environmental education programs, wildlife rehabilitation centers, zoos, and aquariums do it remarkably well. But it is hard to imagine any single activity doing it better than seining. Used by Native Americans to reap the bounties of our

Bill Wheeler

**New Jersey Audubon Society naturalist Hal Miller leads a group in seining Cape May Harbor for marine creatures like flounder, eels, and crabs.**

waterways, seine nets—in this case forty feet long, held on either end by a young explorer—sweep across harbor shallows a few feet deep. All the senses are equally engaged—from the rich, life-cycle smell of a mudflat or a salt marsh, to the timeworn sounds of laughing gulls, to the refreshing feel of sand and saltwater on your legs. There's even a beach plum to be tasted.

"Lots of fish and crabs use the marsh and this area as a nursery ground," says Kim Hannum of the Nature Center of Cape May. "You see lots of young fish. Instead of grown flounder, you see baby flounder; instead of grown croaker, you see baby croaker. You see little baby bluefish, and you see everything from young crabs to mature crabs carrying babies."

The nature center also offers weekly "back bay" tours, in which a pontoon boat pulls a small otter trawl through the marshes of the bay, catching creatures like sea urchins, sea stars, and seahorses and bringing them on board the boat for participants to touch. After all, foremost among the senses is touch—the tentative grasps at smaller crabs, the slither of a fish in the net, the immense bounty of smaller life in every square foot of water.

### Underwater Planet

New Jersey's coast is home to the oyster toadfish—arguably the ugliest creature in the sea, with skin covered by mucous and warts, and with bulging eyes and fleshy whiskers. There is the red beard sponge, which can tolerate pollution and is capable of reorganizing its form after being sliced apart in a lab. The lookdown fish appears exactly as its name suggests: a dramatically sloping face yields to a body so thin it appears two-dimensional. And the Atlantic long-fin squid resembles a toy version of the famed octopus of the tropical coral reefs.

"I'm always shocked by the diversity of what lives in the water," says seashore explorer Joe Reynolds. "You think about these sea creatures like the Forbes sea stars, and it's almost like you went to a different planet. No creature on land is anything like it. They will take a clam shell, open up the shell a little bit, then their stomach comes out of their mouths and digests the clams. Yet you can find it right here along the Jersey Shore. When you think about it, our waters are really the last wilderness we have around here."

It really is a meeting of worlds out here where sand meets surf. Every find is extraordinary, scarcely encountered on any given day in our modern age. Those animals live below the water, and we live above it. The snails, the shrimp, the little minnows may seem common enough. But picture what a mermaid would think upon finding a squirrel, or a pigeon, or an earthworm. In that light, our most common species are truly remarkable. Like a Marvel comic book mutant hero, the summer flounder has both of its eyes on the same side of its head. The spider crab, with its relatively small body and dramatically long and slender legs, looks like a "daddy longlegs" spider at fifty times the size. The northern lobster may be a delicacy on our dinner plates, but it is very much a predator on the ocean floor. And the American eel has that eventful life cycle taking it all the way to the Sargasso Sea.

One typical seining catch stands apart, however. Horseshoe crabs, which resemble bronze shields propelled by menacing, jagged tails, are appealing for reasons far beyond their novelty. These ancient creatures have crawled the ocean floor since the Triassic era of the dinosaurs. Prehistoric flying pterodactyls may have fed on the eggs of horseshoe crabs—just as modern birds do today.

Every June, New Jersey's Delaware Bayshore hosts a natural spectacle of global significance, involving one of the largest populations of horseshoe crabs in the world. Thousands of them breed there, lending an archaic look to beaches and sand bars. These living fossils, more closely related to spiders and scorpions than true crabs, spawn each day. Their eggs, in turn, attract vast numbers of shorebirds, such as the threatened red knot.

### Around the World in 180 Days

Surprisingly, the most extraordinary story on this stretch of beach does not belong to the horseshoe crab. Like many of us, red knots—a plump shorebird with mottled brown wings and a bright salmon-colored head and belly—plan their early summers around a stopover at the Jersey coast. The difference is that their commute doesn't take an hour; instead, it is one of the longest migrations in the animal world. The red knots' 10,000-mile one-way journey takes them from sand flats at the furthest tip of South America, Tierra del Fuego, to the icy tundra of far northern Quebec.

Reeds Beach in Cape May offers a tempting stopover on New Jersey's Delaware Bayshore. Nearly one million shorebirds gather here each year, more than anywhere else in the Western Hemisphere. But the red knots' two- to three-week summer visit is far from a leisurely vacation. The shorebirds must eat enough horseshoe crab eggs to store energy for their return to the Arctic breeding grounds. For decades, that bayshore food source was a fait accompli. Now, however, red knots cannot count on limitless horseshoe crab eggs to tide them over.

That is why I crouch down on this May afternoon, chilly and uncomfortable on the damp sand behind the viewing platform at Reeds Beach. So do former state Endangered and Nongame chief Larry Niles, biologist Amanda Dey, and a dozen volunteers. We spend the next few hours waiting . . . and waiting . . . and waiting. Though flocks of red knots forage along the beach, they display an innate knack for avoiding our nets. We need them right here, where the volunteers secured a long net to capture the birds for banding, then covered the net with sand.

While a volunteer was digging one of those holes, he found a group of buried horseshoe crab eggs. I excitedly looked in the hole to find opaque green jellybeans. It astonishes me that this rugged, primitive creature could have survived eons on earth completely dependent upon such a fragile means of reproduction. Yet in modern times the horseshoe crab is not the only species depending on its eggs.

"The red knots are banking on a huge food resource at Delaware Bay, with the eggs so rich in protein that they can move on after only a week's stopover in some cases," says Dey, who has studied the red knots in Chile's Tierra del Fuego, in the Canadian Arctic, and during annual surveys here in Cape May. "When we went up to the Arctic, it's a pretty harsh place, and those fat reserves they take from the bay are really critical for them to survive in that environment. It's not a far stretch to suggest that birds leaving the bay unprepared may not be reproducing and may not be surviving."

Prior to the New Jersey biologists' study, there was no clear understanding of how the shorebirds lived during the remainder of the year. So Niles and Dey—a husband-and-wife team and both with New Jersey Fish and Wildlife at the time—decided to find out. Their journeys took them by plane over remote Arctic locations like Southampton Island near the Arctic Circle, King William Island, and the Northwest Passage. Let's just say it wasn't your typical New Jersey wildlife study.

"We regularly encountered polar bears. They weren't aggressive animals, even though we are food for them, the size of their prey," says Niles. "Everything is flat, you can see for miles, so you keep your distance. One year we had to have a twenty-four-hour watch. There were polar bears in three different directions—they came ashore and just stopped. One stayed there in the same spot for three days. We had guns and kept watch, but nothing came of it."

On the Cape May bayshore, the last high tide in May once brought the horseshoe crabs ashore to lay their eggs in numbers that rivaled any mass wildlife event across the world. Local fishermen had long harvested some of the crab eggs as bait for eels. By the early 1990s, a burgeoning market for eel and conch fishing spelled the end of the sustainable harvest.

"Trucks would come up onto the beach to harvest the crabs, taking thousands of the biggest, oldest, most reproductively viable crabs in a few hours," says Dey. "Horseshoe crabs take ten years to mature, so that's the worst way to harvest them—and that's what they were doing."

The red knot population is down to a quarter of its former size, with New Jersey Audubon estimating a total population of approximately 20,000 red knots. Dey and other scientists and volunteers time their visit to the Delaware Bayshore in late May and June to survey red knots and horseshoe crabs, as well as two other at-risk shorebirds: ruddy turnstones and sanderlings. They rent a cottage along the Reeds Beach bayfront—we will call it the scientists' shore house—and take turns preparing meals. Many of the volunteers come from Citizens United to Protect the Maurice River, but others are from as far away as Surinam, Kenya, Argentina, and the Netherlands. The red knots truly are a global species.

With red knot numbers declining severely each year, officials in the states along the Delaware and Chesapeake bays—Delaware, Maryland, and Virginia, as well as New Jersey—faced the question of whether to limit horseshoe crab harvests. With a push from conservation groups, New Jersey took the proactive lead in this regional ecological battlefront. The state passed a moratorium on harvesting horseshoe crabs in March 2008, to last until sustainable numbers return. The other three bayshore states have yet to follow that lead, likely hesitant about political opposition among the horseshoe crab, conch, and eel fishing lobby.

### Coordinated Chaos at Reeds Beach

The lengthy wait has left me short of time. I am about to leave when I hear the sound of a gunshot and see volunteers sprinting to the narrow bay beach. For a moment it looks like total chaos. But the sound was the net firing out like a cannon, and everyone here is on a mission—from putting a blanket over the net to calm the birds "like covering a parrot cage," as Dey puts it, to placing the birds in "keeping cages" to be weighed and banded. If it is chaos, it is certainly well coordinated.

I join in, picking up horseshoe crabs caught in the net and carrying them down to the surf. Even though I've seen them countless times, their bizarre shape and prehistoric armored shell never cease to amaze me. It is one thing to survive as an oddity, a curio, but it is another thing entirely to survive as a vital link in a global food chain spanning continents and hemispheres.

The season proves successful, the first time in over a decade that some red knots were ready to return to the Arctic as early as May 27 and 28, according to Niles. Many horseshoe crabs spawned, laying abundant eggs, and the red knots were able to fatten up quickly. Once they were plump enough, the knots were off to the Arctic.

"There's a deck on the back of the place we rent, and for three nights we could see birds lifting off the bay, gradually getting higher. Maybe thirty flocks a night leaving for the Arctic," says Niles. "It was remarkable—it was the end of the season, we had a sense of pride about it. Other years, you might see that once, and it was an event."

With the ban on harvesting for several years, New Jersey horseshoe crabs can grow to maturity and expand their numbers toward their previous levels. But until Delaware, Maryland, and Virginia follow suit, according to Dey, it will be difficult for the horseshoe crabs and red knots to recover fully.

"Time really is the issue here," she says. "Barring an indefinite full moratorium, I think we'll see the horseshoe crab managed at a very low level. I'm sure the crab population can persist at a low level, but not in enough numbers to really help the birds."

In the meantime, the red knots continue their timeless annual flight across the hemisphere. Ten thousand miles to go—next stop, the Arctic.

# Bald Eagles on a Bayshore Bayou

# 19

Ten thousand feet in the sky, an eagle can see a rabbit walking—I wonder what kind of world that must be.

—Dr. Len Soucy, Raptor Trust

In the cold, bright sunlight of a winter morning, I walk along a trail made of oyster and clam shells. The trail leads along an extended berm, also made of shells. Towering mounds of clamshells sit nearby. The only buildings left standing are oyster and clam processing plants. The names of these towns—Bivalve and Shell Pile—are themselves a tribute to oysters and clams.

Even that is understating the case. For miles and miles, this whole stretch of the Delaware Bayshore was built on shellfish. Bivalve was once called the "Oyster Capital of the World." But for the past sixty years, that capital has been crumbling like a shell in the pounding surf. Now all that's left of the industry here in Bivalve are those two buildings. Little remains elsewhere along the bay, either. But as the people moved away, nature strengthened its grip on the bayshore.

I stand atop the clamshell berm, looking over a horizon of salt marsh in three directions. To the east flows the southernmost stretch of the Maurice River before it surges into Delaware Bay. Along the southern coast of New Jersey, I am far removed from the state's stereotypical cities and suburbs and highways and strip malls. Here, the only noise is the squawking of gulls and terns. This is a place for revery, for deep contemplation of a bygone era, for—

*What was that?!?*

The sudden cool of a great shadow envelops me, and I turn and look to the sun. A bald eagle flaps its mighty wings, then glides for a few beats. Its white head is unmistakable. Because the salt marsh is so vast, the land so flat, I can watch the eagle's stately passage—straight across the Maurice River—for what feels like ages. The flight confirms the lesser significance of the land I stand upon. The bayshore's eagles rule an entirely different realm. Theirs is a world of water and sky.

## Everybody's All-American

Now in the midst of a dramatic recovery across the nation, the bald eagle presents an all-American tale of triumph over seemingly insurmountable odds. When this magnificent bird was chosen as the national emblem in 1782, it ranged from Florida to Alaska. Two hundred years later, only one active nest remained in New Jersey. The bald eagle was long hunted for sport, and it suffered from habitat loss, but the effects of the chemical DDT nearly put the finishing touches on the eagle's decline. In 1973, President Richard Nixon signed the Endangered Species Act, with the bald eagle among the first animals listed and protected.

Biologists in New Jersey launched a bald eagle management program that sought to protect the handful of birds that remained, while replenishing the breeding population with young eagle chicks from elsewhere raised in captivity and released into the wild. The eagle's regeneration started slowly, but gained momentum in South Jersey in the 1990s. From there, eagles spread out around much of the state. With a second chance at survival in the Northeast, bald eagles have adapted to the highly developed landscape.

"They do surprise us sometimes in the places they choose for nesting," said Kathy Clark of New Jersey Fish and Wildlife. "You see an eagle nest in Camden, on Petty's Island, and you think they made a mistake. It's always a balance, as with all wildlife, between areas that are pretty wild and undisturbed and places that are more on the edge of human uses. It's eye-opening, though, as you start seeing it from an eagle's perspective."

In the central part of the state, bald eagle sightings from Milltown to South Amboy led Joanne Williams and the Highland Park Environmental Commission to team up with the Edison Wetlands Association in 2007 to create a sightings report for Middlesex County, one of the most highly developed regions in the country.

"I was driving through Donaldson Park and saw this huge bird flying over the road, so big and close that I didn't even need my binoculars," said Williams. "I was really just shocked, pleasantly so. Prior to that, I had always joked with my husband that maybe we'll see a bald eagle—as if it was so unlikely it would be like seeing a pink flamingo."

Even Clark, who has tracked bald eagles since their nadir, retains a sense of wonder about their recovery from near extinction.

"It's still unbelievable to me, it really is," she said. "Who would've thought this could happen in New Jersey?"

## Eagles by Pontoon

Though bald eagles are now found statewide, nowhere beats the Delaware Bayshore of Cumberland County for encountering them in their natural habitat. And nothing immerses you in their world more fully than a "Bald Eagles on the Maurice River" boat tour. My dad, daughter, and I see this firsthand on an early April morning.

The *Osprey*, a thirty-seven-foot pontoon boat, is waiting on a simple dock in downtown Millville, a former center of the glassmaking industry that now boasts a thriving arts district. The dock sits near a bridge between a police headquarters and a Wawa. Here the Maurice River—pronounced "Morris," as Captain David Githens and other locals helpfully correct visitors—seems more an urban waterway than anything wild and scenic.

It takes only a few minutes to erase that impression completely. Githens has scarcely introduced himself before his first cry rings out: "Bald eagle straight ahead!" As the raptor crosses overhead in the gusty blue sky, its white head is crystal clear.

The Maurice River is the color of iced tea, as Githens puts it, because of the tannin, or decaying leaves and tree branches, further upstream in its spring-fed tributaries. Both freshwater and tidal, the Maurice drains areas of the Pinelands into Delaware Bay, running twenty-eight miles on a very winding course. On our boat tour, the small homes on either side give way to the classic South Jersey habitat of pines and deciduous trees topping clay soils with a root-exposed riverfront edge. Perfect for bald eagles.

"Delaware Bay has a lot of landscape similarities to Chesapeake Bay, which has the highest productivity of eagles in the lower forty-eight states," says Clark. "The salinity of the tributaries, fresh tidal, the habitat mix of agriculture and forest alongside these tidal tributaries, the fish population with both resident and migratory fish. It's like magic. It is so similar to Chesapeake Bay, plus it's in fairly close proximity to it."

Along with the Cohansey River, the Maurice probably has the most eagles in the state, according to Jane Galetto. Galetto founded Citizens United to Protect the Maurice River, a nonprofit group that has advocated for the river for more than two decades.

"Some think the Cohansey has more now because the Maurice osprey population is so strong. This year, four different eagles in the state took up residence on osprey platforms—and the ospreys kicked them out," says Galetto. "It's the idea of a chihuahua that can bully a labrador. The osprey is a lot more agile in flight and feisty and acrobatic. I've seen

Tam Stuart

**The Maurice River is one of the best places to spot river otters, which are common but hard to see in many rivers throughout the state.**

an osprey doing a complete backflip from its nest as if from a diving board."

We pass a number of nesting platforms on our way downstream and on our return, and every single one is occupied by an osprey. We see sandpipers, yellowlegs, fish crows, and swallows aplenty. Mink and river otter have been spotted on these trips, along with the more common muskrat. As we peer over the pontoon's front railing, it's easy to picture an otter family slip-sliding down a muddy riverbank. The Maurice River gets more remote as it goes on, twisting through paddies of wild rice and countless coves and inlets, with little but the occasional fishing cabin or duck blind to recall civilization. This river hosts the largest wild rice paddy in New Jersey and the state's only stands of the globally endangered sensitive joint-vetch, an intertidal plant with fernlike leaves.

"The Maurice River is such a unique part of New Jersey," says Githens. "People come on these trips because of the eagles and other birds, and they may not realize how beautiful an area this is. They end up really enjoying the river as much as they do the eagles."

Thanks to the work of Galetto and others, Congress declared the Maurice a Wild and Scenic River in 1993, one of only three New Jersey rivers to receive that federal designation offering protection from harmful developments. (The state's other two Wild and Scenic Rivers are the Musconetcong in the west and the Egg Harbor in the Pinelands and southern coast.)

The scenic habitats along the Maurice's winding course include the thirty-foot-high sandy cliffs lining the river's edge. They seem almost out of place on the otherwise flat South Jersey plain, but they offer a striking vista. Topped with towering pines, these embankments provide ideal habitat for the belted kingfisher. We see three kingfishers—a majestic fish-eating bird, a foot tall with a shaggy blue crown and a long, sturdy beak—skipping overhead and another one landing on an overlook. Such habitat is rare, according to Githens. Kingfisher populations are dwindling in many places—but they thrive here on the Maurice.

This trip aims for bald eagles, however, and it lives up to its promise. Our first nest is the kind of difficult sighting I expected: high atop a pine along a side creek. Scarcely recognizable and half hidden by another tree, the owner looks less like a bald eagle than a silhouette on a safari stakeout.

The second nest, though, surpasses anything I could have imagined in New Jersey. Like a vision from Alaska's Chilkat Bald Eagle Preserve, a massive nest occupies the tallest tree on a wide stretch of the Maurice, head and shoulders over the rest of the treetop line. The residing bald eagle is so clear and gorgeous that I almost miss the even better sighting—that eagle's mate perched on a branch halfway up a pine, just downstream from the nest. That eagle allows our boat to approach before taking off, its hooked yellow beak so prominent on the all-white head. With the mightiest of wingbeats, the eagle swoops past the front of the boat to the amazement of the passengers, then soars off northward in a straight line over the river, diverting our attention away from the nest. On our return voyage, the eagle is back on that same perch.

### The Bayshore Bayou

Every February, Galetto and Citizens United celebrate the Maurice River's raptor residents with an annual Cumberland County Bald Eagle Festival. More than a thousand people enjoy nature displays and vendor booths, joined by expert-led birding tours of top Delaware Bayshore birding locations. The festival's popularity belies the fact that many New Jerseyans overlook the bayshore because it is off the beaten path. As maritime industries based on oysters, shipbuilding, and glassmaking declined over time, people moved away in droves.

"The bayshore is a habitat that is a hybrid of the New Jersey Pine Barrens and the Delmarva peninsula," says Pete Dunne, a longtime naturalist and author. "They're separated by a bay, and both have coastal marshes that are very lush and rich. It is a people-less area, buffered to the north by the Pine Barrens, to the south by the bay. It's a little slice of New Jersey's past heritage protected in economic amber. People here aren't worried about another depression because they never came out of the last Depression."

Birding is extraordinary on the Delaware Bayshore. Purple martins—our largest swallows, their bodies a rich purple-black—gather in mind-boggling numbers of 40,000 to 60,000 in the phragmite marshes around the Mauricetown Bridge every August, prior to beginning their migration to Brazil and other areas of the tropics. The bayshore forests offer some of the few places in New Jersey to see southern species like summer tanager, yellow-throated warbler, and the vibrant golden-yellow prothonotary warbler.

For Dunne and many others, birds of prey are the unparalleled highlight of the Delaware Bayshore. Bald eagles and osprey stand out, and occasionally someone will spot a golden eagle. Plenty of other wildlife abounds.

"Winter is wonderful. There's a place called Jakes Landing, and if you drive to the end of the road for the last half hour before sunset, you can look down to the river and possibly see river otter. Nothing is guaranteed, but otter are all over the place," says birder Paul Kerlinger. "You'll see northern harrier definitely, possibly rough-legged hawk, and sometimes short-eared owl. Then at dusk, the great horned owls start calling, and sometimes even a barred owl. Then you have a beautiful sunset—it's just a beautiful place."

## Full Moon at Turkey Point

For me, another bayshore sunset beckons: the Owl Watch at Turkey Point. In this sparsely populated region, I am stunned to find more than a hundred cars lined up along the road to Turkey Point. It is a testament to the popularity of the Bald Eagle Festival, for which this is the day's final event. A wooden footbridge spanning the creek is crowded with birders and photographers, as is the adjacent viewing tower. Such a crowd might feel claustrophobic at most nature events, but here it is hardly noticeable. The scene steals the show. In hues of orange and purple, the sun slowly sets, reflecting across creeks and silhouetting the few trees of the marsh. A full moon looms above, and a chill sets in. The owls, though reported nearby, are no-shows for the night. No matter—this sunset scene makes the owls an afterthought.

A female northern harrier, a stately brown raptor with a broad white stripe across its tail, courses low over the channels in the dimming light. An American bittern rises up suddenly from the marsh, dipping abruptly like a fighter jet performing aerial acrobatics before diving back into the marsh and disappearing into the reeds. Thick-necked and stout, a stationary bittern hardly seems aerodynamic, but its performance tonight proves sleek and graceful.

This shy and reclusive bird is seldom seen. Yet over a hundred birders have seen the American bittern here tonight. Even better, this one rose close enough to the group to be seen clearly with the naked eye—no binoculars needed. After all, the Delaware Bayshore belongs to the American bittern, to the bald eagle, to the dusk owls. The former "Oyster Capital of the World" might soon lay claim to another title, one involving the birds of winter.

# The Mysteries of the Pine Barrens 20

**FIRE**  Where stunted pines of burned-over forest are revealed in darksome pools, the Jersey Devil lurks.

—Folklorist Henry Charlton Beck

When I was an eight-year-old living in Toms River, our suburban development had just one entrance and exit. On all other sides our modest homes were surrounded by the edges of the Pine Barrens. Sandy trails wound through the pines, the ground just firm enough for dirt-bike tires to grip. My friends and I spent many summer days exploring what to us seemed like deep, limitless forest. One afternoon we found a flat board on the forest floor and raised it to expose a dark hole, wide enough for a person to enter.

As we weighed our options, someone mentioned the Jersey Devil. That was all it took. Ten minutes later, we were safe in my kitchen, hearts pounding, ready for a break from the pines.

The pine forest around that suburban development has now been bisected a dozen times over with tract homes, split up into tiny pockets of woods. But the Jersey Devil, as it has for nearly three centuries, continues to terrorize the denizens of the Pine Barrens in tales told late at night in a bedroom or over a flickering campfire. How fitting that with all of New Jersey's captivating wildlife, our most famous creature doesn't even exist.

Or does it?

## Shout at the Devil

Although the details are somewhat vague after centuries of legends recounted with the help of a potent jug of Pine Barrens moonshine, the essential story is timeless. In the year 1735, a Pine Barrens farmer known as Mother Leeds, struggling with the pain of her thirteenth pregnancy, swore, "Let it be a Devil!" Soon after, as a violent thunderstorm raged outside, Leeds gave birth to the Jersey Devil. Depending on the tale, the creature took the form of a demon, a cloven-hoofed goatlike creature, or a winged, fire-spewing dragon. Ever since, the Jersey Devil has wreaked unholy havoc throughout the Pine Barrens and beyond, with sightings and terrors reported from Salem to Paterson, from Barnegat to Somerville. Reports continued as recently as the 1960s, with incidents in Mays Landing and Batsto.

Assuming for a moment that we don't take the story at face value, what wild creature could be the subconscious inspiration for this myth? What fleeting sight on a fog-shrouded Pine Barrens eve was translated by a terrified imagination as the Jersey Devil? What unearthly wail echoed through the lonely pines and caused a heart to pound in fear?

There are a number of possible real species—though perhaps I should say *scientifically accepted* species, so as not to offend the legend. The black bear has long been a visitor to the Pine Barrens, though infrequently enough to remain uncommon and thus mysterious here. Same goes for the bobcat, which, though modest in size, is certainly capable of emitting a bone-chilling shriek. The white-tailed deer, aggressive packs of wild dogs, the sandhill crane, and even raccoons offer additional possibilities. Domestic goats have been known to climb small trees and issue strange bleating noises, and they possess the horns and cloven hoofprints demanded by a Jersey Devil wanna-be. Certainly, not every "sighting" stemmed from the same misidentification, but each of these animals could have added to the lore that has built up over the last two and a half centuries.

For me, the great blue heron is the top suspect. Only the heron possesses all of the traits of this most unusual culprit. Its towering height, massive six-foot wingspan, plumed crown, gangly body, and long legs all add up to an intimidating encounter for the lone sojourner traveling through the pines at dusk on a moonless night. Most of all, the great blue heron's flight is inherently ghostly. Its huge wings flap with the slowest of rhythms, its head eerily hung low and its long legs trailing. Its bearing, as it unexpectedly rises from the dark hollows of a bog when evening arrives, is that of a forest witch.

## The Pygmy Pines

Even if we presume that the Jersey Devil is mere folklore, no place in the state holds more mysteries than the Pine Barrens. Start with the vegetation. Four forests of pygmy pines dot the Pine Barrens. Driving along Route 539, I come across the two largest stands: the Eastern Plains and the Western Plains. The pines scarcely reach the top of my head. It is like wandering through a tree nursery filled with yearlings and immature saplings—only here, the pines are decades old. New Jersey's pygmy pines stay short, no matter how old they grow. These forests make up for their lack of height by growing closely together, making it difficult to walk through them. That dense foliage provides shelter for rare snakes like the pine snake and eastern timber rattlesnake, which might otherwise be picked off by raptors flying overhead. It also offers one of the few places to find plants like the broom crowberry.

Pygmy pines also provide habitat for the prairie warbler. This songbird relies on the dense foliage of pines and shrub oak close to the ground, along with bright sunlight and high concentrations of insects. According to Emile Devito of the New Jersey Conservation Foundation, who has studied the Pine Barrens for more than two decades, New Jersey's pygmy pines host the greatest concentration of prairie warblers in the world and offer good habitat for the declining brown thrasher. Before it was hunted to extinction last century, the heath hen also populated these pygmy pines. Similar to the prairie chickens of the Midwest, with pointed upright "horns," the heath hen thrived on the scrubby vegetation.

Outside of New Jersey's Pine Barrens and a remnant pine barren in the Hamptons on Long Island, there are no other pygmy pine forests in the world. The pygmy pines are just one of many unique ecosystems within the Pine Barrens. To protect that singularity, Congress designated this region the Pinelands National Reserve—the nation's first such designation—in 1978, protecting 1.1 million acres from overdevelopment. As the largest undeveloped natural area on the eastern seaboard, the Pinelands have also been designated as an International Biosphere Reserve, the only such area in the region to be so recognized.

## Light My Fire

The reason for the Pinelands' unique habitat is, quite simply, fire. Frequent wildfires shaped the overall Pine Barrens ecosystems and enabled special areas like the pygmy pines to evolve. Only fire can effectively release the seeds of many pinecones, and only fire can create open patches of land for young pines to take root and grow. The Pine Barrens' celebration of fire goes even deeper, as Devito observed one April day. He visited a stretch of the pines along the Forked River just two days after an intense forest fire ravaged 23,000 acres. Everywhere Devito looked, smoke from the black, charred ashes of the pines filled the air. Yet the recovery had already begun. Ants were rebuilding their hills, bringing up golden patches of sand from three feet below the surface. Devito noticed another movement.

"A flock of about seventy-five yellow-bellied sapsuckers migrating from the south had either seen the smoke or noticed the burned area, and they descended to the forest floor, hopping around and eating the ants, utilizing the forest fire," says Devito. "That's amazing, and that's New Jersey. Why is the Pine Barrens special? That's why. You have no chance of experiencing something like that anywhere else in the eastern megalopolis."

The ants and the sapsuckers depend on the forest fires of the Pine Barrens, and so do a number of rare butterflies. The Arogos skipper, in fact, cannot live without it. The skipper—light orange with large black eyes—has evolved so that its caterpillars cannot live on anything except rare Pine Barrens reedgrass, a plant that requires regular wildfires that burn into wetlands. Such fires are now much less frequent because controls minimize this very natural element. When fires do occur now, they are often too hot and too destructive.

Dave Golden of New Jersey Fish and Wildlife has studied the endangered species of the Pine Barrens and finds the butterflies' survival ability to be remarkable.

"With their overall rarity, the fact that the butterflies can hold on in these tiny colonies and survive is very impressive," says Golden. "Some of these species, like the Arogos skipper and frosted elfin, have a flight season that's all of two and a half to three weeks. That's their entire life as an adult."

Another species that depends on Pine Barrens habitat is the pine snake. The only snake that digs its own nest, the pine snake needs the open sand dune areas scattered throughout the Pine Barrens. New Jersey's population of pine snakes is the northernmost in the world—by about

500 miles. There are no other pine snakes in the wild until you get as far south as North Carolina. In many ways, this stunning snake—up to six feet long, with a gorgeous brown-and-white color scheme—is a prototype for the Pinelands wildlife, facing the same challenges as so many species. To begin to know the Pine Barrens, I must first meet the pine snake.

### Tracking the Pine Snake

Steady and slow before, the beeps now come fast. If the beeps are like playing the childhood game of "hot and cold," then we are on fire right now. Dave Golden, herpetological consultant David Burkett, my dad, and I hike through the Pine Barrens in search of this old male pine snake. Golden holds a radio transmitter aloft, and we trudge along a sand track through gnarled pines that, fortunately, are not too thick and dense. Golden and Burkett are in the third year of a seven-year study of the pine snakes in this stretch of habitat. The latest threat from mall and sprawl in Stafford Township is just a quick drive away down a classic Pine Barrens rutted, white-sand road. Like the timber rattlesnake and other Pine Barrens snakes, the pine snake has declined in numbers as roads and houses have encroached.

Burkett peers down at a short pine shrub.

"Here he is."

"He" is six feet of coiled brown-and-white checkered scales lying in wait behind the bush. Golden and Burkett examine the snake, measure it, and mark its location. I get the chance to hold this marvelous creature in my hands. It is docile, moving gently around my arms. The snakes I have held before were either relatively small ones in the wild or domestic boa constrictors owned by friends or wildlife shows. Holding a six-foot-long pine snake in the Pine Barrens—in the very spot where only five minutes ago it was quietly waiting for its next meal to approach—is a very different experience. With its declining numbers and precarious status in the wild, this simple act feels freighted with real meaning.

Joanna Burger of Rutgers University understands that meaning better than anyone. She has studied pine snakes in the wild for twenty-five years.

"You study their hibernation behavior, and the published information has the oldest pine snakes living to fifteen years," says Burger. "I've held some in my hand that I've held for seventeen of the past twenty-three years. It's really exciting to measure and weigh the same pine snakes over the years, to see that their longevity record is more than what was even thought possible."

David Wheeler holds a pine snake tracked through the Pine Barrens by state wildlife biologist Dave Golden and herpetologist David Burkett.

Bill Wheeler

Golden and Burkett finish collecting their data, and we set the snake free. It slithers off, its six-foot-long body gliding effortlessly over pine needles and sandy clearings.

"You can see from tracking that they take on a certain personality—each snake has unique characteristics," says Golden.

"Yeah, even in the prey they eat—one likes baby rabbits, another likes squirrels. One of the cool things about tracking is that you can see them in their real behavior," says Burkett. "Otherwise people just see them when they pick up a board or alongside a road. I once saw one thirty feet up in a squirrel nest."

"I even saw a timber rattlesnake up in a tree," adds Golden. "The beeping went on forever—then suddenly it's right here at eye level." He smiles and adds, "The only thing worse than being bit in the foot is being bit in the neck!"

Both the pine snake and the timber rattlesnake are in jeopardy in the Pine Barrens. Yet the rarest snake in New Jersey may be the corn snake. It is tough to know for certain, notes Golden, because the corn snake—red and orange like Indian corn, and up to six feet long—spends so much of its time underground. These three threatened snakes are often found sharing a den along with more common snakes like the rat snake, king snake, and black racer. Through tracking efforts like Golden's, New Jersey Fish and Wildlife is actively working to ensure the pine snake's survival in its preferred open pine-oak habitat.

Many inhabitants of the Pine Barrens depend on those protections. Bear and bobcats pass through here, even though the pines offer such sizable predators little prey. The white-tailed deer of the Pine Barrens—like the pygmy pines—never reach the size of their suburban and northern forest counterparts. And the endangered Pine Barrens tree frog calls out from the acidic waters of vernal pools, a gorgeous lime-green creature with purple eye stripes running down its sides. New Jersey's Pinelands host one of only a handful of remaining populations of this tree frog. Still, despite the protections in place throughout much of the Pinelands, the future is far from guaranteed for dependent species like the Pine Barrens tree frog and pine snake.

"The most significant threats are roads and habitat loss," says Golden. "The measures being put in place seem to be working—but if you take away those protections, we could lose the pine snake."

# The Mysteries of the Pine Barrens     21

**WATER**   If you get off the paved roads in the Pine Barrens, go hiking on a sand trail or go kayaking, you can essentially have the entire world to yourself. You feel like you're the only one in the entire world.   —Emile Devito, New Jersey Conservation Foundation

I paddle my canoe through a beautiful array of Pine Barrens vegetation. Groups of lily pads dot the coves, and green stream banks are rendered scenic by the splashes of yellow and pink from marsh flowers like the globally endangered Pine Barrens gentian, with its deep violet lily-like petals. The Pinelands also hold more than a dozen species of spectacular orchids, pollinated by bees and flies. These flowers never fail to elicit reactions to their jaw-dropping, sensual appearances.

Anywhere else, plants and trees and grasses provide a passive background, a context in which animals can live, forage, and breed. But the plants of the Pine Barrens deliver far more than a pretty backdrop. Here plants are a big part of the action. In the Pinelands—in scenes that could be straight out of The Rocky Horror Picture Show or a Stephen King story—plants eat animals.

Yes, we have carnivorous plants in New Jersey.

The leaves of a plant called the sundew are coated with hairs holding a sticky drop of carbohydrate that acts as glue. When an unfortunate gnat or mosquito comes in to check out the glistening drop of supposed dew, it ends up staying for dinner—the sundew's dinner. Digestive enzymes eat the insects alive.

On an August trip through the Pine Barrens, I walk along a cranberry bog near a place called Hog Wallow. Vast green flats are boxed in by grassy walls, or berms, which keep the water inside at just the right level during the cranberry growing season. Outside those walls, a pond is dotted with an incredibly colorful array of yellow spatterdock wildflowers, lily pads, and sphagnum moss.

A group of pitcher plants sits unobtrusively along the higher edge of the slope, like a table setting of modest, handspun vases. But this plant's dark secret lurks within. Though nondescript enough to be overlooked by a human visitor caught up in the colors of the blooming flowers around it, the pitcher plant is far more attractive to many insects than the gaudy wildflowers. Pitcher plants produce enzymes similar to those of the sundew, only here they sit in a pool within the plant's vaselike pitcher.

"The leaves have reddish veins that look like dying meat, like an animal carcass, and they give off an odor associated with carrion," says Emile Devito. "Flies are fooled into thinking it's the perfect place to lay eggs. But once they land, they can't fly out again because their wings are wet. When they try to crawl out, the hairs on the pitcher plant are like a giant bed of nails pointing backwards to the fly."

### Canoeing a Land of Extremes

The very name Pine Barrens conjures the vision of a flat, empty, continuous stretch of pines, pines, and more pines. The flatness is accurate—the terrain does not even reach 100 feet above sea level. But the "Barrens" part of the name couldn't be further from the truth for the people who know it best, like Devito and naturalist Joanna Burger of Rutgers University.

"The Pine Barrens are kind of a forgotten habitat, appearing at first glance to be monotonous," says Burger. "There are changes seasonally, but just more subtle. They are wild, and they're not as traversed, not as many hiking trails. It's a bit of wilderness right here in New Jersey."

David Wheeler

**Paddlers take a break from canoeing the Wading River through Wharton State Forest and the Pinelands National Preserve.**

For Devito, that wilderness is a product of the most primal of elements: sand and fire and water.

"The Pine Barrens are biologically so incredible; it is really a place of extremes for the Northeast. It is hot as blazes in the summertime, dry as a desert, and it can be snowy and cold in the winter. Here we are in the balmy Northeast, and you can have incredible lightning storms, you can have scorching heat where the sand is 125 degrees at the surface. You literally can get sunburned on your adam's apple because the sunlight reflects off the sand. It is as elemental as it gets."

I have seen the sand, and I have seen how many organisms are dependent on wildfires, but I am missing one of the elements. I need to see the Pine Barrens from the water. After all, the Cohansey aquifer lies underneath much of the region, holding 17 trillion gallons of water. This water seeps up from the ground as springs, bogs, and creeks. Water, too, is essential to the Pine Barrens experience.

On a memorable canoeing trip in my early twenties, a friend and I paddled upstream through the Pine Barrens on the Toms River. We were amazed to find rich wildlife habitat just inland from such a highly developed area. Recent rains had turned the creek into a forceful, twisting river with threatening snags at every turn. We tipped a couple of times and were smacked broadside by a fallen tree extending out across the creek. As novice paddlers navigating the dangerous bends in the reddish-colored water, we felt we were learning some deeper truth, like a journey into Joseph Conrad's heart of darkness.

Now older and (hopefully) wiser, I undertake a trip down the Wading River near Chatsworth with my dad and daughter that turns out to be a very different journey. The Pinelands offer an abundance of great canoeing options, and on this day we choose a three-hour trip through Wharton State Forest. The gently flowing Wading River twists and turns its way downstream, each curve presenting a wholly new scene. As we alternate between bright sun and tree-sheltered cool shade, the habitats tend to follow suit—all of it providing classic Pinelands scenery. We see ample birdlife, including nesting swallows on the underside of a bridge, as well as a medium-sized turtle and a small mammal rushing into the water ahead of the canoe.

### The Magic Eye

Near the end of our canoeing trip, a movement on the water's surface catches our attention. An eastern ribbon snake is swimming across the creek. Two feet long, with yellow pinstripes running the length of its dark, remarkably thin body, it holds its tiny head aloft, like a miniature sea serpent from Old World legends. It passes behind us just an arm's length from the canoe, gracefully twisting its whole body into an ever-shifting ess shape like a sidewinder. Then it disappears into the brush of the bank.

Howard Chew of Mick's Canoeing can attest to the wildlife sightings that occur on a canoe trip through the Pine Barrens.

"I go out kayaking in the evening hours, spot beaver on occasion, and get in right before dark. Some eagles are spotted, and hawks are pretty prolific here. At Martha's Pond on the Oswego, the river widens out, you have small cedars and islands in the area, and it's a truly beautiful spot. With Wharton State Forest, the Pinelands Preserve, there're no developments—it's all natural. It's like the last really scenic and wild area in New Jersey."

There is one encounter that I'm probably glad to have missed, at least from a canoe with my daughter on board. But it sure is awe-inspiring to envision. Devito was leading a group of botanists to a Pine Barrens stream known for its pitcher plants as well as its thriving timber rattlesnake population. The stream meandered through a scenic bog with wild-flowers lining the water's edge and an upland pine forest on the other side.

"We walked up quietly to this big tree that had fallen down, and this big rattlesnake was so incredibly camouflaged that we didn't even see it. Then all of a sudden—holy mackerel! Like one of those visual tricks, you're staring at it for ten seconds and didn't even see it.

"The hair on your neck stands up, a chill goes down your spine. It's this gigantic rattlesnake staring at you the whole time."

# Part Five

## The Heartland

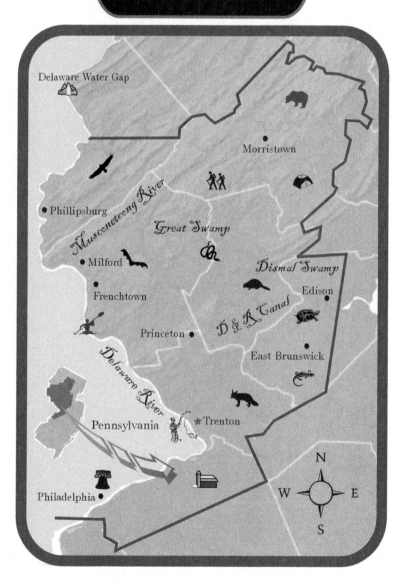

# Wild Nights in Suburbia

People love being involved, the three-year-olds
picking up salamanders and the moms especially
saying, "I can't believe I'm holding it!"
—Richard Wolfert, East Brunswick
Environmental Commission

Follow this recipe, which dates back 300 years to its earliest practitioners and is offered here in its most current version by David Moskowitz of the East Brunswick Environmental Commission:

1 rotten banana
1 pound of brown sugar
1/2 bottle of dark rum
Dark beer

Mash together all ingredients.

Place mixture in the direct sun, until concoction ferments into a ridiculously sweet goo.

Using paintbrush, generously apply mixture to trees at dusk.

After a brief waiting period, walk around with a flashlight, spotlighting the trees.

To best complement this main course, Moskowitz recommends choosing a cloudy, humid night with a chance of thunderstorms. Side dish options include a blacklight or a sheet stretched between two trees, backed by a mercury vapor light.

Now your "Moth Night" is complete. You will be served an abundance of moth species, from the pawpaw sphinx, to the great leopard moth, to the grateful midget.

Bon appétit!

Moskowitz hosts this public event at the end of each summer at Butterfly Park in East Brunswick, helping dozens of people experience another side of nature in the suburbs. On the night I visit, with kids in tow, families and nature buffs alike throng the narrow trails. Rocks painted with colorful butterflies soon give way to live winged creatures. A cacophonous soundtrack of crickets and cicadas and katydids lends the proper nighttime feel.

Even in this eleven-acre park surrounded by suburban developments, more than a hundred different species of moths can be spotted, along with another two dozen butterfly species. Tonight, a dozen sightings span the array of sizes and colors and patterns—from thumbnail-sized brown moths camouflaged perfectly against the speckled bark of trees behind them, to sturdy cream-colored moths that stand out vibrantly on the glossy green leaves along the trail.

The sweet-smelling, sticky mixture proves a success, as does the backlit white sheet that starts its own collection. People ask Moskowitz about the different moths, but more frequent is the question: "What does it taste like?"

"It tastes like an absolutely sickly-sweet alcoholic drink," says Moskowitz. "If you ordered it in a bar, you would definitely send it back."

Enjoy! And please use responsibly.

### Rain, Please

It's not often that I find myself praying for rain on the way out the door. No, when I'm about to spend three-plus hours standing outside on a chilly Sunday evening in March, I usually prefer to stay dry. I'm kind of picky that way.

So if it seems odd that I let out a quick cheer when a few raindrops appear on my windshield as I navigate treacherous backroads in Warren County—well, there's a good reason. Without the rain, there are no salamanders crossing the road. And without salamanders or frogs, New Jersey Fish and Wildlife scientists and a truckload of committed volunteers—and me—have no reason to be out here in the chilly twilight.

I arrive at the site, and my windshield is dry again. I fear that those lone raindrops were just a big tease. It could be a long night. The questionable conditions, fortunately, do little to deter the participants' good cheer.

"C'mon to the party," says one volunteer in a raspy voice with the cadence of an aging hippie. "It's a regular midsummer night's dream!"

He and a dozen other volunteers gather on the road. A forested slope rises steeply to our left. Sod farms span out in the valley to our right. The quickly dimming light lends a mysterious quality to the silhouetted flock of geese coming in for a landing far out on the meadow. Gray clouds alternate with the bright white remnants of the day just ended, topping distant dark mountains and pasture. Somewhere in the distance, a great horned owl hoots. Near the road, a lone spring peeper calls without end like a soapbox preacher. Perhaps he is divining the future for his fellow amphibians, and for us.

After all, this is their migration. We are just here as bouncers, keeping cars and trucks from crashing their party. Tonight, rain is the only question mark. The temperature is in the ideal range, mid- to upper forties. As planned, the night grew dark when the sun went down. (Whew—that's a relief!) So that's two out of three needs for the crossing to begin.

All we need is rain. One volunteer checks the Doppler radar weather forecast on his phone every few minutes.

"There's a system over Lehigh Valley now, but it's moving our way pretty quickly."

Another volunteer reminisces about the good old days.

"2002—that was the best year. We got a torrential downpour."

### Salamander Crossing

The volunteers take their places. For the next few hours, each person will walk a roughly fifty-foot stretch along the dotted yellow traffic line in the middle of the road. Any amphibians that pass through will be tallied by number and species. Should any critters happen to cross during the few times a driver ignores the warning signs, the volunteers will jump in to save a life. The salamanders and frogs cross the road to get from their upland wintering areas to the vernal ponds on the other side, where they can safely lay their eggs. These vernal ponds, or temporary pools, dry up for part of the year. That means no fish are present to eat the amphibian eggs.

"We focus not only on salamanders, but on amphibians as a whole because they are ecological indicators," says Kris Schantz of New Jersey Fish and Wildlife, who started the migration night surveys in 2002 and has run them every year since. "They play an important role in helping us understand the ecosystem health, water availability, and water quality. If there are problems with the water, we will see it in them first."

Schantz, along with Mike Anderson from New Jersey Audubon and MacKenzie Hall from the Conserve Wildlife Foundation of New Jersey, works with municipalities to coordinate these rural road closings for two or three nights each year. Because road closings are so difficult to organize for the vast majority of migration paths, Schantz is calling for a permanent solution: culverts underground. Such systems are in place in Massachusetts and Europe but have not yet been tried in New Jersey, which has more roads per square mile than anywhere else in the country. Culverts would do wonders here.

The first three-hour shift is ending without a single crossing. I say my goodbyes and begin walking back to the car. And then—"Spring peeper!"

"Salamander!"

A volunteer shines his beam on the spotted salamander, a good six inches of stunning dark blue dotted with yellow spots. A few feet away, the spring peeper—a tiny tree frog no bigger than my thumb, with a beautiful darkened X pattern across its olive-colored back—slowly makes its way across the road. It feels great to see these brave individuals, who appear to be testing the conditions for the rest of their groups—perhaps they are the amphibian equivalent of "guinea pigs." I can drive home fulfilled, though Schantz and many of the volunteers will be on the road all night long.

"The volunteers have been a huge help, and we couldn't do it without them," she says. "It's amazing because we have people signing up to work all night, even though we ask for only a three-hour shift."

## Hiding in Plain Sight

It takes real dedication to volunteer for the state survey, but there's another opportunity for everyone to experience a salamander migration firsthand. Each March and April in East Brunswick, five months before Moth Night, the town closes down a half mile of Beekman Road to drivers for a handful of rainy nights. Scores of local residents gather to observe the migration, watching spotted salamanders and spring peepers cross the road, along with occasional red efts and red-backed salamanders.

This unique public event started in the early 2000s when environmental scientist David Moskowitz found his first dead salamander on the road. He told then-mayor William Neary about it, and the mayor was surprisingly receptive to closing the road. Each year since, the road has shut down for up to nine nights, depending on the quality of each mass movement.

"On many nights, we actually have a parking problem, so many families want to come out," says Moskowitz. "Our message is that the perfect analogy of the vernal pool is the oasis in the forest. If you lose a vernal pool, you lose all those species that go into a vernal pool."

Richard Wolfert of the Environmental Commission has attended every salamander crossing, save one night when he had a 102-degree fever. As he puts it, "Someone's gotta be the host." For both Moskowitz and Wolfert, the event's public impact extends far beyond a salamander crossing the road.

"The first response is, 'Wow, look at that—I've never seen anything like that before!' It's the newness of it," says Wolfert. "But people love being involved, the three-year-olds picking up salamanders and the moms especially saying, 'I can't believe I'm holding it!'"

A long-time science teacher, Wolfert founded a nature Web site called "New Jersey Nature Notes" to help spread the news about events such as this one. The East Brunswick group offers a variety of other tours, such as birding trips, community gardens, and Moth Night. The salamander crossing attracts the most participants, largely because it seems like such a different world in the middle of suburban East Brunswick. During my visit to the crossing, the frog calls echo so loudly that I might as well have entered a tropical rainforest.

"The spring peepers even on the road are loud. But in the woods at the base of the vernal ponds, you can barely hear the person next to you," says Wolfert. "It's so loud, it's like being at a crowded restaurant. Then, when I make a concerted effort to actually see the spring peeper that I know is within twelve inches of my face—I cannot find it! They blend in so well."

Perhaps that's why amphibians in New Jersey are so intriguing. They seem to hide in plain sight. Dave Golden of New Jersey Fish and Wildlife can attest to that. He has studied the endangered Eastern tiger salamander, the state's largest salamander at over a foot long. This magnificent creature, with dark and light alternating bars like its namesake, spends eight months of each year underground and even breeds under the ice.

Golden enjoyed a dramatic amphibian encounter close to home. With bright yellow eyes framing vertical pupils, the eastern spadefoot looks more like a character in a stop-motion Claymation film than an actual animal. This bizarre toad species is irruptive, meaning that the individuals all come out at once, breed in one night, and then go back underground. Eastern spadefoots might not come out again to breed for years at a time.

"There is a wet area across from my house, and I heard eastern spadefoots calling. I found hundreds calling in this ponded area," says Golden. "The next night I went out, and the pond was still there, but the spadefoots were all gone. Instead there were tadpoles. Soon after, when they started to hatch, there were 1,000 tadpoles in about a one-foot-by-one-foot area. You're talking 500,000 spadefoot tadpoles in that pond."

## A Night in the Bog

Nighttime brings a wholly different landscape to suburban New Jersey. That's when the real action begins. Owls, nighthawks, and bats patrol the evening skies, and coyotes, red foxes, raccoons, Virginia opossums, and striped skunks prowl the forests and suburban neighborhoods. This kind of New Jersey nightlife never sleeps. The seldom seen flying squirrel may be the most exotic animal in the evening menagerie. Its huge eyes fit its nocturnal lifestyle, and its furry skin flaps on each side help it glide from tree to tree.

"I get northern flying squirrels at my bird feeder all the time, eating the sunflower seeds at night. They are actually very common, but they are extremely nocturnal," said Moskowitz. "They have these big eyes—they look just like little beanie babies."

Even in the suburbs, you are never far from somewhere a bit wilder. So my dad and I join Moskowitz on an evening journey into Helmetta Bog in southern Middlesex County. Time is short before the setting sun whisks away the last glimmers of daylight. Moskowitz steps down from the wooded berm into the cranberry bog, and we follow, step by sodden step. This cranberry bog was abandoned in the late 1800s. Nature has since reclaimed and transformed it into stunning and expansive habitat, now partly protected as federal priority wetlands within the 1,700-acre Jamesburg Conservation Area.

"Nature took over, and the old water-control ditches once used to maintain water levels now function as working streams," says Moskowitz. "The berms were used as large dams, almost like they made the bog into a giant bathtub for the cranberries to grow. Now they serve as upland areas and trails in the middle of the marsh."

We cross streams on fallen trees and use the relatively stable tussocks of marsh grass rather than wading directly through the water. Like every bog, Helmetta holds acidic water from decomposed plant matter. Underfoot, pickerel frogs and grasshoppers dive for cover among lily pads and tree stumps sawed off by beavers, while swamp darner dragonflies dart between arrow arum and pitcher plants.

The falling leaves of autumn reveal bare trees, perhaps the best time of the year to view the hard-to-spot species of wildlife most active around dawn and dusk. Blurs of copper speed to and fro across the swamp. On closer look, I realize they are cedar waxwings—their tan heads crested like blue jays and masked black—catching evening meals of flying insects. The booming voices of tree frogs and crickets provide a primordial soundtrack for the dusk action.

New Jersey's eight species of owls, including the short-eared owl, hunt small rodents, birds, reptiles, and amphibians.

Brenda Jones

### A Pine Barrens Outlier

"Helmetta is part of what is called a Pine Barrens outlier," says Moskowitz. "The Pine Barrens' northern terminus is southern Monmouth County, then you go through this area in between that is not Pine Barrens habitat. And then you hit the Pine Barrens outlier, which is essentially this island of Pine Barrens vegetation, Pine Barrens geology, and Pine Barrens species. You get pitcher plants, carnivorous sundews, carpenter frogs, a number of dragonflies, whip-poor-will. It's really a fantastic wilderness just a stone's throw from the New Jersey Turnpike."

With the crimson sun falling below the distant tree line, we step across spongy sphagnum moss to ascend a raised berm. After decades of natural recovery, the berm now holds a dense canopy of pitch pine and birch. The dimming light scarcely reaches through the canopy, lending a prehistoric feel to the forest floor of moss and ferns. Ancient reptiles like snapping turtles and painted turtles still crawl out of the bog to lay their eggs on the berm.

A night hike is hardly complete without cameos by those famed creatures of the night, owls and bats. As flocks of red-winged blackbirds fly overhead toward their nightly roost in a stand of tall pitch pines across the bog, a little brown bat swoops down every so often to catch one of the many insects in the cranberry bog. It sounds obvious, but unless you are outside at night, you have little chance of seeing many of New Jersey's nocturnal species.

"We're creatures of sight, and I like the idea that when you're out at night, you have to rely on your other senses and really listen to what's around you. It takes you a little bit out of your comfort zone," says Moskowitz. "You take an area you don't think twice about during the day, and you make it into an extremely new world when you're out there at night. It's literally a completely different experience."

When darkness fully descends over the bog, Moskowitz returns the group to the twenty-first century by setting up his sound system: an MP3 player and portable speakers that broadcast digital recordings of owl calls across the swamp. We have our bat; now we want an owl. After several sequences of the pre-recorded owl song, Moskowitz calls it out himself. A faint response echoes back across the bog. Tense seconds pass, then the eerie sound—akin to the high-pitched whinny of a horse—comes back louder. An eastern screech owl is nearby.

As we scan our flashlights across the black depths of this primeval scene, there seems to be no better setting for a nighttime hike than the cranberry bog. In fact, the ancient Celts and Germanic pagans of the Iron Age believed bogs to be a portal to the otherworld, a place to encounter the divine. On this night in Helmetta, this cranberry bog—with its bats and owls and sounds of the deepest darkness under a red autumn moon—is another world indeed.

# The Croc Hunter 23
# of the Diz

There's an unlikelihood that something this amazing exists in a densely settled area so close to New York City. Who would think that, just a half mile from crowded neighborhoods and backyard grills, you could have the solitude of a pristine wildlife refuge big enough to get lost in?
—Environmental author Tony Hiss

Have you heard the one about the Dismal Swamp? So a sculptor and a baker walked into this swamp . . .

Huh?

This one, though, is no joke. It's the story of how two everyday people can make a world of difference right in their own backyard. How Johnny Shersick, an ice sculptor, and Bob Spiegel, a pastry chef, became the self-appointed guardians of the Dismal Swamp.

In the late 1980s Spiegel and Shersick became outraged when a politically connected developer sought to pave over the Dismal Swamp, a beautiful nature sanctuary near their homes. Neither Spiegel nor Shersick was trained in environmental science or ecology, but to them, their backgrounds were irrelevant. Learning on the fly, the duo used rallies, protests, flyers, and public meetings to limit the destruction of a place that was nothing at all like its forbidding name—an unfortunate relic of the time when swamps were considered best suited for filling in.

One night Spiegel and Shersick tried a new "gonzo" tactic. Concerned residents stood wall-to-wall at a planning board hearing in Edison to comment on plans to bulldoze the Dismal Swamp's woods, wild meadows, and wetlands for a new housing development.

"There will be no impact from our development. Nothing important lives in the swamp anyway," said the developer condescendingly in response to a softball question from a planning board member.

Spiegel, dressed in a suit and tie, stood up in righteous anger.

"You can't lie anymore—tell the truth!"

"Sit down! There is no public comment period at this meeting."

"We are going to give you public comments, and you're going to listen to us!" shouted Spiegel, as the crowd's murmuring grew more pronounced. "There are a lot of things living in the swamp, and this is one of 'em!"

With that, Shersick uncovered the washtub under his seat and dramatically stood up holding a snapping turtle—fifty-eight pounds of prehistoric, fearsome reptile.

"Bob was getting everyone all riled up, yelling and going on," recalls Shersick with a grin under piercing blue eyes. "And just as he had the crowd going crazy—he gave me my cue."

The planners jumped back in horror, the crowd roared with delight, and a dozen uniformed policemen swarmed in. Holding back a smile, one officer politely told Shersick to take the turtle outside. By the end of the night, Spiegel and Shersick had rescued the Dismal Swamp from the bulldozer.

### Green Gonzo

Bob Spiegel's confrontational style got results. It also put him directly in harm's way. When a powerful developer wanted to clear-cut a forest atop a historic Revolutionary War site, Spiegel convinced a judge to issue a stop work order. Spiegel and a town official served the order, but the bulldozer operator ignored them. Spiegel faced down the bulldozer—and got smacked in the ribs by the giant metal scoop. He spent three days in the hospital with a bruised diaphragm.

"I felt like a lone protester in Tiananmen Square, except here it was a bulldozer, not a tank," says Spiegel. "Only the bulldozer didn't stop."

Much of the forest survived—and the local media reported the man-against-bulldozer confrontation. "All I kept thinking about was the fact that 150 patriots lost their lives there to try and defend that site against the English during the battle of Oak Tree," Spiegel told a local newspaper. The reporter noted that the interview took place "as he lay in his hospital bed on the third floor in the cardiac unit attached to monitors and wearing only a hospital gown."

The newspaper's cover photo showed Spiegel and a dozen supporters decked out in colonial regalia at the top of Oak Tree Hill, waving Old Glory and the Union Jack. Yes, Bob Spiegel did things a bit differently than the average environmentalist. Maybe he wasn't exactly John Muir founding the Sierra Club—but it worked.

## Suburban Wilderness

If you were to create the most inauspicious place to encounter the wilds of New Jersey, you would create the Township of Edison. Named to honor the "Wizard of Menlo Park," Thomas Alva Edison, the town is the prototype of modern suburbia. Located nearly smack dab in the center of the state, it has no walkable downtown, just a mishmash of quiet residential neighborhoods, strip malls, and chain restaurants along Route 1. Home to 100,000 people—largely commuters along the Northeast Corridor rail line, the Garden State Parkway, and the New Jersey Turnpike—Edison's two claims as a destination confirm the stereotypes of suburban New Jersey: the Menlo Park Mall and the Metro Park corporate office complex.

Yet Edison is also a microcosm of New Jersey as a whole. It is a melting pot city and a sleepy suburb. It retains the old smokestacks of industry, and it hosts the new corridors of technology. It nurtures a few remnants of its farming past, and it still offers untrammeled nature. Those last two features come together in the Dismal Swamp Conservation Area—more than 1,240 acres spread across Edison, South Plainfield, and Metuchen.

Out here in the Dismal Swamp, it is easy to forget we are surrounded by one of the most densely populated areas in the nation. These wetlands are considered so ecologically important for wildlife diversity and flood control that the U.S. Fish and Wildlife Service designated them a national priority. Along with the abundant reptiles and amphibians, nearly 200 species of birds can be found in the Dismal Swamp, including threatened species such as black-crowned night-heron and American bittern. Coy-

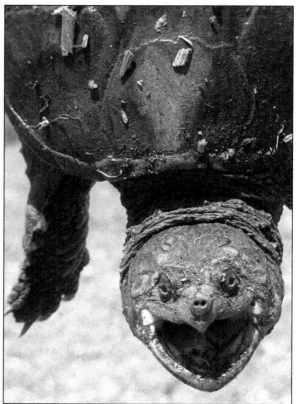

The largest freshwater reptile in New Jersey, the snapping turtle can weigh as much as seventy-five pounds.

Melanie Worob

otes are rarely seen, but their eerie howls can be heard at night in the Diz, as locals call it.

"You don't hear them all the time, but every once in a while, if an ambulance goes through with the siren going, you can hear the coyotes howling along in response," says Spiegel.

No one knows the wildlife of the Dismal Swamp like Johnny Shersick. Born and raised in the area, he is the person the authorities consult when they need help with a wildlife problem. When the Metuchen police receive a call from a worried resident about an injured Cooper's hawk that crashed into an apartment window, they call Shersick. Spiegel calls him "the Croc Hunter of the Diz" for his fearless ability to wade into any body of water and safely handle a seventy-pound snapping turtle. And on this July afternoon, it's turtle time.

## Snappers in the Swamp

Parking on an industrial side street in South Plainfield, we hike down a dirt path directly into a stand of eight-foot-high phragmites. Goldenrod and bergamot blossom along the trail. The ground gets wet, then earth fully gives way to water. Our group of seven is now separated into the haves and have-nots—those with hip waders and those with only knee-high boots. The unfortunates cling to clutches of reeds, choosing each foothold with the utmost caution, every fallen tree a godsend, clumps of dead reeds now the safest place to anchor for a moment.

Johnny Shersick never breaks stride going from earth to water. Before the landlubbers can even take notice, he's out in the middle of the "Everglades of Central Jersey." These Helen Street Wetlands are the deepest, biologically richest ecosystem within the Dismal Swamp Conservation Area. I look up at the feathery reeds and down at the water rising over my knees, and I realize that, right here, suburbia is a distant second to swamp. Dozens of tree stumps line these waterways, gnawed down to triangular stakes by beavers, as if Vlad the Impaler had paid a visit.

Shersick explores for a while, stalking through the lily pads, stepping with purpose. Walking stick in hand, he moves deliberately, each step an exploration, each placement of the stick a survey point on his mental grid of the swamp.

Then he sees what he's looking for. Bubbles. The slender Shersick, wearing sunglasses and a tightly pulled grey ponytail, looks at us and breaks into a smile.

"Here it is—it's gonna be a big one," he says in a raspy voice.

A steady stream of bubbles rises up near Shersick to break the otherwise flat surface. He takes several long, deliberate steps until he stands next to the bubbles. The self-taught naturalist reaches down into the water, carefully. After half a minute—with the group hushed, our breaths halting and our eyes locked on him—he slowly pulls out a prehistoric reptile the size of a large shoebox. It looks like the result of a mad scientist's experimental breeding of an everyday pond turtle with an armored dinosaur relic. This aggressive reptile lives up to its name, too, kicking its legs and clamping down violently on Shersick's walking stick. Like a magician pulling a rabbit from a hat, Shersick has made a snapping turtle appear from the muck and mire of deep swamp.

### Lost in the Flood

For the last six years I have worked with the nonprofit Edison Wetlands Association at the Triple C Ranch in Edison, a farm on a bumpy rural road that dead-ends in the middle of the Dismal Swamp. I feel blessed to look out at nature from my office window, far removed from the traffic and construction that rule the streets just beyond the swamp. The last farm in

Edison, the Triple C Ranch could have just as easily become a strip mall or sprouted cookie-cutter condos, because for decades the Dismal Swamp was viewed as little more than a dumping ground, a wasteland just waiting to be "improved."

The Triple C Ranch maintains its own monument to the battle to preserve it: a sewer drain that sits six feet above wetlands, next to a nature trail. It marks the height of the fill a developer once sought to dump in order to build a golf course. Spiegel, Shersick, and others defeated that project, but the one unbeatable opponent is Mother Nature. Flood control takes on a very tangible meaning here. An especially heavy rain puts entire streets under water. I have had the unforgettable experience of canoeing down Tyler Road, the entrance road for the ranch, and passing the mailbox at eye level. If more wetlands are paved over and developed, the flooding will only get worse for neighbors of the Dismal Swamp.

Environmentalist Tony Hiss, a long-time writer for *The New Yorker*, first explored the Dismal Swamp on a 2005 tour with Shersick, Spiegel, and me.

"The Dismal Swamp is part of a seven-mile-long, hidden biological corridor of habitat going all the way up to Ashbrook Reservation in Scotch Plains," Hiss told me afterward. "It's intricately connected within the inner suburbs of the region, yet this extraordinarily large and unspoiled site has the exact same feeling it must've had for Native Americans thousands of years ago before permanent settlements occurred."

Indeed, the Dismal Swamp's prehistoric sites from the early Archaic period date back at least 5,000 years. Amateur archaeologists have discovered scattered fire pits and stone tools such as arrowheads, scrapers, and axe heads. In many ways, the Dismal Swamp served as a grocery store for the Lenape hunter-gatherers passing through the area. Over time, their semi-permanent camps gave way to farm settlements across the state. Then the farms yielded to development—except for the Triple C Ranch.

Now the public's primary gateway to Dismal Swamp hiking trails, the Triple C Ranch is the only place in the area for scout troops and student field trips to encounter the bright-red, lobster-like crayfish that thrives in slow-flowing creeks, among other natural sights. For most of its neighbors, the Dismal Swamp is still a hidden treasure.

"So many people come up to me and say, 'I've lived here my whole life and I had no idea this was here—but it's absolutely beautiful,'" says Spiegel.

Little by little, the place's reputation is starting to outgrow its forbidding name. In late 2009 Governor Jon Corzine formed a Dismal

Swamp Preservation Commission and signed the bill at the Triple C Ranch.

"It's the largest undeveloped tract of natural habitat in northern Middlesex County," says New Jersey State Assemblyman Peter Barnes, who led the state effort to regionalize the area's protection. "If someone dropped you off in the Dismal Swamp and you didn't know, you'd never think you were in northern Middlesex County. It's so tranquil and peaceful."

### Amphibian Alley

Preserving what's left is a major priority for environmental groups like the Edison Wetlands Association, which is working to expand hiking trails and bird blinds within the Diz. About half of the Dismal Swamp is now protected, but development threatens the remainder. A big milestone came in 2008, when NY/NJ Baykeeper and the Port Authority of New York and New Jersey teamed up to preserve the seventy-acre South Plainfield Holdings property in the heart of the Diz.

On a summer ecotour, we give that property a much more apt name: Amphibian Alley. In upland meadows, American toads hop away with every few steps. Bullfrogs and green frogs plunge into the safety of pools of water. In Aztec Pond, we find a baby snapping turtle no bigger than a mouse, as well as thousands of tadpoles and a large fishing spider stalking the water's surface. We even find a spotted turtle in the wet ruts of an off-road vehicle trail—another threat to the Dismal Swamp's ecology.

Despite its suburban location, the habitat can be unforgiving. Meadows of sawgrass tear up the legs of one hiker who dared to wear shorts, while brambles, thickets, and sinking mud offer different challenges. Bushwhacking through ten-foot-high phragmite stands at the height of summer growth, I find it impossible to see more than a few feet away. Struggling to free my boot from the mud's vacuum-like pull, I am glad for my familiarity with this place. No real trail exists, and few landmarks seem helpful in this winding waterworld. The Dismal Swamp is closer to true wilderness than I imagined could exist in Edison, New Jersey.

At one point, environmentalist Sara Imperiale and I walk through a dark forest clearing filled with birdsong and enter a sun-baked dead-end lined with high-rise condominiums to one side and manicured ballfields to the other. We step out of the woods, and the driver of an idling car looks at us as if Bigfoot had just emerged from the great enchanted forest.

### An Eager Beaver

On a September evening, I stop by the Triple C Ranch with my daughter, Kayla. We bring flashlights out of the car for a quick walk around Turtle Pond, a small watering hole that sits next to Bound Brook, a stream with headwaters deep in the Diz. Had this been early spring, the decibel-splitting chorus of spring peepers would have surrounded us. Instead a lone bullfrog calls out, and the occasional bat flits across the darkened sky, keeping the mosquitoes in check. The green heron and wood ducks from earlier in the afternoon are long gone.

Then I spot ripples on the water. We scan our flashlights across the surface—could it be?

A beaver!

It swims along the surface for a few minutes before we lose sight of it. We walk over to a corner of the pond where a timeworn animal trail connects the pond and the brook. I call it the "Turtle Turnpike" because I often find a snapping turtle or stinkpot or painted turtle crossing from one water body to the other. Sure enough, the beaver peeks its head out from the pond. Upon seeing our flashlights, it retreats back into the water. On any day anywhere in America, this sighting would conclude a memorable wildlife encounter. The American beaver was nearly gone from New Jersey a century ago, trapped and hunted for both its fur and its habit of damming streams. In the Dismal Swamp, beavers were gone for decades before they returned in the late 1990s.

Tonight, however, that sighting is just the start of our encounter. The beaver seems to grow more comfortable by the moment, chewing on some young shoots as Kayla and I watch with awe. It swims back to the crossing and climbs slowly out, keeping a close eye on us, just ten feet away. After a few halting steps toward the brook, it pauses, allowing us to take in its sheer girth. This beaver likely weighs close to fifty pounds and is so thick that its back rises up two feet from the ground. It looks like a giant, buck-toothed ball of fur the size of six-year-old Kayla.

Satisfied we mean no harm, the beaver continues down the trail, dragging its black tennis racket of a tail behind it. Then, with a subtle splash that hardly corresponds to its size, the beaver drops into the darkened brook. It is early in the evening, and the American beaver still has much work to do.

# Serpent Eden in the Great Swamp

# 24

On my guided tours, I always welcome them to Great Swamp International Airport—because that's what this would've been.
—Judy Schmidt, Friends of Great Swamp

A few feet in front of me, a snake swims through the shallows like a sea serpent. To my left, a snake slithers under the boardwalk trail. Not far from there, a dark snake drapes itself over the branches three feet above the water. Then a movement catches my eye, and I look down. Just six inches from my foot, separated by the boardwalk ledge, a banded northern water snake slowly slides out of its coil around a tree stump island and glides smoothly into the water.

This tree stump is one of countless "islands" here. Just as in a mangrove forest in the Everglades, islands here can consist of a single tree growing out of the swamp water, its roots blanketed with moss and fallen leaves until it becomes an island hammock. Others can be twenty to thirty feet across, holding up to a dozen different basking snakes. Looking at one of the tree islands, I realize that what appeared to be another blackish snake coiled around the tree roots is actually two—no, three snakes! Looking like a modern-day Medusa, many heads appear to spring from the coils of a single body.

If this were a zoo exhibit, an open-air area where northern water snakes and other snakes bask, feed, and swim—called, let's say, Serpent Eden—it would be a famous attraction. Experts would tout it as innovative and daring. But it's not a zoo—it's the Great Swamp National Wildlife Refuge. Only nature—and the visionaries who laid out the boardwalk trails—could come up with something this enthralling.

## Amazon as Airport?

Driving past the horse farms and well-manicured lawns of Basking Ridge and Bernardsville hardly prepares you for arriving at an outpost of Amazonia. Yet as you walk into the Great Swamp National Wildlife Refuge on a sunny mid-April day, you might as well be entering some timeless jungle in the tropics.

Brenda Jones

©Brenda J Jones

**The northern water snake can be found in huge numbers each spring at the Great Swamp National Wildlife Refuge in Morris County.**

This refuge could have been something far different. Judy Schmidt of Friends of Great Swamp leads frequent public tours here and makes sure visitors understand what was nearly lost.

"On my guided tours, I always welcome them to Great Swamp International Airport—because that's what this would've been. People got together and wrote letters, turned over 3,000 acres to the Department of the Interior, and they made it a wildlife refuge."

In 1959 the Port Authority of New York and New Jersey planned to build an airport on this land. A local housewife named Helen Fenske led an informal grassroots group in defeating the proposal, a monumental victory that was recognized across the nation for its significance. In 1964 Congress designated the Great Swamp National Wildlife Refuge as the first federal wilderness area east of the Mississippi River. And that informal citizens group became the New Jersey Conservation Foundation.

One small portion of the area did become home to fliers, but of a different sort. Dr. Len Soucy founded the Raptor Trust in Millington in 1968 as a unique rehabilitation center for injured, sick, and orphaned raptors and other wild birds. More than 4,000 birds have been treated here, everything from sparrows to eagles. Along the way, this sixty-acre treatment center became something else entirely—a public sanctuary just down the road from the Great Swamp entrance, with around seventy live raptors on display for families to see up close.

"Forty thousand people walk around my backyard for nothing," says the gruff but passionate Soucy with a laugh. "What the hell kind of business am I running?"

## The Raptor Trust

My family and I are among those visitors on a spring afternoon, and we find an exciting variety of raptors on display, including the golden eagle, bald eagle, American kestrel, merlin, and broad-winged hawk. In one enclosure, both a turkey vulture and black vulture hop eerily along a beam, displaying that menacing posture and deathly appearance that caused plenty of nightmares in ancient times. A peregrine falcon plays with a leather belt stretched across its perch, then fluffs its wings and jumps around animatedly.

This bird's behavior is enjoyable to watch in its own right, but knowing Georgette's story makes it downright inspirational. She was born atop the George Washington Bridge—hence her name. She and her sister jumped out of the nestbox at only a few weeks old, plummeting 100 feet down to the Interstate 95 highway pouring traffic across the Hudson River. Her sister died, but Georgette had a stroke of luck. She bounced off wires and landed on the narrow walkway along the highway. A few feet in any direction and Georgette would have ended up dashed onto the road or drowned in the Hudson. A Port Authority officer found her, couldn't believe she had survived the fall, and called—who else?—the Raptor Trust. Georgette had broken all her wing bones and her sternum, but Soucy's expert surgeries helped her recover to become a goodwill ambassador at the Raptor Trust. Soucy prefers to release recovered birds into the wild, but Georgette and the other birds on display could not survive on their own.

On the day we visit the raven is the unlikely star, its raucous calls echoing so loudly through the center that it overshadows the more beloved birds. The trust cares for eagles, hawks, and a variety of owls ranging from the large snowy owl and great gray owl to the tiny eastern screech owl. To Soucy, all of the birds are miraculous.

"Raptors have fascinated me all my life—it's something to do with their nature, their freedom," he says. "I'm jealous they can fly and I can't. Ten thousand feet in the sky, an eagle can see a rabbit walking—I wonder what kind of world that must be."

## Owling in the Sunlight

You wouldn't expect to go to a zoo or aquarium and then step outside the property and see one of its main attractions—a tiger or shark, let's say—in the wild. But at the Raptor Trust, located right in the heart of the Great Swamp, you can do exactly that. It's like going backstage to see the stars of the show in their natural environment.

I leave the Raptor Trust in search of one of those stars—the long-eared owl. Practically the definition of *nocturnal*, owls are usually seen at dawn or dusk, high up in the trees. Even then it takes a lot of luck. Seeing an owl midday is rare. About the only chance you have is the old birder tactic of finding a group of crows or blue jays mobbing a perched owl. They aggressively hover, scream, and generally annoy the heck out of an owl until it leaves its roost, or daytime resting spot.

Yet on the day of my winter visit to the Great Swamp, the refuge's long-eared owls are the worst-kept secret in the New Jersey birding world. It is an irruption year, meaning that owl numbers have exploded in response to an uptick in the population cycles of their prey in the wintry north. All of the trees are bare at this time of year, except coniferous—or evergreen—trees like the red cedar. Those trees offer cover and so are favored roosting spots for owls.

"It's tough to get a really good look at a long-eared owl if you don't know the location of a reliable roost," says Bill Lynch, an avid birder and graduate student in Rutgers University's ecology department. "The long-eared owls at the Great Swamp this winter were particularly unique because they were literally roosting right over the road."

Along with my fellow wildlife adventurer—six-year-old Kayla—we walk around the metal gate blocking the bridge at the end of Pleasant Plains Road, enjoying the scenic view of the stream in both directions. We walk the middle yellow line along a street with just one home and minimal traffic, fields and forest lining either side.

A birder approaches, headed back to the parking lot. Although my usual plan is to figure it out as I go—like any red-blooded American male—today I break down and actually ask for directions.

"Are the owls there?"

"Yep—one of them is," he answers with a smile.

"How far down are they?"

"As you look down the street from here, they're about where the street disappears."

I see the bend in the road, and we head off in that direction. As we near that spot, I pay more attention to the passing trees, mostly bare deciduous trees with a few scattered evergreen pines and cedars. Then I see it. A roundish dark shape in the loose outline of the tree, just above eye level, ten feet away on the conifer next to the road—it's a long-eared owl!

The owl, about a foot tall, faces away from me, looking toward the forest. I admire its gorgeous white-and-brown speckled coat. Kayla is only mildly impressed—until the owl turns. Now we see its strikingly tall ear tufts highlighted darkly against the faint background of distant sky. The long-eared owl earns its name.

"Wow, that's cool, Daddy," Kayla says as quietly as an excited kindergartener can say anything. "I didn't know you could see an owl during the day."

Me neither. I feel fortunate to see this owl. Some birders this season were even luckier, spotting two different owls in that same cedar.

"My guess is that the Great Swamp birds found a comfy spot and decided to stick with it," says Lynch. "Fortunately—and somewhat surprisingly—they weren't permanently scared off by birders trying to get a close look or dogs being walked down the road."

The owls have company in the trees and skies over the Great Swamp. Along another segment of Pleasant Plains Road visitors can enjoy an overlook with two public spotting scopes that once surveyed a vast heron rookery, though it was abandoned a few years back. Now this site frequently brings sightings of the threatened red-headed woodpecker. Northern shrikes—a rare, dark-masked gray bird normally found in Canada's boreal forest—are often sighted at the bridge crossing we passed. The rare and mighty golden eagle has been spotted in the Great Swamp, and another visitor from the north, the pine siskin, occasionally winters here.

### Kingdom of Reptiles

Birds rule the winter in the Great Swamp, but spring awakens the reptiles and amphibians from their underground hibernations. Sometime around the first week of June each year, a host of turtles pours forth to lay eggs near Pleasant Plains Road, including the threatened wood turtle, a stream- and wetlands-dependent turtle with an intricately etched carapace, or shell. Two other endangered species, the bog turtle and the blue-spotted salamander, are also found here.

On my snake tour, I see another at-risk turtle. A spotted turtle, its gorgeous dark shell dotted with tiny yellow spots, is basking on a mossy tree island a few jumps away from the boardwalk trail. It has claimed its own private island in this reptile archipelago kingdom. Like the protagonist of the Dr. Seuss tale (and early Red Hot Chili Peppers song), *Yertle the Turtle*, this spotted turtle is "the king of the pond . . . the ruler of all that he sees."

For me, however, nothing can top the snakes. Just about everywhere I look, I find snakes and snakes and snakes, three and four and five in a group. Though the vast majority of sightings are northern water snakes, I even see a garter snake slithering across the leaves of the forest floor.

Snakes sunning and writhing in a mass of serpentine leisure. Swimming snakes. Snakes rearing their heads. A snake in the grass. Snakes on a plane. (Okay, maybe not that last one.)

It's enough to make another visiting suburban dad pushing a baby stroller feel like a modern-day Indiana Jones. As for his kids in tow? Awe and surprise, in a parade of exclamations:

"There's another one!"

"On the tree, on the tree!"

"He's swimming through the water!"

### Frog versus Snake

Later, after I tell friends about this fantastic place, more than one person asks if the snakes are too close for comfort in the Great Swamp. Rest assured, I explain, no snakes were on the elevated boardwalk trails. New Jersey Fish and Wildlife biologist Dave Golden regularly sees those kinds of reactions from people in his work with timber rattlesnakes in the Pinelands.

"The biggest misconception about snakes is that people are afraid to turn around and walk away from them because they think a snake will chase them—so they end up in a standoff. The snake is afraid of you. I tell the public it's not a rabid dog—it isn't going to chase you."

The Great Swamp may be the one place where public access has helped improve the habitat for the wildlife. The snakes and turtles here are acclimated to human visitors. Yet the raptors and other wildlife that might otherwise swoop in and snatch a snake for a quick meal steer clear from the heavy foot traffic of park visitors. In the Great Swamp, a person really is the snake's best friend.

As I walk the trails later, snakes seem to be everywhere. Every branch, every root, any log in the water—each becomes another snake. A different little creature puts any thoughts of danger in perspective. A chunky bullfrog squats on the edge of a tree island half in the water. Just a few feet away, a midsized water snake stares at the oblivious frog. I eagerly await the face-off. It is obvious that this snake is about to enjoy a healthy dinner.

"This is gonna be like Animal Planet," says that man with the baby carriage.

Instead, the bullfrog flinches at the snake, which immediately backs up, then slinks away.

If a snake could put its tail between its legs in embarrassment, this one would have.

# Night Falls on New Jersey's Bats

# 25

Between me and the moonlight
flitted a great bat, coming and
going in great whirling circles.
Once or twice it came quite
close, but was, I suppose,
frightened at seeing me, and
flitted away across the harbour to
the abbey. —Bram Stoker, *Dracula*

It is just before dusk when I turn off the lonely country road. I pass a small, dated village of old farmsteads in Milford, an area once known as Bat Town. A few homes in from the main road, I pull my truck into a narrow driveway and park beneath a red barn with white trim. The rising moon, nearly full, will soon add a mysterious dim glow to the grazing fields below. Behind the barn, woods line a brook bordering the pasture.

I prepare myself to enter Bat Wing Farm. One thousand bats await.

There is something about bats that nearly always elicits a reaction from people—be it fascination or repulsion. The bat is a little bit *different* from most other animals.

The only flying mammal in the world? Check.

Hangs upside down and sees the world from a perspective wholly different from yours or mine? Check.

Uses sonar rather than its eyes to navigate? Check.

Devilish reputation passed down over centuries? Check.

One of our best friends in the animal kingdom? Check. Really.

"Bats can eat 3,000 insects per night, if you're talking about small insects like mosquitoes," says MacKenzie Hall, who surveys the state's bats for Conserve Wildlife Foundation of New Jersey. "Nursing females will eat their own body weight in insects each night—4,500 mosquito-sized insects a night."

Far from being the satanic monster of Dracula legend, bats actually provide a great service to modern-day humans. They keep insect populations in check and eat agricultural pests that otherwise cost our economy millions of dollars every year. Considering that bats are the longest-lived mammals for their size in the world—they can live up to thirty years in captivity—they offer human civilization an extremely effective form of pest control free of charge.

New Jersey's nine species of bats include three migratory species that pass through on their way south for the winter. State surveys focus on the year-round breeding bats. The big brown bat's larger body size enables it to tolerate winter's freezing temperatures, but all other breeding bats in New Jersey need caves and former mines for their winter dens, or hibernaculum. Only there can the shared warmth of thousands of little bodies sustain bats through a northern winter. The Indiana bat, an endangered species that for years was the primary bat of concern for wildlife biologists in New Jersey, has been found to hibernate in densities of up to 484 bats per square foot. Living so close together was always a blessing for bats. Now it may be their curse.

## Exploring a Bat Cave

A decade ago I explored a bat cave. No, not in Transylvania—in New Jersey. One of several abandoned mines that bats use as hibernacula, Roomy Mine in Ringwood's Norvin Green State Forest is a classic. A hike from Weis Ecology Center brought me to a rocky outcrop. After doing the limbo through the three-foot-high entrance, I found myself in a round, open foyer. Shafts of light descended onto the shelflike clefts along the walls. At the far end, the twisting, narrow tunnel began. Six feet high with an arched top, the passage was just wide enough not to feel claustrophobic. Crouched in this dark and mysterious cave, I could see why ancient Mayans believed caves to be portals to the underworld, a shadowy transition between life and death.

The wet, hard ground held shallow puddles of mud and guano, the technical term for bat droppings. The walls of Roomy Mine are pierced with deep, narrow holes bored by manual drills during the iron mine's heyday in the 1840s and 1850s. These cozy alcoves are ideal for little brown bats to tuck away for their daytime naps or long winter hibernations. The tunnel's gradual turns allowed my flashlight beam to illuminate only about ten feet of cave in front of me. As I stood peering into the darkness, I caught my first glimpse of flight. Hardly larger than a monarch butterfly, the shape flitted into and out of the light. Holding the beam steady, I saw another bat and ducked into a crouch to stay out of its way.

Though the experience was exhilarating for me, I later learned that, for the bats' sake, it is much less intrusive to skip cave exploring. Bats can be viewed safely at a number of locations where they enter and exit their caves near dusk, such as Hibernia Mine in Morris County. State wildlife officials installed a gate at Hibernia in 1994 to allow the bats safe refuge in the mine, while an observation platform enables the public to experience the spectacle of hundreds or thousands of bats without disrupting their hibernation or daily routines. But if the hibernacula have long provided strength in numbers, they now serve as ground zero for white-nose syndrome.

## A Biblical Plague

Mick Valent of New Jersey Fish and Wildlife surveys and counts the bats in Hibernia, Weis, and other mines across the state. Valent had been aware of white-nose syndrome in other states, which was causing mortality as high as 100 percent in the caves in which it was found. As late as November 2008, there was no sign of it in New Jersey's hibernacula. A month later, on New Year's Eve, Valent got the call he had been dreading: a volunteer at the Mount Hope mine in Rockaway had seen bats flying outside.

In a healthy hibernaculum, bats will pick the warmest spot in the cave or mine, as far from the entrance as possible, to spend the winter. Bats seek to hibernate throughout the cold season, storing precious energy to last the winter. A bat flying around outside the cave is a bat that is destined to die.

When Valent visited Mount Hope a few days after that call, his heart sunk. Bats were indeed flying outside the mine. White-nose syndrome had arrived in New Jersey. Soon after, Valent went into Hibernia Mine.

"That's when it hit me the hardest. It was like night and day from before—bats were clustered by the entrance. Every five minutes there was a steady stream of bats flying out. We saw dead bats near the entrance, and there was fungus on the bats."

A month later, Valent found thousands of dead carcasses on the floor of the mine. He counted around 750 bats remaining alive. A typical, healthy year would have yielded up to 30,000 bats. White-nose syndrome had struck the bats of New Jersey with the terrifying force of a biblical plague. Their long-term survival was suddenly in question.

Even among those who harbor no strong feelings for bats themselves, there is recognition that they consume hordes of insects every night. Without tens of thousands of bats to keep them in check, just how quickly would our mosquitoes multiply?

May we never learn the answer.

## Bat Wing Farm

When Caroline Ratti and her family purchased their home in rural Milford more than a decade ago, one item was not listed on the real estate forms: a colony of 1,200 little brown bats roosting in the barn's attic.

"The first day we came here, we were sitting right there on the deck having dinner, and out they all came," says Ratti, as chimney swifts spiral over our heads. "I said, 'Ouch!' It was a little eye opening. Of course, I found out later that this area around the corner used to be called Bat Town."

It is just before dusk as we stand outside talking on this summer night. Though rain has fallen almost every day for two straight weeks, no one in our group complains of a single mosquito bite over the course of the night. Hall leads us into the barn, where the ammonia-like scent of guano wallops us as we walk through the door. Small piles of guano sit on the floor, and a few early bats fly about the eaves. In her mid-twenties, Hall doesn't hesitate to pick up a desiccated young bat, which died after it fell out of its roost.

"Most bats can't fly from a standing position, so if they fall, they're probably not going to make it," says Hall, her long blond hair pulled into a ballcap. "Vampire bats are the only bats that can run and jump around, and they're not found anywhere close to here."

The sun goes down, and we climb the wooden ladder to the pitch-black barn attic. Miner's helmet atop his head, Mick Valent checks the harp trap, which funnels the bats into a holding pen on their way out the barn window. One at a time, he hands the bats to Melissa Craddock, a Conserve Wildlife Foundation biologist, who places them individually into brown paper bags. I look out into the blackness, then briefly turn on my flashlight beam—illuminating a few bats.

Pitch black again. I hear the whiz of wings close by. Then another whooshing sound. It's an eerie feeling to have bats flying right next to my head but invisible in the darkness. I feel blind as a bat—no offense intended to any bats in the vicinity, which are not blind at all, of course.

The sheer volume of the bats hits home a minute later. I snap photos with my digital camera in the dark depths surrounding me, then I check the display. The images are picking up four, five, nine bats in each photograph—all within a few feet of the camera. It's spooky, like some kind of horror movie concept. When Hall walks to the end of the barn and briefly shines her flashlight on the thousand-plus bats still remaining in the far corner, the big picture is complete. Whatever serious troubles bats are having throughout the state, this barn belongs solely to them. This is truly their belfry. (Sorry, I couldn't resist.)

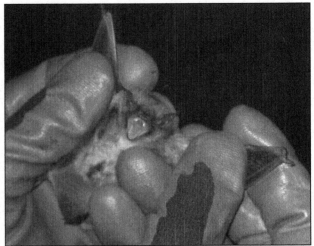

David Wheeler

A little brown bat is tested for white-nose syndrome, a disease that is killing thousands of bats in the northeastern United States.

### Passing a Test

We climb back downstairs to the barn workshop, where Valent, Hall, Craddock, and Charles Hofer weigh, measure, and band each bat. Perhaps most important, they check for any sign of the white-nose fungus. The fungus isn't really a "yes or no" question, as Valent explains, because bats that had the full-blown syndrome would already be dead. Instead, they measure the bats' symptoms, using a scale to estimate any areas of depigmentation, or loss of color, on their wings. Thankfully, no bats tonight show a score of concern. A similar banding a few weeks earlier at Supawna Meadows National Wildlife Refuge along the Delaware River near Salem also showed few bats with serious signs. The Conserve Wildlife Foundation summer survey at roosts across the state found most bats to be reproducing successfully, so perhaps there is reason for cautious hope.

Valent lets the bats fly off one at a time after each is measured and banded. I try to snap photographs of each one, but the bats move quickly. No bat flies off in the same direction as the one before it. Bats somehow occupy a world different from that of other animals, moving to a rhythm all their own. The band, which Valent places lightly on a single wing, will help the biologists track each bat back to a specific hibernacula.

"Bats can travel many miles, so by following a bat with a transmitter, we can follow them to their roost sites and foraging," says Valent. "Bands will help in tracking them at their hibernacula, and we can say, 'We got this bat at Milford, New Jersey.'"

The brown paper bags, a single little brown bat in each one, sit on the floor in the corner. High-pitched squeaks ring out constantly, sounding nearly identical to mice. A reminder of just how tiny these bats are—so far apart from their Hollywood reputation—comes as a housecat wanders over, intrigued by the chirping, moving bags. The housecat looms over the bats like a Siberian tiger alongside a bunny. And people are afraid of the bats?

"Bats are one of those animals, like rattlesnakes and big cats, that get a bad rap. Many people are unduly fearful of them. It's something inherent with us—whether it's the animal's behavior, its appearance, its nocturnal character—we have a knee-jerk reaction to be afraid of them," says Hall. "Now with white-nose syndrome, people are starting to see bats as vulnerable. You see how infinitesimal they are—these little squeaky things, practically weightless. It softens the heart."

A few weeks later, when I see a few bats flitting around the twilight sky as I take my two-year-old son for a walk around a suburban field in Piscataway, the encounter suddenly feels weighted with meaning. If the importance of bats was taken for granted before, now each and every bat carries a part of the species' future on its tiny wings. Any bat sighting now brings questions like:

Does this one hibernate in one of the impacted caves or mines?

Does it have white-nose syndrome?

Most of all, will it survive the coming winter?

That last one is the million-dollar question for New Jersey's resident bats. Only time will provide our answer. Unless you are a big fan of mosquitoes, may bats forever rule our nights.

# A Journey in Time from Farm to Field    26

As the long shadows deepened and the blue vanished from the sky, a procession of coal boats, each with its green light forward, passed silently in review and disappeared around the bend.

—"A Tale of the D&R Canal," *Century Magazine*, 1887

"**Y**ou need five ingredients: habitat, timing, luck, skill, and temperature. You put those five together and you will have a phenomenal day," says Dominic Rizzo. "We might have the others, but we still need the temperature to get up about 10 more degrees."

We are in search of reptiles on the Delaware & Raritan Canal on an early May morning. Rizzo is concerned that the turtles and snakes will not fully emerge to soak up the rays if the day remains mild, so he demands that the sun come out—immediately. As for me? I am already satisfied. Melanie Worob and I hadn't even crossed the footbridge over to the towpath when I saw a long brown water snake slithering through the canal below. My snake quota has been met for the day. Everything else will be reptile gravy.

Built in 1834, the Delaware & Raritan Canal transported troops, goods, and cargo for the North during the Civil War. Steamships later carried coal from Pennsylvania that powered New York City's industrial boom. But as railroads expanded, the D&R's importance diminished, and it closed for good in 1932. Today, however, the canal is alive with new activity—bicyclists, hikers, fishermen, birders, and families pushing baby strollers along the towpath that runs the length of the canal. Mule teams trudged the same track as today's joggers, and the mule tenders' barracks remain standing in Griggstown, where families now rent canoes to enjoy the water.

With river on one side and canal on the other, this greenway offers an outdoor novice the chance to see nature and wildlife on more than 3,500 easily accessible acres. Where else can you ride a bike for miles on end and rarely cross a street while passing turtles, songbirds, waterfalls, and living history? The D&R became a state park in 1974, and the canal serves as a water supply resource. It also continues its role in international trade—albeit with an improbable bill of goods. The D&R Canal is now the established home of a variety of reptiles, including a number of exotics, or species that are not naturally found here.

## Be the Reptile

A self-taught herpetologist, Dominic Rizzo guides visitors along the canal the way a friendly neighbor might lead a walking tour around the block.

"Over there is where the softshell turtles can often be found concealed on the riverside—but they're quick to go into the water because they lack a hard carapace. It's almost impossible to get a good view of them. . . ."

"I was in the bush looking for turtles when not five feet away, a turkey popped out, screamed at me, defecated on the ground, then walked away. . . ."

"I've seen an eel flip itself across the towpath. It looked like a breaded chicken strip because of the clay substrate covering it. It was tired of the canal side and wanted to get to the river. Why did the eel cross the towpath? To get to the other side."

Goateed and with close-cropped hair, Rizzo is affable, motor-mouthed, quick to laugh, and thrilled to be outside looking for rep-tiles—all good qualities for someone who has spent the last few years giving reptile presentations to school kids for a living. Rizzo first got hooked on reptiles as a toddler when his uncle gave him a stuffed "Tommy the Turtle." As Rizzo puts it, the stuffed animal was like a "gate-way drug" that led to living, breathing reptiles.

After years of experience, Rizzo now sees the terrain as the reptiles do. Turtles dive into the water when we approach, and he notes that cer-tain species—red-eared sliders, red-bellied turtles, and cooters—soon come up for air just a short distance away. "They say, 'I wanna see what scared me,'" he explains.

When I ask what species of turtles are found here, Rizzo rattles off more than I knew were possible in New Jersey. He mentions the Wichita map turtle, river cooter, false map turtle, red-eared slider, common map turtle, and eastern spiny softshell—most of which are not native to the state. These species have been introduced, most likely released into the wild as castoffs from the exotic pet trade. And each has managed to estab-lish breeding populations on the D&R.

"The canal is unbelievable for exotics—there's really no better place around for them," says Rizzo. "Each lock is independent, and from what I gather, the variety comes from having fast-moving and slow-moving water. The canal gets a fair amount of sunshine, there's a towpath to lay eggs, fields to lay eggs, rock outcrops, tree snags—the canal and the river and side creeks all in one. Plus, there's easy access for cars to drop them off."

On this day, Rizzo catches a baby red-bellied turtle tiny enough to fit in the palm of his hand and a juvenile cooter turtle not much bigger. We release them, of course, but not before we examine them. The red-bellied turtle is so tiny that a mountain bike rut carved into the sandy trail proves to be an insurmountable peak. We also see a muskrat navi-gating the canal, Baltimore orioles, a green heron, and a steady stream of double-crested cormorants.

But Rizzo has higher expectations. Like a New York Yankees fan spoiled by so much success, he worries near the trip's conclusion that our day was not productive enough. After all, this is someone who has seen "a hognose snake, flipping over and doing that dying thing, seen 'em regurgitating toads and bleeding from the mouth."

Someone who has seen "a click beetle—that was really cool. When you touch 'em, they click and pop up in the air!"

A person who was once "trying to catch this turtle, when I look up and there's this bear watching me."

The bar is set markedly higher for Dominic Rizzo on the Delaware & Raritan Canal.

### Sixty Miles on the D&R Canal

Stephanie Fox, the state park naturalist, leads public tours along the canal. For her, the stretch along the Delaware River is without peer. Neotropical migrants come through in great numbers. Cliff swallows build nests underneath the bridges, and fishermen come in droves for the trout, catfish, perch, and crappies. Egrets and American woodcock arrive at the floodplains in spring.

"My favorite spot is the Bulls Island section, at the very beginning of the canal, where a wing dam feeds water into the canal from the river. We get all kinds of wildlife," says Fox. "There are miles of paths and cobblestone walkways full of toads and these big, huge ostrich ferns. It gives you a remote feeling. Every once in a while, you can catch a glimpse of a mink. When people see Bulls Island for the first time, I get to kind of relive it—I live it vicariously through them."

The thirty-nine acres of the Bulls Island natural area support rare nesting birds like cerulean warbler, Acadian flycatcher, yellow-throated warbler, and the northern parula. Sycamores, tulip poplars, and silver maples rise up from the Bulls Island floodplain. The four-foot-high ostrich fern forms dense colonies along the water, its green fronds resembling the tail feathers of an ostrich. Before they mature, those fronds can be cooked as a delicacy called fiddleheads; prepared with hollandaise sauce, they taste something like asparagus—or so I hear.

Speaking of ostriches, another stretch of the canal, along Weston Road in Franklin Township, often hosts a wintering bird as close as we get to that giant in America. In November 2007 three sandhill cranes—gray birds that bear a dramatic blood-red crest and stand up to five feet tall—lingered for at least a week among grassy hills between the canal and a block of industrial warehouses. They returned for most of the next two winters, though some birders—cough, ahem—missed them. (Another group of sandhill cranes shows up annually on certain farm fields in Salem County.)

"Large waders like herons and egrets are fairly commonplace," says birder Bill Lynch. "But to see birds with such a substantial physique browsing the fields of central New Jersey was something different entirely."

A few months after my Rizzo tour, I visit the D&R again with two-year-old William. We have been walking for only a few minutes when he says, in the same voice he might use to point out a squirrel or a sparrow at the bird feeder, "Daddy, a snake." A northern water snake slithers off into the underbrush just twelve inches from William's feet. And I'm not even surprised. Another naturalist has counted more than fifty water snakes along the canal on a single three-mile hike. William and I, over the course of a short walk, see plenty of turtles as well, for I find myself adopting the learned Rizzo method. That is to say, I see things through the eyes of the reptiles.

The branches extending out over the water? Check for snakes.

See a turtle basking on a nearby log in the water? Keep walking—it's your stop that scares them into diving.

And most of all, those clouds need to get lost. We need that sun out here—immediately.

### Exotic New Jersey

The exotic turtles of the D&R Canal have proved to be relatively harmless to the native ecosystem. Like pigeons—known as rock doves in the wilds of their native Western Europe—or house sparrows, these species have adapted remarkably well to an ever more developed United States. Other exotics, such as the ring-necked pheasant and landlocked salmon, were introduced for hunting or fishing purposes and found a niche that they could maintain without too much help.

One species that is exotic in both senses of the word is the monk parrot. More commonly found in Brazil, Uruguay, and Bolivia, monk parrots have established themselves in colonies in New Jersey, not exactly a tropical jungle. Yet the urban landscapes of Edgewater, Ridgefield, and Carteret somehow offer the parrots the right mix of habitat, food, and shelter.

I visit one monk parrot colony in a hardscrabble section of Carteret. Just a few blocks from the Arthur Kill and with Staten Island beyond, this little slice of tropicalia beats to its own rhythm. Attached to a transformer on a power line, the birds' sprawling, unwieldy nest—jam-packed with sticks so no daylight is visible—sits over a vacant lot near warehouses and apartment housing. At first the nest appears abandoned. Then a flash of bright green appears, then another. The parrots' vibrant colors stand out against the bleak gravel lot. Loud and raucous calls echo as two more parrots fly home. Years earlier, I visited the Edgewater monk parrots, the colony's joyous cacophony resounding across Veteran's Memorial Park at near-deafening levels. Their exotic presence in urban Hudson County—and devotion to rebuilding their nests each time a power company tore them down—made them beloved local favorites.

The parrots arrived in the United States in a shipment at JFK International Airport in 1968 and escaped from damaged crates on the runway. One population found a home at Brooklyn's Green-Wood Cemetery, and another group migrated to New Jersey. For more than four decades, the parrots sustained and increased their population without direct help from humans. They were rewarded in 2009 when the state records committee formalized their status: monk parrots are now officially Jersey birds.

Other exotic species in New Jersey, conversely, have adapted in a way that makes us cringe. Their damage is measured both in millions of dollars and in devastating impacts on native ecosystems. Norway rats, the bane of urban existence, came over on the ships of early colonial settlers. European starlings—or, as they are often called, "the rats of the birding world"—were famously introduced to Central Park by a Shakespeare fanatic who wanted every bird mentioned in the Bard's writings to be present in New York City. Starlings exploded in population to compete with native birds and generally wreak havoc on many an ecosystem.

Perhaps no creature has devastated our native habitat more than the hemlock woolly adelgid, an aphid-like pest introduced from Asia that sucks out the juices from the tree's needles, ultimately killing thousands of mighty hemlock trees in New Jersey and the Northeast. Giving the adelgid a run for its money is the Asian longhorned beetle, which conquers with two distinct waves of destruction. First, the beetle destroys maples, elms, and other deciduous trees by boring deep into their heartwood. Then, in humans' efforts to slow the beetle's spread, we cut down any trees near the infected ones. In the case of the "harbor herons" of New York–New Jersey Harbor, an entire Arthur Kill island lost its trees—and with it, the nests of hundreds of herons, egrets, and ibis.

## Wild Amazon

In an era of unparalleled international travel and trade, exotic species continue to threaten already fragile habitats. The nutria, a beaver-like mammal native to South America, was spotted in Lower Alloway Township near the Delaware River in 2007. Introduced by fur farmers in Louisiana and Maryland, the nutria causes tremendous damage to wetlands.

"They are almost like a snow goose—they eat out an entire area. Where you might have had sawgrass and phragmites, you would have nothing but a big mud flat," says state biologist Andrew Burnett, who saw the nutria in Lower Alloway. Burnett believes we are safe for now, thanks to our cold winters. Hopefully, global warming won't give nutria any ideas.

Another threatening water creature is the Asian swamp eel. Hundreds of the eels were found in Gibbsboro's Silver Lake in 2008, and biologists fear the eels could make their way to the Delaware River. With no natural predators and a primeval ability to travel over land to get to another water body, the Asian swamp eel is one scary predator. The voracious eels feed on fish, reptiles, amphibians, and invertebrates—in other words, anything it can catch.

The swamp eel has nothing on two species caught in the Delaware River in 2009: the alligator and the piranha. A four-foot-long alligator eluded capture by state wildlife officials for three weeks in August, lurking in Trenton's Stacy Park between the river and a residential street. The alligator was snared in a backyard dog cage baited with a chicken leg and thigh.

In mid-September, fisherman George Horvath caught a fourteen-inch piranha—an Amazon River species legendary for its razor-toothed attacks that strip an animal to bones in mere minutes—from a Trenton dock. Horvath told a reporter that he had caught another piranha in the Delaware River four years earlier, using his "homemade cornmeal carp bait." The piranhas were likely dumped into the river or a tributary by a pet owner, according to a state spokesman, who assured the press that piranhas could not survive New Jersey's cold winters.

## Hog Wild

And then we have the feral, or wild, hog. In theory, the feral hog is merely a pig that has been set free and reverted to its natural state. But theory doesn't begin to describe the horror-movie quality of this transformation. Only a few months after their release into the wild, hogs become covered with fur. Breeding rapidly—with litters of up to twelve piglets, twice a year—the feral hogs quickly develop longer snouts and longer tusks, the better to root around in the dirt. They become fierce and aggressive. As for the damage they can cause . . . ?

"They put their snouts in the soil and disrupt anything they can. In just one night, it looks like a rototiller ripped up the whole yard," says Cathy Blumig, a seasonal state wildlife worker. "In their stomachs we find rattlesnakes, fawns, tubers, salamanders. They are a problem for farmers and for people protecting rare plants. They also defecate in streams, hurting the water quality and increasing water temperature, which kills trout. For many biologists, they are the greatest environmental threat we face other than habitat being developed."

Feral hogs are now established in New Jersey. Likely released by a farmer who no longer wanted to care for them, the hogs were officially spotted in 2000 in the White Oak Branch Wildlife Management Area in Gloucester County after years of rumors. Estimates range up to 100 hogs, and in 2009 the state allowed a hunt to take place. Former Fish and Game Council biologist Len Wolgast believes the hunt is New Jersey's best bet to control the animals—but he's not betting against the hogs.

"Estimates are difficult because they are mostly nocturnal, secretive, and they move around a lot. This is a very intelligent animal, and they adapt so quickly. They know where to find food sources, they learn to become nocturnal to avoid humans."

George Orwell's *Animal Farm* has come to Gloucester County. Four legs good, two legs bad?

### The Real Garden State

The Garden State earned its nickname the old-fashioned way: New Jersey was America's original breadbasket. The sweet corn, juicy tomatoes, and tangy cranberries grown on our fertile soils filled—and still fill—millions of dinner plates each year. Although developers have cleared many farmlands for condominiums, cul-de-sacs, and strip malls, other New Jerseyans still till the fields and plow the earth. A trip through our rural west is like traveling through the Garden State's past.

As farming dwindled, so did the habitat for grassland birds like the bobolink and the American kestrel. MacKenzie Hall of Conserve Wildlife wants to change that, one farm at a time. Hall is working with federal agencies to help farmers replace pesticides, invasive weeds, and monocultures with productive native grasses. On a hot July morning, I join Hall and two local farmers for a trip back in time, touring two recent grassland restoration projects.

As I near the Warren Rod and Gun Club, I pass roadside signs reading "Preserved Farmland" and "Franklin: A Clean Farmland Community." The club's 300-plus acres sit alongside the Musconetcong River, one of New Jersey's three Wild and Scenic Rivers. The owners of this property once used artificial fertilizer and herbicides to produce corn and soybeans. That changed when a state-funded project planted native grasses such as switchgrass, Indian grass, big bluestem, little bluestem, and a spattering of wildflowers like black-eyed Susan. These grasses reach up to eight feet tall, providing habitat for threatened grassland birds.

"For grassland birds, it's not so much working with them as a species as it is restoring their habitat. Their habitat is so dependent on human influence, as opposed to so many other species that want little or no human interaction. In nature at least, it requires that we be active with the land to prevent it from going back to forest or being developed," says Hall. "Now the most exciting thing is the tie-in with carbon and global warming and alternate energy. Some of the habitats that we're creating for birds are also helping to address those other issues. It has real potential—I get chills thinking about it!"

All of the grasses have potential as biofuels, but switchgrass is particularly easy to harvest. It stands tall for the cutting and handles drought and low fertility in the soil like a champ. The two sustainable uses for switchgrass—as grassland bird habitat and as an alternative source of fuel—are also perfectly compatible. You mow the grasses in winter to maximize the energy, which allows the birds' nesting season to run its course without disruption.

## Sky-High Savannah

On this early summer day, the grasses are at eye level rather than towering over us, as they soon will. The fields are a whirlwind of activity. Swallows spiral overhead, and grasshopper sparrow and indigo bunting flit by. A song sparrow lives up to its name, and an eastern towhee calls from across the meadow. Butterflies lead us down breaks in the dew-covered grasses.

Harold Scaff, a local farmer, manages this project with the state.

"When the hay is ready, we go through with a tractor. The bluebirds line up and dive in, and you've got tree swallows diving in like kamikaze pilots, bringing up the bugs," says Scaff. "Otherwise we get lots of owls—I hear them early morning in the groves. Also birds of prey, red-tailed hawks. The harriers work the fields in winter. They even take rabbits, and they're known to drown their prey."

Hall, who leads the grassland project for the state, agrees.

"Nature is a bitch. You know that when you see a garter snake with a half-eaten toad in its mouth, and it's still squealing. It's not for the faint of heart."

Nature always boils down to the question of predators and prey. Three birds—bobolink, grasshopper sparrow, and eastern meadowlark—tend

The red fox is one of the primary predators for grassland nesting birds like the bobolink and grasshopper sparrow.

©Brenda J Jones

Brenda Jones

to be most common in grasslands. Those birds are hard-wired to choose the centers of grasslands to avoid any predators. Because native grasses grow in clumps, the spaces between those clumps help grassland nesters avoid flying predators like red-tailed hawks, American kestrels, and Cooper's hawks. Those gaps also allow birds to forage for insects and weed seeds safely.

One predator, though, is difficult to avoid even when native grassland habitat is restored. The wily red fox is a challenging foe for grassland nesters. As we leave one farm for another—native grasses extending up a gorgeous hillside, an old silo rising up over huge bales of switchgrass, each one taller than twelve feet—we drive a rural backroad over a one-lane bridge. I slow my car before getting on the bridge, and out of the corner of my eye, I spot an orange shape on the grassy slope to my right. A young red fox sits there, curiously watching our caravan pass.

On any other day, I would be pleased without reservation to see this clever survivor. Today, though, I see it through the eyes of the grassland birds. Take away those birds, and the fox will still have plenty of prey to ensure its survival. But take away those native grasses, and those birds will be homeless. Here's to switchgrass, and Indian grass, and bluestems big and little—and here's to the birds that love them.

# Delaware Water Gap 27

## A WONDER OF THE WORLD

The Delaware River really
supports every aspect of our
life—but only when it's clean,
healthy, and free-flowing.

—Maya Van Rossum,
Delaware Riverkeeper

Now this is the life. I am out in nature, leisurely riding the downstream current under cumulus clouds, passing by wooded islands, half in Pennsylvania and half in New Jersey. The summer sun beats down, but the water keeps me comfortable and refreshed. Dozens of birds—cedar waxwings, swallows, vultures, egrets—cross the sky above. Small fish and large ones, catfish and crayfish, zip under me. I am a floating coach potato, sprawled out on an inner tube, one of hundreds out here today on the Delaware River south of Frenchtown.

I veer off from the mid-river current and explore an island shoreline. As rafters stream past, I wade through a reedy shallow so filled with tadpoles that each step sends half a dozen wriggling in different directions. At least two different species of frog and toad tadpoles are present, perhaps far more. Some are the size of a pinhead, others speckled with green and the size of a dime. Fish shoot between the algae clusters, and vibrant damselflies, as blue as robin eggs, hover over the surface in pairs, like a luxury aerial fleet of insect airliners. Another island brings a green heron flying this way, a great blue flying the other way, and a dozen cedar waxwings spiraling in all directions. Cliffs rise up on the New Jersey side from the otherwise flat banks, a scenic outcropping that beckons the paddlers.

Sure, it's a tourist trap in one sense. We have buses picking us up and dropping us off, and we have waiting lines for the tubes. Most of all, we have the Hot Dog Man vendor boat at the halfway point of the trip. Lo and behold, the Big Apple on the Delaware! Dozens of us stand in line knee-deep in the Delaware River, awaiting hot dogs, cheeseburgers, chips, and candy. If this is a wilderness journey, it certainly has quite a high comfort level. But if you look away from the sun-tanning girls on the tubes nearby, you might find wildlife and nature on the Delaware

David Wheeler

**A family enjoys a tube ride down the Delaware River, certainly the most relaxing of all Wild New Jersey adventures.**

River. This trip both plays to the stereotypes of New Jersey—and defies them.

The Delaware River begins with a trickle high up in the Appalachian Mountains of New York. It winds its way through the Catskills, then separates New York from Pennsylvania. After reaching High Point, the Delaware runs along the Kittatinny Ridge between New Jersey and Pennsylvania before surging through the Delaware Water Gap. Originally named for a colonial governor of Virginia, Baron De La Warr, the Delaware is the longest undammed river on the East Coast, flowing 410 miles and reaching tidewater at Trenton. Its brackish estuary begins at Camden, and its Pea Patch Island holds the largest heron rookery on the Atlantic seaboard north of Florida.

Today we get but a glimpse of this natural majesty. Too soon, our tubes are collected, and we are riding north, packed into an old bus and dripping wet. The river dream ends, and we return to the land. In New Jersey, no daydream floats on by quite like the Delaware River.

"The Delaware River really is the lifeblood of the region. It gives us drinking water, it gives us food, it gives us jobs," says Maya Van Rossum, who has served as the Delaware Riverkeeper since 1996. "When it's properly cared for, it protects us from flooding, strengthens our economy, provides recreational opportunity, and allows us to recharge. The river really supports every aspect of our life—but only when it's clean, healthy, and free-flowing."

## A Real Cliffhanger

I cling precariously to the trunk of a pitch pine, suspended nearly half a mile over a vast gorge. With pinecones jutting against my face, I peer through the dense needles. The scene so far below looks like a child's intricately detailed playset. Tiny matchbox cars crawl along a road, and toy boats sputter along a narrow stream. Model train tracks follow the ribbon of water at the foot of a mountain.

That road far below is Interstate 80, and that narrow stream is the mighty Delaware River. The tracks are the Delaware-Lackawanna Railroad traversing the Pennsylvania side under towering Mount Minsi. Minsi is a mile west of me, a world apart across the awe-inspiring Delaware Water Gap. As for me, on the windswept edge of the massive Mount Tammany, I might as well be an action figure dangling at the mercy of a rowdy child.

Overlooking postcard views of the Delaware Water Gap, Mount Tammany has led me to the edge of a slab of rock angling 45 degrees over the highway and the U-shaped river below. The rolling fog drapes Mount Minsi in mystery, lending an aura of far west to the Delaware Water Gap National Recreation Area. All I have right now is this scene of a lifetime— and a white-knuckled grip on this pitch pine. I sure hope its roots are strong.

## Dam It

Established as a National Recreation Area in 1965, the Delaware Water Gap is now the eighth most popular National Park unit in America—just ahead of the Grand Canyon. A quarter of the nation's population lives within a six-hour drive of the Water Gap. Five million people visit the Gap each year, enjoying its forty miles of untamed river by canoe, kayak, tube, and boat, and with fishing pole. Others hike, birdwatch, and rock-climb its 67,000 acres in New Jersey and Pennsylvania. Vacationers once came here in droves on railroads from New York City and Philadelphia. It was even touted as one of the "Wonders of the World." Yet, strangely enough, when the Gap was named a National Recreation Area, the reason was not its scenic beauty or its wilderness expanse. The plans were to drown the whole area.

A dam was proposed for the Tocks Island area as early as the 1930s, and Congress authorized the dam in 1962. Thirty miles of river would have been lost, and 30,000 acres of river valley would have been drowned under the vast reservoir. To be sure, reservoirs provide a reliable drinking water source, and many of them—such as Merrill Creek and the

Manasquan Reservoir—are enjoyed for public recreation. But destroying a national treasure like this to build a reservoir would have been shameful. You don't drown a global beauty.

Fortunately, those plans were defeated—after the residents of Millbrook Village and other hamlets along the river had been forced to leave.

"Tocks Island was a hot-button for a lot of people," says Jeremy Phillips of the Pocono Environmental Education Center. "On the one hand, it is what created this National Recreation Area, which is a great thing. But a lot of people lost their homes. They were going to dam it up, then they found the rock layer couldn't support it. But they had already bought people's properties."

Alan Ambler of the National Park Service concurs.

"A combination of environmental issues, federal budget problems, and engineering factors all combined to make the dam infeasible. The costs kept going up and up during the time of the Vietnam war, when the federal budget was facing real shortages. It ended up being one of the very first environmental battles that took place in the country."

The Delaware Water Gap thankfully remains in its natural state, with clean mountain water flowing through by the billions of gallons. The Delaware River's excellent water quality is particularly impressive for a waterway that was all but dead half a century ago.

"In the 1940s and 1950s, we had an oxygen dead zone from Philadelphia to Camden—twenty miles long, top to bottom, bank to bank," says Van Rossum. "The fish could not migrate through, the shad could not get to the upper reaches, dock workers would get deathly ill with yellow fever, cholera, and the like. The pollution was so thick, it could clog ship engines and peel paint off their hulls. You could even smell the river from a plane."

Those days are long gone, thanks to the Clean Water Act and activists like Van Rossum. The Upper Delaware River is now a Wild and Scenic River, with some of the cleanest water in the eastern United States. The river is one of the best eel-fishing corridors in the nation and the Northeast's only natural shad river, where the migrating fish can reach upriver spawning grounds.

### Glacial Geology

As you approach the Delaware Water Gap from the east, the mountains tower over Interstate 80. From the parking lot near Kittatinny Point, the trail ascends Mount Tammany's steep boulders. The smells of pine and oak and hickory forest wash over me as the sound of rushing water echoes deep along the wooded ravine. My dad and I clamber over rock terraces laid across the mountain's edge. A mile and a half of hiking brings views unparalleled on the East Coast.

Each view is an award winner—but a better one somehow awaits after each mountain switchback. Upward we climb, until a boulder-strewn meadow entices me to a mountainside plateau. The fog rolls in and washes away the cliff's edge, the Delaware River, the mountains on the Pennsylvania side. I explore farther, and I end up clinging to that 45-degree angled slab of rock. If New Jersey's mountains lack the continental scale of the Rockies, they make up for it with an abundance of drama. Here, the geology of New Jersey's northwestern Kittatinny Ridge is quite apparent.

That geological history is hard to fathom for those of us who count in human years. When the ancestral continents of North America and Africa—yes, you read that right—collided more than 400 million years ago, the edges pushed up the ancestral Appalachian Mountains. Erosion wore away much of the rock, leaving only the hardest gray sandstone and conglomerate rock—what is now the fantastic Kittatinny Ridge—for the human era in New Jersey. Stretching forty-three miles along the Delaware River from the Water Gap all the way up to High Point and the New York border in the north, the Kittatinny is a natural wonderland of glacial ponds, plummeting rivers, deep forests, mind-blowing views, and steep promontories. Even the neighboring great valley holding the homes, businesses, and farms of New Jersey's northwest was carved out by an Ice Age glacier a mile deep.

The last and best overlook, following a narrow footpath through dense vegetation and over a pile of recent bear scat, brings me out to Indian Head. This vulture's-eye view, shared with the raptors spiraling overhead on the crosswinds, extends to a Delaware River island and a classically arched footbridge to the south.

The trail turns inland here, trading windswept mountainside for wooded interior. From here, you can follow the Mount Tammany Fire Road trail northeast along the Kittatinny Ridge. That ridgetop hike leads to Sunfish Pond, a popular migration point carved out by a glacier in the most recent Ice Age and considered by many nature lovers to be the most scenic spot in the state. The Kittatinny Ridge is dotted with no fewer than fourteen of these glacial ponds—yet another remarkable geological remnant in this wild northwestern corner of New Jersey. Little surprise that this trail is ranked among the top hikes in the nation.

# The Road to Crater Lake  28

It really is just a matter of being out there and
trying to figure out a mystery. Predators and
carnivores are so elusive; you can go years without
seeing them. But we know they're out there.
—Conservation biologist Charlie Kontos

**M**y dad and I begin our descent from the other side of Mount Tammany, a gradual 2.5-mile hike through Worthington State Forest and its vast array of habitats. Meadows host scattered trees growing out of a sea of grass. A hemlock grove gives way to a hardwood forest, which in turns yields to a shrubby clearing still recovering from a forest fire. Dozens of warblers and songbirds flit from tree to tree along the path, which connects us with the Appalachian Trail. The "AT" crosses fifteen miles of gorgeous terrain in the Delaware Water Gap National Recreation Area on its winding course along the East Coast.

About 100 feet below us, the terrain drops off into a ravine to connect with another trail running parallel. We find a spot to trek off the beaten trail and hike-slide down the mountain slope. Halfway down, I spy the singular form of a pileated woodpecker—perhaps New Jersey's most beautiful bird and one my dad has never before spotted. We watch it fly across the ravine, then alight on a hemlock high on the slope above. It is a thrilling encounter, and more likely here on the Kittatinny Ridge than anywhere else in the state.

We reach Dunnfield Creek, a crystal-clear mountain stream twisting and turning through boulders and rocks, pouring through rapids, and plummeting down waterfalls every few minutes. We hike amid the forest floor ferns along the bottom of the ravine, the canopy of mighty old-growth hemlocks towering high above the slopes on either side. The sky-high hemlock and mixed hardwood canopy provides the shade needed to maintain the water temperature demanded by the creek's most beloved inhabitants—the brook trout. Designated a Wild Trout Stream, Dunnfield Creek hosts a healthy population of brook trout, the official New Jersey state fish. Dunnfield's habitat is reminiscent of Tillman Ravine in Stokes State Forest—only this ravine goes on and on.

Bill Wheeler

**David Wheeler surveys the Delaware Water Gap from a vantage point high on Mount Tammany.**

Dunnfield Creek is, indeed, a magical place. A waterfall crashes down a chasm into a carved-out circular pool of rich blue water, looking like an arctic meltwater lake. The rapids carry the creek over moss-covered rock slabs. Frogs splash into the water a step ahead as we walk downstream. Lichens and mushrooms grow out of fallen logs. Three huge boulders form a gateway with a narrow chute of water pouring through, like the marbles of the gods.

Another wide and picturesque waterfall crashes under a trail footbridge, near a gnarled root system that forms a natural stairway fifteen feet high attached to the cliff. When you can climb up a mountain slope using roots of a single tree as your grips and footholds, you know you are in a very special place. Tolkien's Middle Earth has arrived in New Jersey. (Let me check with Gollum—where is that confounded ring?)

## The Kittatinny Ridge
Like the rest of the Kittatinny Ridge, this is rugged terrain. The Kittatinny provides habitat for timber rattlesnakes, fence lizards, and prickly

pear cactus. Northern goshawks, barred owls, ruffed grouse, and red-shouldered hawks nest in the Kittatinny's dark oak and maple forests. Peregrine falcons and ravens have returned to nest along the cliffs, and the rare golden eagle, its seven-foot wingspan flanking a bronzed head, is sometimes seen majestically surveying the river far below. More than a hundred bald eagles migrate here each year to spend the winter atop the towering riverside trees at Poxono Island. Other winter visitors include grosbeaks, pine siskins, and common redpolls, while migrants like golden-crowned kinglets, blackburnian warblers, and solitary vireos pass through each spring.

"The Kittatinny Ridge is one of the larger raptor flyways east of the Mississippi, with very good migration passing along that ridge," says Alan Ambler of the National Park Service. "We have a very large avian population in general. The natural corridor of protected space both along the ridge and along the river offers a natural migratory route."

Arguably New Jersey's most scenic region, the Kittatinny is enjoyed by both weekend sightseers and experts alike. Mick Valent of New Jersey Fish and Wildlife counts himself among its aficionados.

"My favorite area is the Kittatinny Ridge. It extends from the Water Gap to High Point, and it's almost all protected land. You have Worthington, the Delaware Water Gap National Recreation Area, a couple of Wildlife Management Areas; you even have Nature Conservancy areas. And then you get into Stokes and High Point. Even from the air, when I was up in a plane highlighting the area, it's expansive.

"You have bobcats, bears. It's where the fisher are, where the moose was. You have eagles, most of the threatened and endangered hawks; you have owls. Kittatinny is just incredible."

I'm sorry, did he say moose? In New Jersey?

"We got a call one day about a moose in Culvers Lake. 'Oh, here we go,' I said. 'Here's another crackpot,'" says Valent. "Then a conservation officer saw him—it was real. It turned out the moose wandered down from the Adirondacks. I could see him getting to the Catskills, then there's a lot of good habitat between there and northwest New Jersey."

The moose crossed Route 206, went into Stokes State Forest, crossed the Delaware River into Pennsylvania near Dingmans Ferry, and ultimately re-crossed the Delaware into New York. The Adirondack Mountains, the farthest south a moose is typically encountered, are five hours north of here by car. Yet a moose—seven feet tall, and weighing over half a ton—made it to New Jersey.

## Old Mine Road Safari

Back in the car after my favorite hike in New Jersey, I feel a nearly satiated bliss from the untarnished natural beauty I just enjoyed. Sitting at a stoplight, my dad and I face a decision: begin the long drive back, or continue to the Delaware Water Gap? We could easily call it a day, but there's still some daylight left. Plus, we are just a few minutes from Old Mine Road, where black bear and bobcat sightings are reported with some regularity. Although bears are relatively common in northwestern New Jersey, the bobcat is seldom seen anywhere. Still, bobcats are found more often here than anywhere else.

"I was up at the Delaware Water Gap, driving in my car when I came over the crest of a little hill, and standing in the road was a bobcat," says David Moskowitz of the East Brunswick Environmental Commission. "It was about twenty-five feet in front of me, just standing there looking at me. The bobcat stood in the road for about five seconds, then ran off the side of the road."

Hmm, bobcats and bears? Easy decision. Even though bobcats are the longest of long shots, the chance for a black bear cannot be passed up. My dad hasn't seen a black bear in the wild since that bear family encounter years ago in Wawayanda. I make a right and drive up that mountain ridge road, Old Mine Road, which is so narrow at its southern terminus that a stoplight closes traffic in alternating directions for minutes at a time. The road is remote, and we pass few other drivers.

Old Mine Road was not always so removed from the mainstream. Fur traders and Dutch copper miners once used this well-trod Native American trail, which follows the ridge all the way up to Port Jervis, New York. During the French and Indian War in the 1750s, the Kittatinny and Water Gap area served as the English colonies' northwestern frontier. Old Mine Road was the farthest outpost of a colonial supply route called Military Road, stretching all the way to the New Jersey colonial village of Elizabeth.

On this late afternoon, Old Mine Road is traversed by another group. Hundreds of giant millipedes are crossing the road, their long black bodies easily visible on the asphalt. White-tailed deer graze in a meadow lining the Delaware River, and wild turkey forage in a clearing just in from the road. The river peeks in every so often between the forest groves.

The gorgeous drive along Old Mine Road feels like a safari-type voyage through a classic national park of the American West. Shade and sunlight alternate from the forest canopy overhead, taking us from cool to warm and back again as the minutes pass.

### The Wilderness Prophet

Soon after turning our car off of Old Mine Road toward Crater Lake, I pull to the side of the road to admire an indigo bunting, a songbird with bright blue feathers that glimmer in the sunlight. In my rearview mirror, I see a man walk out of the woods and approach our car. He is a serious nature photographer, judging from the expensive camera in his hand.

"How'ya doing? What are you looking for?" he asks.

"Bear—you seen any?"

"I've seen a bunch of them. I saw a mother bear and two year-old cubs. I got great photos." He clicks through the digital photos—and they are impressive—but his own enthusiasm is for the warbler migration coming through at this very moment.

As an afterthought, the photographer mentions another local sighting he recently heard about from multiple people—a mountain lion. The sightings—real, imagined, or simply mistaken—of mountain lions in the Delaware Water Gap region have been steady and consistent over the last few years. Experts remain highly skeptical.

"We know they're moving east, but not in high density and not females—mostly only young males, which we expect," says Christopher Spatz of the Eastern Cougar Foundation. "It's happening in Wisconsin and Illinois, but the pictures stop in Minnesota. East of there, why don't we have any roadkills? Also, with 3,000 remote hunting cameras, why are they not showing up? Given the road density, if they're out there, one would get hit, or show up on camera, or get shot."

Charlie Kontos, for one, is not convinced the mountain lion is definitely absent. The studies previously undertaken to find cougars in New Jersey, he says, relied on cameras that had slow trigger times and were not necessarily placed in the best cougar habitat to begin with. It is also possible that any cougars spotted were transient, coming through the Catskills, through the Kittatinny Ridge, then moving on.

"Out in the Water Gap on Old Mine Road, where it is miles with no one else around, you look across the river and over the border and think maybe it's possible that cougars could return," says Kontos.

Though he doubts that the reported sightings prove an established mountain lion population, Spatz certainly agrees that the vast, open habitat and terrain could support cougars if they were able to make it here from their stronghold in the American West.

"You've got a prey base, one of the densest populations of deer in North America. We know now from the last twenty years that they can live in suburbs. In Colorado, cougars are living side by side with people.

For them to make it to New Jersey naturally, it would take a long, long time. But northwest New Jersey could absolutely support a population."

For Kontos, those big uncertainties are part of what makes all top carnivores so fascinating.

"It really is just a matter of being out there and trying to figure out a mystery. Predators and carnivores are so elusive; you can go years without seeing them. But we know they're out there."

I hand the camera back to the photographer.

"Good luck," he says. "The bears are out there. You just gotta look deeper into the forest."

We wish him well, and I drive off. My dad and I smirk at each other. *We know what we're doing,* we say to each other smugly. *We don't need to look deeper.*

Then each of us silently puts his ego aside, making an effort to look beyond the roadside edge that moves past as a steady blur. Instead, we focus more intensely on what is behind it all, scanning deeper into the forest.

A few minutes later, we stare down a stream running through a wetlands area, with dark green skunk cabbage lining the wet meadow. Around forty yards in from the road, lo and behold, a huge adult black bear stares back at us. He stands and forages for a while, his massive head and ears outlined in dark brown-black over a field of deep green. When he turns to the side, we see the huge expanse of his body. We quietly step out of the car for a clearer view—keeping plenty of distance. This is one big bruin. My dad's mouth is agape, and I cannot suppress a huge grin.

Finally, the black bear bounds away. We don't have to say much on the way out of Crater Lake. The wilderness prophet was right—we just had to look deeper. It is a fitting end to a year in the field. My dad has his black bear. As for me, my Wild New Jersey journey is complete.

Well, not exactly—I still haven't seen a bobcat in the wild . . .

# NATURE CENTERS IN NEW JERSEY

Animal Kingdom Zoo, Bordentown: http://www.animalkingdomnj.net/

Atlantic City Aquarium, Atlantic City: http://www.oceanlifecenter.com/aquarium.asp

Bamboo Brook Outdoor Education Center, Chester Township:
http://www.morrisparks.net/aspparks/bbrookmain.asp

Bennett Bogs Nature Preserve, Cape May

Bergen County Zoological Park, Paramus:
http://www.co.bergen.nj.us/bcparks/zoo.aspx

Bergen Museum of Art & Science, Paramus: http://www.thebergenmuseum.com

Cape May Bird Observatory, Cape May: http://www.birdcapemay.org/

Cape May Bird Observatory School of Birding, Cape May:
http://www.birdcapemay.org/school.php

Cape May County Zoo, Cape May:
http://www.capemayzoo.org/capemayzoo.org/Welcome.html

Cape May National Wildlife Refuge, Cape May:
http://www.fws.gov/northeast/capemay/

Cohanzick Zoo, Bridgeton: http://www.cityofbridgeton.com/zoo.html

Cooper Environmental Center, Cattus Island County Park, Toms River:
http://www.fieldtrip.com/nj/82706960.htm

Cora Hartshorn Arboretum and Bird Sanctuary, Short Hills:
http://www.hartshornarboretum.org/

Down Jersey Folklife Center, Millville: www.wheatonvillage.org

Edwin B. Forsythe National Wildlife Refuge, Oceanville:
http://www.fws.gov/northeast/forsythe/

Elizabeth D. Kay Environmental Center, Chester:
http://www.morrisparks.net/aspparks/edkmain.asp

Essex County Environmental Center, Roseland: http://www.njaudubon.org/
SectionCenters/SectionEssex/Introduction.aspx

Fairview Lake Environmental Education Center, Stillwater:
http://www.fairviewlakeymca.org/environmental-education/
environmental-education-main-page.html

Great Swamp National Wildlife Refuge, Basking Ridge:
http://www.fws.gov/northeast/greatswamp/

Great Swamp Watershed Association, New Vernon: http://www.greatswamp.org/

Greenbrook Sanctuary, Alpine: http://www.njpalisades.org/greenbrook.htm

Hackensack Meadowlands Environmental Center, Lyndhurst:
www.meadowlands.state.nj.us/

Hilltop Conservancy, Verona: http://www.hilltopconservancy.org/

Huber Woods Park Environmental Center, Rumson:
http://www.monmouthcountyparks.com/page.asp?agency=133&Id=2635

Insectropolis, The Bugseum of New Jersey, Toms River:
http://www.insectropolis.com/

Island Beach State Park, Seaside Park: http://www.islandbeachnj.org/

Jacques Cousteau National Estuarine Research Reserve, Tuckerton:
http://www.jcnerr.org/

James A. McFaul Wildlife Center, Wyckoff:
http://www.co.bergen.nj.us/parks/parks/mcfaul.htm

Jenkinsons Aquarium, Point Pleasant Beach: http://www.jenkinsons.com/aquarium/

John J. Crowley Nature Center, Paterson

Lakota Wolf Preserve, Columbia: http://www.lakotawolf.com/

Liberty Science Center, Liberty State Park, Jersey City: http://www.lsc.org/

Liberty State Park Interpretive Center, Jersey City:
http://www.state.nj.us/dep/parksandforests/parks/liberty_state_park/
liberty_education.html

Linwood-MacDonald Environmental Education Center, Branchville

Lorrimer Sanctuary, Franklin Lakes:
http://www.njaudubon.org/SectionCenters/SectionLorrimer/Introduction.aspx

Manasquan Reservoir Environmental Center, Howell:
http://www.monmouthcountyparks.com/page.asp?agency=133&Id=2627

Mercer County Park Commission, Trenton:
http://www.state.nj.us/counties/mercer/commissions/park/

Mercer County Wildlife Center, Lambertville: http://www.wcinc.org/

Merrill Creek Reservoir, Washington: http://www.merrillcreek.com/home.html

Monmouth County Parks System:
http://www.monmouthcountyparks.com/index.asp

Montclair Hawk Watch Nature Preserve, Montclair:
http://www.njaudubon.org/SectionBirdingSites/MontclairHawkWatch.aspx

Nature Center of Cape May, Cape May:
http://www.njaudubon.org/SectionCenters/SectionNCCM/Introduction.aspx

Newark Museum Mini Zoo, Newark:
http://www.newarkmuseum.org/museum_default_page.aspx?id=138

New Jersey Adventure Aquarium, Camden: http://www.adventureaquarium.com/

New Jersey Coastal Heritage Trail, Newport: http://www.nps.gov/neje/index.htm

New Jersey Marine Sciences Consortium Education, Fort Hancock:
http://njmsc.org/gofish.html

New Jersey Pinelands National Reserve, New Lisbon:
http://www.state.nj.us/pinelands/

New Jersey state parks:
http://www.state.nj.us/dep/parksandforests/parks/parkindex.html

Old Farm Sanctuary, Independence Township:
http://www.njwildlifetrails.org/SkylandsTrails/Sites/tabid/445/Scope/site/
Guide/SKYLANDS/Site/221/Default.aspx

Palisades Interstate Park Commission, Alpine: http://www.njpalisades.org/

Pequest Trout Hatchery and Natural Resource Education Center, Oxford:
http://www.state.nj.us/dep/fgw/pequest.htm

Plainsboro Preserve, Cranbury:
http://www.njaudubon.org/SectionCenters/SectionPlainsboro/Introduction.aspx

Popcorn Park Zoo, Forked River: http://www.ahscares.org/

Poricy Park, Middletown: http://www.poricypark.org/

Pyramid Mountain Natural Historical Area, Kinnelon:
http://www.morrisparks.net/aspparks/pyrmtnmain.asp

Rancocas Nature Center, Mount Holly:
http://www.njaudubon.org/SectionCenters/SectionRancocas/Introduction.aspx

Raptor Trust, Millington: http://theraptortrust.org/

Rocky Springs Wildlife Rehabilitation Center, Washington: http://www.rswrc.org/

Sandy Hook Bird Observatory, Highlands:
http://www.njaudubon.org/SectionCenters/SectionSHBO/Introduction.aspx

Sandy Hook's Ocean Institute, Highlands:
http://ux.brookdalecc.edu/staff/sandyhook/index2-2.html

Scherman-Hoffman Wildlife Sanctuary, Bernardsville:
http://www.njaudubon.org/SectionCenters/SectionScherman/TheSanctuary.aspx

Sluice Creek Nature Preserve, Middle Township: http://www.njaudubon.org/Section-
AboutNJAS/OurNaturePreserves.aspx

Somerset County Environmental Education Center, Basking Ridge:
http://www.somersetcountyparks.org/parksFacilities/eec/EEC.html

South Mountain Wildlife Rehabilitation Center, Essex County:
http://www.southmountainwildlife.org/

Space Farms Zoo & Museum, Sussex: http://www.spacefarms.com/

Stony Brook Millstone Watershed Association, Pennington:
http://www.thewatershed.org/

Supawna Meadows National Wildlife Refuge, Pennsville:
http://www.fws.gov/supawnameadows/

Trailside Nature and Science Center, Mountainside: www.unioncountynj.org/trailside

Triple C Ranch Environmental Education Center, Edison:
http://www.edisonwetlands.org/

Tuckerton Seaport: http://www.tuckertonseaport.org/

Turtle Back Zoo, West Orange: http://www.turtlebackzoo.com/tbzoo/index.jsp

Upper Raritan Watershed Association, Gladstone: http://www.urwa.org/index.html

Wallkill River National Wildlife Refuge, Sussex:
http://www.fws.gov/northeast/wallkillriver/

Walpack Valley Environmental Education Center, Walpack:
http://nynjctbotany.org/njkttofc/walpack.html

Warren E. Fox Nature Center, Mays Landing:
www.aclink.org/PARKS/mainpages/nc.asp

Weis Ecology Center, Ringwood:
http://www.njaudubon.org/SectionCenters/SectionWeis/Introduction.aspx

Wetlands Institute, Stone Harbor: http://www.wetlandsinstitute.org/

Wild Baby Rescue Wildlife Rehabilitation Center, Blairstown:
http://www.wildbabyrescue.org/

Woodford Cedar Run Wildlife Refuge, Medford: http://www.cedarrun.org/

Woodlands Wildlife Refuge, Pittstown: http://www.woodlandswildlife.org/

# SUGGESTED READING

## General and Introduction

Beans, Bruce E., and Larry Niles, eds. 2003. *Endangered and Threatened Wildlife of New Jersey*. New Brunswick: Rutgers University Press.

Beletsky, Les. 2006. *250 North American Birds in Song*. San Francisco: Chronicle Books.

Boyle, William J., Jr. 2002. *A Guide to Bird Finding in New Jersey*. New Brunswick: Rutgers University Press.

Brown, Tom, Jr. 1978. *The Tracker*. Upper Saddle River, N.J.: Prentice-Hall.

Burger, Joanna, and Michael Gochfeld. 2000. *25 Nature Spectacles in New Jersey*. New Brunswick: Rutgers University Press.

Conserve Wildlife Foundation of New Jersey. http://www.conservewildlifenj.org/.

Dunham, Judith, ed. 1999. *American Safari*. New York: Discovery Travel Adventures.

Elia, Vince, Thomas Halliwell, Rich Kane, and Joan Walsh. 1999. *Birds of New Jersey*. Bernardsville: New Jersey Audubon Society.

Field & Stream. 1999. *The World of Incredible Outdoor Adventures*. Minneapolis: Creative Publishing International.

Golden, David M., and Vicki Schwartz. 2002. *Field Guide to Reptiles and Amphibians of New Jersey*. Trenton: New Jersey Division of Fish and Wildlife.

Jones, David. 1999. *North American Wildlife*. New York: Whitecap Books.

Krafel, Paul. 1999. *Seeing Nature: Deliberate Encounters with the Visible World*. White River Junction, Vt.: Chelsea Green Publishing.

Little, Elbert L. 1980. *National Audubon Society Field Guide to Trees: Eastern Region*. New York: Alfred A. Knopf.

Melham, Tom. 1976. *John Muir's Wild America*. Washington, D.C.: National Geographic Society.

National Geographic Society. *Magazine*. http://ngm.nationalgeographic.com/.

New Jersey Audubon Society. http://www.njaudubon.org/.

———. "Voice of New Jersey Audubon." http://www.njaudubon.org/Tools.Net/Sightings/VoiceOf.aspx.

New Jersey Birding listserve. http://birdingonthe.net/mailinglists/NJBD.html.

New Jersey Bird Records Committee. http://www.njbrc.net/index.html.

New Jersey Conservation Foundation. http://www.njconservation.org/.

New Jersey Department of Environmental Protection. Green Acres Program. http://www.nj.gov/dep/greenacres/.

New Jersey Division of Fish and Wildlife. http://www.state.nj.us/dep/fgw/.

———. 2004. "Black Bear in New Jersey: Status Report." Trenton: New Jersey Division of Fish and Wildlife. http://www.state.nj.us/dep/fgw/pdf/2004/bear_report04.pdf.

_____. "Raptors in New Jersey." http://www.state.nj.us/dep/fgw/ensp/raptor_info. htm.

_____. "Wildlife Management Areas." http://www.state.nj.us/dep/fgw/wmaland. htm.

New Jersey Division of Parks and Forestry. "New Jersey State Parks, Forests, Recreation Areas and Marinas." http://www.state.nj.us/dep/parksandforests/parks/ parkindex.html.

New Jersey Sierra Club. http://newjersey.sierraclub.org/.

Pettigrew, Laurie. 1998. *New Jersey Wildlife Viewing Guide*. Helena, Mont.: Falcon Press.

Richard, Bryan. 2004. *The Encyclopedia of North American Animals*. London: Parragon.

Sibley, David Allen. 2000. *The Sibley Guide to Birds*. New York: Alfred A. Knopf.

_____. 2001. *The Sibley Guide to Bird Life and Behavior*. New York: Alfred A. Knopf.

Stanfield, Charles A. 2004. *A Geography of New Jersey: The City in the Garden*. New Brunswick: Rutgers University Press.

United States Fish and Wildlife Service. http://www.fws.gov/.

_____. 1997. "Significant Habitats and Habitat Complexes of the New York Bight Watershed." http://library.fws.gov/pub5/begin.htm.

Walter, Eugene. 1996. *The Smithsonian Guides to Natural America: The Mid-Atlantic States*. New York: Random House.

Weidensaul, Scott. 2005. *Return to Wild America: A Yearlong Search for the Continent's Natural Soul*. New York: North Point Press.

Whitaker, John O., Jr. 1996. *National Audubon Society Field Guide to North American Mammals*. New York: Alfred A. Knopf.

Wild New Jersey blog. http://www.wildnewjersey.tv/.

Wilson, Edward O. 1999. *The Diversity of Life*. New York: W. W. Norton.

### Chapter 1 Wawayanda Wilderness: A Quest for Black Bears

Appalachian Trail Conservancy. http://www.appalachiantrail.org.

Bryson, Bill. 1998. *A Walk in the Woods: Rediscovering America on the Appalachian Trail*. New York: Broadway Books.

Burguess, Kelcey. 2009. "Black Bears on the Fly: Avoiding Conflicts, Managing Encounters." Presentation for Central Jersey Trout Unlimited meeting, Dunellen, N.J., June 16.

Muir, John. 1901. *Our National Parks*. Boston: Houghton Mifflin.

New Jersey Audubon Society. "New Jersey Birding & Wildlife Trails: Skylands Trails." Bernardsville: New Jersey Audubon Society. http://www.njwildlifetrails.org/ SkylandsTrails/Trails.aspx.

New Jersey Division of Fish and Wildlife. "Know the Bear Facts: Black Bears in New Jersey." Trenton: New Jersey Department of Environmental Protection. http:// www.state.nj.us/dep/fgw/bearfacts.htm.

New Jersey Division of Parks and Forestry. Wawayanda State Park. http://www.state. nj.us/dep/parksandforests/parks/wawayanda.html.

New Jersey Herald. 2009. *Bear With Us*. Newton, N.J.: New Jersey Herald.

United States Fish and Wildlife Service. Walkill River National Wildlife Refuge. http:// www.fws.gov/northeast/wallkillriver/.

### Chapter 2 The Carnivore Corridor of Stokes Forest

Baron, David. 2003. *The Beast in the Garden: A Modern Parable of Man and Nature*. New York: W. W. Norton.

Busch, Robert H. 2004. *The Cougar Almanac: A Complete Natural History of the Mountain Lion*. Boston: Globe Pequot Press.

Eastern Cougar Foundation. http://www.easterncougar.org/.

Johnston, Sid. 2010. "Cougar Sightings Remain Unsubstantiated." *The Record* (Bergen County), January 15.

Keane-Ross, Anne. 2006. "Mountain Lions Believed Prowling in New Jersey." ABCNews.com, December 5.

New Jersey Division of Fish and Wildlife. "Bobcat, *Felis refus*." http://www.state.nj.us/dep/fgw/ensp/pdf/end-thrtened/bobcat.pdf.

———. Endangered and Nongame Species Program. http://www.state.nj.us/dep/fgw/ensphome.htm.

New Jersey Division of Parks and Forestry. Stokes State Forest. http://www.state.nj.us/dep/parksandforests/parks/stokes.html.

"The New Jersey Fisher Experience." http://www.njfishers.org/.

Parker, Gerry. 2001. "Status Report on the Canada Lynx in Nova Scotia, Final." http://www.gov.ns.ca/natr/wildlife/biodiversity/pdf/statusreports/sr_lynx.pdf.

Reid, Elwood. 2003. "Stalker." *Outside Magazine*, May.

Rutgers University. Grant F. Walton Center for Remote Sensing and Spatial Analysis. Landscape Change Research. http://crssa.rutgers.edu/projects/lc/.

## Chapter 3   High Point's Call of the Wild

Aventure Québec nord. 33, chemin de la Coulée, Lac Beauport, Québec G0A 2C0.

Blumenthal, Ralph. 1998. "Weekend Warrior: Warming Up to Snow-Shoeing." *New York Times*, March 6.

High Point Cross Country Ski Center. http://xcskihighpoint.com/.

Iditarod, Alaska. http://www.iditarod.com/.

Kontos, Charlie. 2009. "Wild New Jersey Exclusive: Carnivore Expert Calls for Greater Land Preservation." *WildNewJersey.tv*, March 24.

Lakota Wolf Preserve. http://www.lakotawolf.com/.

London, Jack. 1906. *White Fang*. New York: Macmillan.

McBride, Tony. 2006. "Coyote Management: An Integrated Approach." *New Jersey Fish and Wildlife Digest Hunting Issue*.

New Jersey Division of Fish and Wildlife. "Coyotes in New Jersey." http://www.state.nj.us/dep/fgw/coyote_info.htm.

New Jersey Division of Parks and Forestry. High Point State Park. http://www.state.nj.us/dep/parksandforests/parks/highpoint.html.

New Jersey Sled Dog Club. http://www.njsdc.com/main.html.

Way, Jonathan G. "Eastern Coyote (Coywolf) Research." http://www.easterncoyoteresearch.com/.

"When the Dogs Go Racing By." http://www.njskylands.com/oddogsled.htm.

## Chapter 4   The Mountain Kingdom of Rattlesnakes

Bartlett, Richard D. 1987. *In Search of Reptiles and Amphibians*. New York: E. J. Brill.

DeMasters, Karen. 1999. "The Great Outdoors: Timber Rattlesnake Puts Development on Endangered List." *New York Times*, March 14.

Franklin, Benjamin [An American Guesser, pseud.]. 1775. Letter to the editor. *Pennsylvania Journal*, December 27.

New Jersey Division of Fish and Wildlife. "Snakes of New Jersey." http://www.state.nj.us/dep/fgw/ensp/pdf/snakes.pdf.

———. "Timber Rattlesnake Conservation." http://www.state.nj.us/dep/fgw/ensp/tmbratlr.htm.

New Jersey Meadowlands Commission. 2009. "The Meadowlands Blog: Awesome Milk Snake." June 25. http://www.meadowblog.typepad.com/mblog/2009/06/awesome-milk-snake-click-for-photo.html.

## Chapter 5   Volcanic Cliffs over the Big Apple

Brinkley, Douglas. 2009. *The Wilderness Warrior: Theodore Roosevelt and the Crusade for America*. New York: HarperCollins.

Burrows, Edwin G., and Mike Wallace. 1999. *Gotham: A History of New York City to 1898*. New York: Oxford University Press.

Cronin, John, and Robert F. Kennedy Jr. 1999. *The Riverkeepers*. Austin: Touchstone.

Dalzell, Robert F., and Lee Baldwin Dalzell. 2007. *The House the Rockefellers Built*. New York: Henry Holt.

Davis, E. Emory, and Eric Nelsen. 2007. *New Jersey's Palisades Interstate Park*. San Francisco: Arcadia Publishing.

Greenbrook Sanctuary. http://www.njpalisades.org/greenbrook.htm.

Hudson Riverkeeper. http://www.riverkeeper.org/.

King, Moses. 1892. *King's Handbook of New York City 1892*. Boston: Moses King.

Luhr, James F., ed. 2003. *Smithsonian Earth*. New York: Dorling Kindersley.

Miller, Peter. 2009. "Before New York: Rediscovering the Wilderness of 1609." *National Geographic*, September.

New Jersey Division of Fish and Wildlife. "Foxes in New Jersey." http://www.state.nj.us/dep/fgw/speciesinfo_fox.htm.

Stegemann, Eileen C. 1994. "Sturgeon: The King of the Freshwater Fishes." *The Conservationist*, August.

"To Save the Palisades, Rockefeller and Other Rich Men Back of Bill to Stop Blasting." 1906. *New York Times*, January 13.

Valent, Mick. 2009. "Can You Help the Allegheny Woodrat?" Conserve Wildlife Foundation of New Jersey, *Explorations* (October). http://www.conservewildlifenj.org/explorations/fall09/Valent.html.

## Chapter 6   Urban Jungle on the Hudson

Carson, Rachel. 1962. *Silent Spring*. Boston: Houghton Mifflin.

Clark, Kathleen. 2002. "Soapbox: A High Flier among High Rollers." *New York Times*, July 21.

Clark, Kathleen, Ben Wurst, and Mick Valent. 2009. "Peregrine Falcon Research and Management Program in New Jersey, 2009." Trenton: New Jersey Department of Environmental Protection. http://www.state.nj.us/dep/fgw/ensp/pdf.pefa09_report.pdf.

Lovelock, James. 2006. *The Revenge of Gaia*. New York: Basic Books.

New Jersey Division of Fish and Wildlife. Jersey City Peregrine Cam. http://www.state.nj.us/dep/fgw/peregrinecam/.

United States Environmental Protection Agency. 1972. "DDT Ban Takes Effect." Press release, December 31. http://www.epa.gov/history/topics/ddt/01.htm.

"Wild New Jersey Exclusive: Urban Adventure with Peregrine Falcons on a Jersey City Skyscraper." 2009. *WildNewJersey.tv*, June 18.

## Chapter 7   Snowy Owls in the Shadow of Liberty

Clark, Amy Sara. 2009. "Jersey City Community Group Says Plan to Cleanup Chromium Doesn't Go Far Enough." *Jersey Journal*, April 8.

Friends of Liberty State Park. http://www.folsp.org/index.htm.

Hackensack Riverkeeper. http://www.hackensackriverkeeper.org/history.html.

Hanley, Robert. 1989. "Chromium and Worry Rise in Jersey City." *New York Times,* June 26.

Kuser, John E., and George Zimmerman. 1995. "Restoring Atlantic White-Cedar Swamps: Techniques for Propagation and Establishment." *Tree Planters' Notes 46,* no. 3 (Summer). http://www.rngr.net/publications/tpn/46-3.

Mates, William J., and Jorge L. Reyes. 2006. *The Economic Value of New Jersey State Parks and Forests.* Revised edition. Trenton: New Jersey Department of Environmental Protection. http://www.njstatelib.org/digit/p252/p2522004.pdf.

New Jersey Audubon Society. 2006. "New Jersey Birding & Wildlife Trails: Meadowlands and More Trails." Bernardsville: New Jersey Audubon Society. http://www.njwildlifetrails.org/MeadowlandsTrails.aspx.

New Jersey Division of Parks and Forestry. Liberty State Park. http://www.state.nj.us/dep/parksandforests/parks/liberty.html.

New Jersey Meadowlands Commission. Parks. http://www.njmeadowlands.gov/environment/parks.html.

Schmidt, Margaret. "On the Water, Recreating History." *Jersey Journal,* June 14.

Warren, Lynne. 2002. "Snowy Owls: Muscle & Magic." *National Geographic,* December.

Weisman, Alan. 2007. *The World Without Us.* New York: Thomas Dunne Books.

### Chapter 8    The Meadowlands: Nature Reborn

Conniff, Richard. 2001. "Swamps of Jersey: The Meadowlands." *National Geographic,* February.

Genovese, Peter. 2008. "I Am NJ: Bill Sheehan." NJ.com,, October 5. http://blog.nj.com/iamnj/2008/10/bill_sheehan.html.

Hackensack Riverkeeper. "The Paddling Center at Laurel Hill Park." http://www.hackensackriverkeeper.org/canoeproject.html.

_____. "Who Is Hackensack Riverkeeper?" http://www.hackensackriverkeeper.org/who.html.

Jacobs, Andrew. 2002. "Ex-Trash Heap to Be Big Urban Park." *New York Times,* May 13.

Lutz, Joshua. 2008. *Meadowlands.* Brooklyn: powerHouse books.

"The Meadowlands Nature Blog." http://meadowblog.net/.

New Jersey Meadowlands Commission. "Meadowlands Tours." http://www.njmeadowlands.gov/environment/tours.html.

Sullivan, Robert. 1998. *The Meadowlands: Wilderness Adventures on the Edge of a City.* New York: Scribner.

Waterkeeper Alliance. http://www.waterkeeper.org/.

Wheeler, David. 2001. "A Meadowlands Oasis: Laurel Hill." *E/The Environmental Magazine* (July). http://www.emagazine.com/view/?322.

"Wild New Jersey Exclusive: Meadowlands Sunset Pontoon Tour through the Thriving 'Swamps of Jersey.'" Part 1. 2009. *WildNewJersey.tv,* June 23.

### Chapter 9    Commuting by Wing in New York Harbor

Conference House Park. http://www.nycgovparks.org/parks/conferencehousepark.

Greiling, Dunrie A. 1993. *Greenways to the Arthur Kill.* Morristown: New Jersey Conservation Foundation.

JerseyBirds listserv. http://www.princeton.edu/~llarson/njb/jbird.html.

Malwitz, Rick. 2008. "Project Aims to Restore Wetlands Around Turnpike Rest Stop in Woodbridge." *Home News Tribune,* September 7.

Mittelbach, Margaret, and Michael Crewdson. 1997. *Wild New York: A Guide to the Wildlife, Wild Places, and Natural Phenomena of New York City*. New York: Three Rivers Press.

National Biodiversity Parks. http://www.nationalbiodiversityparks.org/.

New York City Audubon. "Harbor Herons Project." http://www.nycaudubon.org/projects/harborherons/.

NY/NJ Baykeeper. http://www.nynjbaykeeper.org/index.php.

Parsons, Katharine C. 1996. "Recovering from Oil Spills: The Role of Proactive Science in Mitigating Adverse Effects." *Colonial Waterbirds* 19(1): 149–53.

Rahway River Association. http://www.rahwayriver.org/.

Rogers, Heather. 2005. *Gone Tomorrow: The Hidden Life of Garbage*. New York: New Press.

Wheeler, David. 2008. "Reclaiming New York's Blighted Waters." *Gotham Gazette*, April 7. http://www.gothamgazette.com/article//20080407/212/2482.

**Chapter 10   The Raritan's Industrial Wilderness**

Atlantic Divers, Egg Harbor Township, N.J. http://www.njwreckdivers.com/.

Dubose, Lou. 2003. "Superfund Man." *Mother Jones* (January). http://motherjones.com/politics/2003/01/superfund-man.

Durkas, Susan. 1992. *Impediments to the Spawning Success of Anadromous Fish in Tributaries of the NY/NJ Harbor Watershed*. Highlands, N.J.: American Littoral Society Baykeeper.

Edison Wetlands Association. http://www.edisonwetlands.org/.

Friedman, Alexi. 2009. "Environmentalists Press for Raritan River Cleanup." *Star-Ledger*, May 17.

Galiano, Rich. "Scuba Diving—New Jersey & Long Island New York." http://njscuba.net/index.html.

Ivins, Molly. 2003. *Bushwhacked*. New York: Random House.

Mitchell, John G. 2001. "Urban Sprawl: The American Dream?" *National Geographic*, July.

New Jersey Audubon Society. 2001. "Voice of New Jersey Audubon." October 10. http://www.njaudubon.org/Tools.Net/Sightings/SightingsArchive.aspx.

———. 2004. "Voice of New Jersey Audubon." December 16. http://www.njaudubon.org/Tools.Net/Sightings/SightingsArchive.aspx.

Patterson, Dana. 2009. "Wild New Jersey Exclusive: Edgeboro Landfill Restoration Offers Habitat for Migrating Birds." *WildNewJersey.tv*, June 16.

Rutgers University. Edward J. Bloustein School of Planning and Public Policy. Raritan River Initiative. www.blueraritan.org.

Wheeler, David. 2007. *The Birds of Middlesex County, New Jersey*. Edison, N.J.: Edison Wetlands Association. http://www.leoraw.com/hpenv/data/BirdsofMiddlesexCounty.pdf.

———. 2009. *The Raritan: New Jersey's Queen of Rivers*. Wild New Jersey Productions. Video. May.

**Chapter 11   Captain Morgan and the Sargasso Sea Voyagers**

Brown, Tom, Jr. 1986. *Tom Brown's Guide to Wild Edible and Medicinal Plants*. New York: Penguin.

Clark, Kathleen, and Benjamin Wurst. 2009. *The 2009 Osprey Project in New Jersey*. Trenton: New Jersey Division of Fish and Wildlife and Conserve Wildlife Foundation of New Jersey. http://www.njfishandwildlife.com/ensp/pdf/osprey09.pdf.

Conserve Wildlife Foundation of New Jersey. Osprey Project. http://www.conservewildlifenj.org/protecting/projects/osprey/.

Gulf of Maine Council on the Marine Environment. 2007. "American Eels: Restoring a Vanishing Resource in the Gulf of Maine." http://www.gulfofmaine.org/council/publications/american_eel_low-res.pdf.

New Jersey Division of Parks and Forestry. Cheesequake State Park. http://www.state.nj.us/dep/parksandforests/parks/cheesequake.html.

"Wild New Jersey Exclusive: The Eels of Cheesequake." 2009. WildNewJersey.tv, April 9.

Worob, Melanie. 2009. Osprey Banding at Cheesequake State Park. Wild New Jersey Productions. Video. August.

## Chapter 12   The Lost World of Jurassic Jersey

Academy of Natural Sciences, Philadelphia. Dinosaur Hall. http://www.ansp.org/museum/dinohall/index.php.

Ambrose, Stephen E. 1996. Undaunted Courage: Meriwether Lewis, Thomas Jefferson, and the Opening of the American West. New York: Touchstone.

Crichton, Michael. 1990. Jurassic Park. New York: Alfred A. Knopf.

"Dinosaurs: Where Jurassic Park Got It Wrong." 2009. The Observer [London], February 8.

Fisk, Alan, Jr. 1995. "Cretaceous Cavortings at Big Brook." Lapidary Journal 49 (August):67.

Flannery, Tim. 2001. A Gap in Nature: Discovering the World's Extinct Animals. New York: Atlantic Monthly Press.

Gallagher, William B. 2003. When Dinosaurs Roamed New Jersey. New Brunswick: Rutgers University Press.

Haddonfield, N.J., Dinosaur Sculpture Committee. http://hadrosaurus.com/.

Haines, Tim. 2001. Walking with Prehistoric Beasts. London: BBC Worldwide Ltd.

Jurassic Park. 1993. Directed by Steven Spielberg. Universal Pictures.

Kleiman, Miriam. 2009. "Amateur Teenage 'Dinosaur Hunter's' Find Ends Up in the National Archive." http://www.archives.gov/75th/stories/featured-stories/dinosaur-hunter.html.

Klinkenbourg, Verlyn. 2010. "Last One: Countdown to Extinction." National Geographic, January.

Knisley, C. Barry, James M. Hill, and A. M. Scherer. 2005. "Translocation of the Northeastern Beach Tiger Beetle, Cicindela dorsalis dorsalis, to Sandy Hook, New Jersey." Annals of the Entomological Society of America 98(4):552–57.

New Jersey Paleontological Society. http://www.njpaleo.org/.

New Jersey State Museum, Trenton. http://www.state.nj.us/state/museum/index.htm.

Pollak, Michael. 1997. "New Jersey Underground: Fossils, Gems and Glowing Rocks." New York Times, May 11.

Quammen, David. 1996. The Song of the Dodo. New York: Touchstone.

Rutgers University. Coastal Ocean Observation Lab. http://rucool.marine.rutgers.edu/.

Yoost, Derek. "New Jersey's Premier Fossil Web Site." http://www.njfossils.net/.

## Chapter 13   Great White Hunter

Bauder, David. 2000. "Benchley Wouldn't Write Same 'Jaws' Today." Associated Press, April 5. http://www.peterbenchley.com/JawsToday.htm.

Benchley, Peter. 1974. Jaws. New York: Doubleday.

Blood in the Water. 2009. Directed by Richard Bedser. Brook Lapping Productions for Discovery Channel's Shark Week.

Campbell, Eric Scott. 2009. "Bull Sharks—or Just Bull—Along Mullica River." *Press of Atlantic City*, August 2.

Capuzzo, Michael. 2001. *Close to Shore: A True Story of Terror in an Age of Innocence.* New York: Random House.

Fernicola, Richard G. 2001. *Twelve Days of Terror: A Definitive Investigation of the 1916 New Jersey Shark Attacks.* Boston: Globe Pequot Press.

Global Shark Attack File. http://www.sharkattackfile.net/.

Handwerk, Brian. 2002. "Great Whites May Be Taking the Rap for Bull Shark Attacks." *National Geographic News*, August 2. http://news.nationalgeographic.com/news/2002/08/0802_020802_shark.html.

*Jaws.* 1975. Directed by Steven Spielberg. Zanuck/Brown Productions.

Jersey Coast Shark Anglers. http://www.jcsa.org/.

Marine Mammal Stranding Center, Brigantine, N.J. http://www.mmsc.org/main.htm.

New Jersey Natural Lands Trust. Clarks Landing Preserve. http://www.nj.gov/dep/njnlt/clarkslanding.htm.

"9 Shark Attack Victims to Testify Before Congress." 2009. *Huffington Post*, July 15.

Reynolds, Joe. "Shore11.org: All Things Green Down the Shore." http://www.shore11.org/joereynolds.

Shark Research Institute, Princeton, N.J. http://www.sharks.org/.

Volker, Darren. Mary Lou Crew Sportfishing Charters. http://www.newjerseycharterboat.com/index.html.

### Chapter 14   The Final Frontier: Birding the Open Atlantic

Boschung, Herbert T., Jr., et al. 1983. *National Audubon Society Field Guide to North American Fishes, Whales, and Dolphins.* New York: Alfred A. Knopf.

Guris, Paul. Pelagic birding and sea life trips. http://www.paulagics.com.

Hull, Jim. Sportfishing boat charter. http://www.rosier.net/.

National Oceanic and Atmospheric Administration. Ocean Explorer. "Hudson Canyon Cruise." http://oceanexplorer.noaa.gov/explorations/02hudson/welcome.html.

New Jersey Audubon Society. Cape May Bird Observatory. Avalon Sea Watch. http://www.birdcapemay.org/seawatch.shtml.

———. "View from the Field." http://www.birdcapemay.org/sightings/2009_10_04_archive.html.

Ocean Wanderers. Pelagic wildlife blog. http://www.oceanwanderers.com/.

Safina, Carl. 2007. "On the Wings of the Albatross." *National Geographic*, December.

Sutton, Patricia, and Clay Sutton. 2006. *Birds and Birding in Cape May.* Mechanicsburg, Pa.: Stackpole Books.

United States Geological Survey. Woods Hole Science Center. "U.S. Geological Survey Studies in the New York Bight." http://woodshole.er.usgs.gov/project-pages/newyork/.

"Wild New Jersey Exclusive: Christmas on the High Seas." 2009. *WildNewJersey.tv*, January 7.

### Chapter 15   Wild Summer at the Jersey Shore

Bonney, Rick. 1985. "The Biggest Day." *The Living Bird Quarterly* (Winter). http://www.birds.cornell.edu/wsb/articles-and-summaries/firstteam/.

Brookdale Community College. Ocean Institute at Sandy Hook. http://ux.brookdalecc.edu/staff/sandyhook/.

Burger, Joanna. 1996. *A Naturalist along the Jersey Shore.* New Brunswick: Rutgers University Press.

Conserve Wildlife Foundation. Beach Nesting Bird Project. http://www.conserve wildlifenj.org/protecting/projects/beachnestingbird/.

Friends of Forsythe NWR. http://www.friendsofforsythe.org/.

Meinkoth, Norman A. 1981. *National Audubon Society Field Guide to North American Seashore Creatures.* New York: Alfred A. Knopf.

Monmouth County Park System. http://monmouthcountyparks.com/.

National Park Service. Gateway National Recreation Area. http://www.nps.gov/gate/index.htm.

New Jersey Audubon Society. Sandy Hook Bird Observatory. http://www.njaudubon.org/SectionCenters/SectionSHBO/Introduction.aspx.

New Jersey Division of Parks and Forestry. Island Beach State Park. http://www.state.nj.us/dep/parksandforests/parks/island.html.

Obmascik, Mark. 2004. *The Big Year: A Tale of Man, Nature and Fowl Obsession.* New York: Simon and Schuster.

Save the Manatee Club. http://www.savethemanatee.org.

Tuckerton Seaport Museum. http://www.tuckertonseaport.org/.

United States Fish and Wildlife Service. Edwin B. Forsythe National Wildlife Refuge. http://www.fws.gov/northeast/forsythe/.

Vinzant, Carol. 2009. "Manatee on the Run." *New York Magazine,* October 4.

Wetlands Institute, Stone Harbor, N.J. http://www.wetlandsinstitute.org/.

World Series of Birding. http://www.birdcapemay.org/wsob.shtml.

"The World Series of Birding." 2000. *The Daily Show.* Hosted by Jon Stewart. July 18.

### Chapter 16   Moby-Dick; or, Call Me Cetacean

American Cetacean Society. "Blue Whale." http://www.acsonline.org/factpack/bluewhl.htm.

Burd, Joshua. 2009. "Whale Spotted Swimming Near Perth Amboy Dies on Beach." *Home News Tribune* (www.mycentraljersey.com), August 18.

Cape May–Lewes Ferry. http://www.capemaylewesferry.com/.

Cape May Whale Watch & Research Center. http://www.capemaywhalewatch.com/.

Clean Ocean Action. http://www.cleanoceanaction.org.

"Dead Dolphin Found Near Bon Jovi's House." 2009. *Associated Press,* April 19. http://cbs3.com/local/Dolphin.Dead.Bon.2.988530.html.

Fox, Karen. 2008. "Whalers: A Link to Our Past." *Cape May Magazine* (Fall). http://capemay.com/magazine/2009/11/whalers-the-link-to-our-past/.

Godfrey, Bill. 2006. "The Cape May Canal." *This Is Cape May* (July). http://www.capemay.com/Editorial/august06/capemaycanal.html.

Gomolka, Gene. 2005. "The Search for the 'Sea Wolves.'" *Naples Daily News,* May 8.

"The History of Cape May." http://www.capemay.com/capemayhistory.html.

Junger, Sebastian. 2002. "The Whale Hunters." *Outside 25: Classic Tales and New Voices from the Frontiers of Adventure,* ed. Hal Espen, 184–97. New York: W. W. Norton.

National Oceanic and Atmospheric Administration. 2009. "Bottlenose Dolphins in the Shrewsbury and Navesink Rivers, NJ." June. http://www.nmfs.noaa.gov/pr/health/njdolphins/.

Payne, Roger. 1970. *Songs of the Humpback Whale.* New York: Columbia Records.

Roman, Joe. 2006. *Whale.* Chicago: University of Chicago Press; London: Reaktion Books.

Siebert, Charles. 2009. "Watching Whales Watching Us." *New York Times Magazine,* July 12.

Stewart, Captain Jeff. Cape May Whale Watcher. http://www.capemaywhalewatcher. com/.

"Wayward Whale Frees Itself from Delaware River Mud." 1994. *Associated Press*, December 9.

"Whale Still Hanging Out on Delaware River." 2005. MSNBC, April 15. http://www. msnbc.msn.com/id/7486673/ns/us_news-environment/.

### Chapter 17 Cape May: The Never-ending Migration

Cape May County Chamber of Commerce. *Jersey Cape Vacation Guide* (annual). http:// www.capemaycountychamber.com/vacationguide/default.htm.

Cornell University. Cornell Lab of Ornithology. http://www.birds.cornell.edu/.

Fox, Karen. 2008. "Higbee Beach . . . Journey Back to Nature." *Cape May Magazine* (June). http://www.capemay.com/Editorial/june08/HighbeeBeach.htm.

Kane, Richard. 1996. "Ecotourism and Conservation: NJAS Opinion." http://www. njaudubon.org/SectionConservation/NJASOpinion/EcotourismandConservation. aspx.

Kerlinger, Paul. "Cape May Times: Birds by the Month." http://www.capemaytimes. com/birds/cape-may-birds-by-the-month/default.htm.

New Jersey Audubon Society. Cape May Bird Observatory. http://www.birdcapemay. org/.

_____. Cape May Rare Bird Alert. http://www.njaudubon.org/Tools.Net/Sightings/ CapeMay.aspx.

_____. Important Bird and Birding Areas. http://www.njaudubon.org/SectionIBBA/ Welcome.aspx.

_____. "Zeiss/NJ Audubon Society Morning Flight Project." http://www.njaudubon. org/Portals/10/Research/PDF/MornFlight.pdf.

New Jersey Division of Fish and Wildlife. Birds of New Jersey. http://www.state.nj. us/dep/fgw/chkbirds.htm.

New Jersey Division of Parks and Forestry. Cape May State Park. http://www.state.nj. us/dep/parksandforests/parks/capemay.html.

United States Fish and Wildlife Service. Cape May National Wildlife Refuge. http:// www.fws.gov/northeast/capemay/.

"Wild New Jersey Exclusive: Interview with David Sibley as 63rd Annual Cape May Autumn Weekend Gets Underway." 2009. *WildNewJersey.tv*, October 23.

### Chapter 18 Triassic Meets Arctic on the Delaware Bay

Eliot, John L. 2003. "Birds That Go to Extremes." *National Geographic*, February.

Githens, Captain David. Birding by boat and tidelands discovery tours from the Cape May Bird Observatory. http://www.birdingbyboat.com/.

New Jersey Audubon Society. Nature Center of Cape May. http://www.njaudubon. org/SectionCenters/SectionNCCM/Introduction.aspx.

Niles, Larry. "The Shorebird Project." http://www.shorebirdproject.blogspot.com/.

Wheeler, David. 2009. "New Jersey Leads the Way in Protecting Red Knots." *Green Jersey*, March 27. http://greenjersey.org/2009/03/27/new-jersey-leads-the-way-in-protecting-red-knots/.

"Wild New Jersey Exclusive: NJ Fish & Wildlife Studies Red Knots on Delaware Bayshore." 2009. *WildNewJersey.tv*, May 19.

### Chapter 19 Bald Eagles on a Bayshore Bayou

Citizens United to Protect the Maurice River. http://www.cumauriceriver.org/.

Clark, Kathleen E., and Larissa Smith. 2009. *New Jersey Bald Eagle Project, 2009*. Trenton: New Jersey Department of Environmental Protection, Division of Fish and Wildlife. http://www.conservewildlifenj.org/downloads/cwnj_14.pdf.

Cumberland County, N.J. Winter Eagle Festival. http://www.moretooffer.com/tcontent/asp.

Duke Farms, Hillsborough, N.J. Bald eagle webcam. http://www.dukefarms.org/Education/Research/Duke-Farms-Eagle-Cam/.

Eliot, John L. 2002. "Bald Eagles Come Back from the Brink." *National Geographic*, July.

Githens, David. "Bald Eagles/Maurice River" boat tour. http://www.birdingbyboat.com/gallery.

National Park Service. 1993. Maurice National Wild & Scenic River. http://www.nps.gov/maur/.

New Jersey Audubon Society. 2006. "New Jersey Birding & Wildlife Trails: Delaware Bayshore." Bernardsville: New Jersey Audubon Society. http://www.njwildlifetrails.org/DelawareBayshoreTrails/Trails.aspx.

Stryker, Noah K. 2008. "A Birding Interview with Pete Dunne." *Birding Magazine* (March). http://www.aba.org/birding/v40n2p20.pdf.

United States Congress. 108th Congress. 1973. Endangered Species Act of 1973. http://www.fws.gov/Endangered/pdfs/esaall.pdf.

United States Environmental Protection Agency. History. http://www.epa.gov/history/

United States Fish and Wildlife Service. 1986. *Habitat Suitability Index Models: Bald Eagle (Breeding Seasons)*. October. http://www.nwrc.usgs.gov/wdb/pub/hsi/hsi-126.pdf.

Wheeler, David. 2007. *Great American Comeback: The Return of the Bald Eagle to Middlesex County, New Jersey*. Edison, N.J.: Edison Wetlands Association; Highland Park, N.J.: Highland Park Environmental Commission. July. http://www.edisonwetlands.org/docs/BaldEagleReport.pdf.

"Wild New Jersey Exclusive: Eagle Festival Soars in Cumberland County." 2009. *WildNewJersey.tv*, February 9.

## Chapters 20–21    The Mysteries of the Pine Barrens: Fire and Water

Beck, Henry Charlton. 1963. *More Forgotten Towns of Southern New Jersey*. New Brunswick: Rutgers University Press.

Burger, Joanna. 2006. *Whispers in the Pines: A Naturalist in the Northeast*. New Brunswick: Rutgers University Press/Rivergate Books.

Citizens United to Protect the Maurice River. 2008. "Plants of Southern New Jersey." http://www.cumauriceriver.org/botany/.

McCloy, James F., and Ray Miller Jr. 1976. *The Jersey Devil*. Moorestown: Middle Atlantic Press.

McMahon, William. 1973. *South Jersey Towns*. New Brunswick: Rutgers University Press.

McPhee, John. 1968. *The Pine Barrens*. New York: Farrar, Straus & Giroux.

Moran, Mark, and Mark Sceurman. 2003. *Weird NJ*. New York: Barnes & Noble.

National Park Service. Pinelands National Reserve. http://www.nps.gov/pine/index.htm.

New Jersey Division of Parks and Forestry. Wharton State Forest. http://www.state.nj.us/dep/parksandforests/parks/wharton.html.

New Jersey History's Mysteries. http://www.njhm.com.

New Jersey Pine Barrens blog. http://www.njpinebarrens.com/.

New Jersey Pinelands Commission. http://www.state.nj.us/pinelands/.

_____. "Pinelands Canoe Liveries." http://www.state.nj.us/pinelands/pasttimes/canoe/.

Piney Power. Pine Barrens information for visitors and residents. http://www.pineypower.com/.

Scheller, Bill. 2009. "Canoeing the Jersey Pine Barrens." *Natural Traveler* (June). http://www.naturaltraveler.com/article.php?article=pine_barrens&issue=2009/06/48.

"Wild New Jersey Exclusive: Tracking Snakes in the Pine Barrens." 2009. *WildNew Jersey.tv*, May 4.

Xerces Society for Invertebrate Conservation. http://www.xerces.org/.

### Chapter 22   Wild Nights in Suburbia

Bangma, Jim, Allen E. Barlow, and David M. Golden. 2009. *Field Guide to Dragonflies and Damselflies of New Jersey.* Trenton: Conserve Wildlife Foundation of New Jersey.

The Bug Guide. http://bugguide.net.

Bugseum of New Jersey, Toms River. Insectropolis. http://www.insectropolis.com/.

Bunnell, John F., and David M. Golden. 2002. *Calls of New Jersey Frogs and Toads.* Audio CD. Trenton: New Jersey Department of Environmental Protection, Division of Fish & Wildlife.

Burger, Joanna, and Michael Gochfeld. 1997. *Butterflies of New Jersey.* New Brunswick: Rutgers University Press.

The Dragonflies and Damselflies of New Jersey. http://www.njodes.com.

Gessner, Jackie, and Eric Stiles. 2001. *Field Guide to Reptiles and Amphibians of New Jersey.* Trenton: New Jersey Department of Environmental Protection, Division of Fish & Wildlife. http://www.state.nj.us/dep/fgw/ensp/pdf/turtles.pdf.

Lange, Karen E. 2007. "Tales from the Bog." *National Geographic*, September.

Morell, Virginia. 2001. "The Fragile World of Frogs." *National Geographic*, May.

Moskowitz, David. 2007. "The Tiny Frog with the Big Voice." New York–New Jersey Trail Conference, *Trailwalker*, March–April. http://www.nynjtc.org/trailwalker/2007/ma07.pdf.

New Jersey Nature Notes. http://www.njnaturenotes.com.

Schrag, Anne M. 2003. "Highways and Wildlife: Review of Mitigation Projects Throughout Europe, Canada, and the United States." January 13. http://www.I90 wildlifebridges.org/HighwaysandWildlifeReport.pdf.

Wheeler, David. 2007. "Dusk Hike through Bog Brings Alternate Perspective." *Star-Ledger*, October 4.

### Chapter 23   The Croc Hunter of the Diz

DePalma, Anthony. 2005. "The Accidental Oasis." *New York Times*, August 21.

"Edison Ranch Location for Movie Shoot." 2008. *Home News Tribune*, May 25.

Halbfinger, David. 2002. "Missing: Lodgers with Big Teeth." *New York Times*, March 6.

Hiss, Tony, and Christopher Meier. 2004. *H20: Highlands to Ocean.* Morristown: Geraldine R. Dodge Foundation.

Niering, William A. 1997. *Wetlands.* National Audubon Society Nature Guides. New York: Alfred A. Knopf.

———. 1991. *Wetlands of North America.* Charlottesville, Va.: Thomasson-Grant.

Walsh, Diane. 2008. "More Space in a 'Glorious Place': Acquisition Adds 69 Acres to Dismal Swamp." *Star-Ledger*, August 21.

Weislo, Jill. 2009. "Wild New Jersey Exclusive: New Jersey's Newest Natural Wonder." *WildNewJersey.tv*, December 23.

Wheeler, David. 2007. "Turtles, Clams, and More Find an Unlikely Haven." *Star-Ledger*, May 3.

## Chapter 24   Serpent Eden in the Great Swamp

Cavanaugh, Cam. 1978. *Saving the Great Swamp: The People, the Power Brokers, and an Urban Wilderness.* New York: Vanguard Press.

Friends of Great Swamp National Wildlife Refuge. http://www.friendsofgreatswamp. org/index.html.

Lynch, Bill. *New Jersey Outdoors.* http://newjerseyoutdoors.blogspot.com/ and http://www.flickr.com/photos/billysbirds/.

New Jersey Audubon Society. Scherman Hoffman Wildlife Sanctuary. http://www. njaudubon.org/SectionCenters/SectionScherman/TheSanctuary.aspx.

Perry, Sandy. 2009. "Jetport Plan 50 Years Ago Led to Founding of New Jersey Conservation Foundation." New Jersey Conservation Foundation. http://www. njconservation.org/html/JetPortPlan50YearsAgo.htm.

Soucy, Dr. Len. The Raptor Trust. http://theraptortrust.org/.

Sutton, Patricia Taylor, and Clay Sutton. 1999. *How to Spot an Owl.* Boston: Houghton Mifflin Harcourt.

United States Fish and Wildlife Service. Great Swamp National Wildlife Refuge. http://www.fws.gov/northeast/greatswamp/.

"Wild New Jersey Exclusive: The Kingdom of Snakes." 2009. *WildNewJersey.tv,* April 21.

## Chapter 25   Night Falls on New Jersey's Bats

Bat Conservation International. http://www.batcon.org/.

Braun, John, and Maria Grace. 2008. *Bats of New Jersey.* Conserve Wildlife Foundation of New Jersey. June. http://www.conservewildlifenj.org/downloads/cwnj_39.pdf.

Hyman, Vicki. 2006. "Bring on the Bats: The Flying Mammals Get a Bad Rap." *Star-Ledger,* August 13.

National Speleological Society. "White Nose Syndrome Page." http://www.caves.org/ WNS/.

New Jersey Audubon Society. Weis Ecology Center. http://www.njaudubon.org/ SectionCenters/SectionWeis/Introduction.aspx.

New Jersey Division of Parks and Forestry. Norvin Green State Forest. http://www. state.nj.us/dep/parksandforests/parks/norvin.html.

"Wild New Jersey Exclusive: Conserve Wildlife Foundation Releases 2009 Bat Count Results." 2010. *WildNewJersey.tv,* January 1.

"Wild New Jersey Exclusive: A Night at Bat Wing Farm." 2009. *WildNewJersey.tv,* August 18.

## Chapter 26   A Journey in Time from Farm to Field

Barth, Linda J. 2002. *The Delaware and Raritan Canal.* San Francisco: Arcadia Publishing.

"Biologist Says Nutria Have Arrived in New Jersey Marshland." 2007. *Associated Press,* December 5.

Boyle, William J., Jr., and Laurie Larson. 2009. "'Old Crooked Toe' and the *Grus* Cranes of Southern New Jersey." New Jersey Audubon Society, *New Jersey Birds* 35, no. 2 (Spring). http://www.njaudubon.org/Portals/10/Research/PDF/NJBSpring 09.pdf.

Brooklyn Monk Parrots. http://www.brooklynparrots.com/.

Delaware and Raritan Canal Commission. http://www.dandrcanal.com/drcc/index. html.

Delaware Valley Ornithological Club. http://www.dvoc.org/Main.htm.

Friedman, Alexi. 2009. "Hunters Shrink New Jersey's Wild Boar Population." *Star-Ledger*, March 1.

Linden, Eugene. 1999. *The Parrot's Lament, and Other True Tales of Animal Intrigue, Intelligence and Ingenuity.* New York: Plume.

Mirsky, Steve. 2008. "Shakespeare to Blame for Introduction of European Starlings to US." *Scientific American Magazine* (June).

Moscatello, Brian. 2003. "Preliminary Review of the Status of Monk Parakeets in New Jersey." New Jersey Audubon Society, *New Jersey Birds* 29, no. 1 (Spring). http://www.njaudubon.org/Portals/10/Research/PDF/MonkParakeets_in_NJ.pdf.

New Jersey Division of Fish and Wildlife. Landowner Incentive Program. http://www.state.nj.us/dep/fgw/ensp/lip_prog.htm.

New Jersey Division of Parks and Forestry. Delaware & Raritan Canal State Park. http://www.state.nj.us/dep/parksandforests/parks/drcanal.html.

Rizzo, Dominic. Rizzo's Reptile Discovery. http://rizzoswildlife.com/.

Rothman, Carly. 2008. "Asian Swamp Eel Threatens Native N.J. Wildlife." *Star-Ledger*, September 24.

United States Department of Agriculture. National Invasive Species Information Center. http://www.invasivespeciesinfo.gov/.

"Wild New Jersey Exclusive: Native Grasses Helping Imperiled Grassland Birds Recover in New Jersey." 2009. *WildNewJersey.tv*, July 9.

## Chapters 27–28    Delaware Water Gap: A Wonder of the World and The Road to Crater Lake

Albert, Richard C. 1987. *Damming the Delaware: The Rise and Fall of Tocks Island Dam.* State College: Pennsylvania State University Press.

Cougar Network. http://www.cougarnet.org/.

Crabtree, Pam, Douglas V. Campana, and John R. Wright. 2002. "Exploring the Archeological Potential of French and Indian War Fortifications." *CRM: Cultural Resource Management* 25, no. 3.

Delaware River canoeing, kayaking, rafting, and tubing. http://www.delawarerivertubing.com/, http://www.kittatinny.com/, and http://www.adventuresport.com/.

Delaware Riverkeeper. http://www.delawareriverkeeper.org/.

Friends of the Delaware Water Gap National Recreation Area. http://www.friendsofdewa.org.

Kopczynski, Susan. 2000. "A Ride Down Old Mine Road." *Spanning the Gap* (Summer). http://www.nps.gov/dewa/historyculture/stories-old-mine-rd.htm.

Lewis, Glen. 2008. "Return to the Old Mine Road." *New Jersey's Great Northwest Skylands.* http://www.njskylands.com/hsoldmine.htm.

National Park Service. 2008. "Attendance Rises in 2007." Press release. February 26.

_____. Delaware Water Gap National Recreation Area and Middle Delaware National Scenic River. http://www.nps.gov/dewa/index.htm.

_____. "How the Gap Formed." http://www.nps.gov/dewa/planyourvisit/upload/sb2Geogap.pdf.

Nature Conservancy. Skylands: Kittatinny Ridge. http://www.nature.org/wherewework/northamerica/states/newjersey/work/art29242.html.

New Jersey Audubon Society. Mount Tammany Cliffs. http://www.njaudubon.org/SectionIBBA/IBBASiteGuide.aspx?sk=3101.

_____. "New Jersey Birding & Wildlife Trails: Skylands Trails." Bernardsville: New Jersey Audubon Society. http://www.njwildlifetrails.org/SkylandsTrails/Trails.aspx.

New Jersey Division of Parks and Forestry. Fort Mott State Park. http://www.state.nj.us/dep/parksandforests/parks/fortmott.html.

_____. Worthington State Forest. http://www.state.nj.us/dep/parksandforests/
parks/worthington.html.

Sayre, Phillip. 1998. "Vertical Water: Where the Falls Are in New Jersey." *New York
Times*, April 5.

Stutz, Bruce. 1992. *Natural Lives, Modern Times: People and Places of the Delaware River.*
New York: Crown Publishers.

Tarlowe, Paul. 2010. "New Jersey's Wildlife Management Areas."
http://www.state.nj.us/dep/fgw/wmarticl.htm.

Trails.com. "Top 100 Trails—Best Trails in North America: Sunfish Pond and Mount
Mohican." http://www.trails.com/tcatalog_trail.aspx?trailid=HDG077-001.

United States Fish and Wildlife Service. Supawna Meadows National Wildlife Refuge.
http://www.fws.gov/supawnameadows/.

Weidensaul, Scott. 1994. *Mountains of the Heart: A Natural History of the
Appalachians.* Golden, Colo.: Fulcrum Publishing.

"Wild New Jersey Exclusive: A Walk in the Clouds at the Delaware Water Gap." 2009.
*WildNewJersey.tv*, May 20.

"Wild New Jersey Exclusive: Worthington Forest—New Jersey's Best Hike." 2009.
*WildNewJersey.tv*, May 22.

Wright, John R. 1999. "The French and Indian War in the Delaware Valley." 1999.
*Spanning the Gap* 21, no. 2 (Summer). http://www.nps.gov/dewa/historyculture/
upload/cmsstgFOJO.pdf.

# INDEX

CPSIA information can be obtained
at www.ICGtesting.com
Printed in the USA
LVOW01s0122210816

501181LV00007BA/33/P

9 780813 549217